THE TARTAR KHAN'S
ENGLISHMAN

Gabriel Ronay was born in Transylvania and came to Britain after the crushing of the 1956 Hungarian Revolution. A graduate of Edinburgh and Budapest universities, he read history and studied Russian, German, Romance languages and Finno-Ugrian philology. While continuing his medieval researches, he worked on the Foreign Desk of *The Times* for 25 years, contributed to the *Sunday Times*, wrote a syndicated column for a political weekly and broadcast regularly on the BBC World Service. He is now correspondent for the Scottish paper *Sunday Herald*.

He has published more than a dozen works on historical topics, both medieval and contemporary. His books have been published in the USA, Britain, Scandinavia and Japan. After the collapse of Communism, he was awarded a high decoration by the President of Hungary for his role in the country's 1956 fight for freedom. Mr Ronay and his wife, Lois Elspeth, have three children and live in London.

ALSO BY GABRIEL RONAY

The Dracula Myth
The Lost King of England

THE TARTAR KHAN'S ENGLISHMAN

Gabriel Ronay

PHOENIX
PRESS

5 UPPER SAINT MARTIN'S LANE
LONDON
WC2H 9EA

To Lois

A PHOENIX PRESS PAPERBACK

First published in Great Britain
by Cassell Ltd in 1978
This paperback edition published in 2000
by Phoenix Press,
a division of The Orion Publishing Group Ltd,
Orion House, 5 Upper St Martin's Lane,
London WC2H 9EA

Copyright © Gabriel Ronay 1978

Maps and diagrams prepared by Peter McClure
Copyright © Cassell Ltd 1978

The moral right of Gabriel Ronay to be identified as the author
of this work has been asserted by him in accordance with
the Copyright, Designs and Patents Act 1988.

A CIP catalogue record for this book
is available from the British Library.

Printed and bound in Great Britain by
Butler & Tanner Ltd, Frome and London

ISBN 1 84212 210 X

Contents

Contents

Illustrations

Maps

Acknowledgements

The author gratefully acknowledges the valuable assistance given to him by the following people and organisations: the British Library; the Austrian Institute; the National Szechenyi Library, Budapest; Professor Gyula Germanus, Budapest; Professor Ya. S. Lurye, Russian Literary Institute of the Soviet Academy of Sciences, Leningrad; Professor Jozef Blaskovic, Charles University, Prague; Don Jure Belic of the bishopric of Hvar, Yugoslavia; Dr Eileen Roberts, St Albans; the Essex Record Office; the Right Rev Richard Chartres, Chaplain to the Bishop of St Albans; E. G. W. Bill, Librarian at Lambeth Palace; and my wife, Lois.

The author also wishes to thank the Trustees of the British Library; the Master and Fellows of Corpus Christi College, Cambridge; the Courtauld Institute; the Israeli Embassy; the National Szechenyi Library, Budapest; and the Dean and Chapter of Worcester Cathedral for permission to print illustrations in their possession.

Most of the key documents relating to the Englishman's peregrinations, his East European missions, and the diplomacy of the Mongol period, have never been translated into English before. They appear here, unless otherwise stated, in the author's translation.

Foreword

IT WAS BY CURIOUS CHANCE that I came across the story of the shadowy Englishman who was the Tartar Khan's chief diplomat and intelligence expert in the middle of the thirteenth century. Although his brand of diplomacy played a key role in the preparation of the Tartar invasion of Europe, the annals of the Eurasian continent do not even record his name.

Strange as it may seem, Dracula helped to pluck him from obscurity. After the publication of my last book, *The Dracula Myth*, I received a great many letters from readers wanting to impart their views and comments. One of them, written by Szabolcs de Vajay, a noted Paris medievalist, asserted that Vlad the Impaler of Walachia, the historical Dracula, was a direct descendant of Genghis Khan.

The prospect of a genealogical link between the bloodthirsty Tartar world-conqueror and the Balkan prototype of Dracula led me to do some desultory research into the 1241 Tartar onslaught on Europe, and its legacy in the eastern half of the continent. Soon, however, I found myself digging deeper into contemporary documents. And then the unexpected happened.

In the annals of Matthew Paris, the learned St Albans chronicler of thirteenth century events, I chanced on a report, dated 1243, on the capture of the Tartar Khan's chief diplomat, together with a group of Tartar officers participating in the siege of Wiener Neustadt in Austria. The Khan's envoy was a 'native of England'.

This astonishing piece of information, based on a solid eye-witness account in the best journalistic tradition, made me forget all about Dracula's genealogy and want to find out more about this mysterious Englishman.

His actions have left their stamp on the face of Europe and their effects are still with us today. But our collective memory is notoriously short and this Englishman, superseded by diplomats of greater perfidy and by greater holocausts, has fallen through the sieve of history.

There were many questions about the Khan's English envoy that needed answering. What made him, a Christian, go over to 'the brood of Anti-Christ' battering their way into the heart of Europe? How was he spotted by the 'talent scouts' of Tartar intelligence? How did he get to the court of the Khan of Khans in the steppes of Mongolia well over half a century before the epic journey of Marco Polo, and why is he not listed, like the Venetian, among the great European explorers? How did he rise so high in the employ of the Tartars and, given his role in the invasion of Europe, why is his name unknown to the historians of the continent? And most importantly, why was he so intent on hiding behind the cover of his protecting anonymity?

That the riddle of the Tartars' Englishman had preoccupied early historians is shown by Purchas's decision to include in his *Pilgrims* 'the confession of an Englishman which had lived among the Tartars, and was drawne along perforce with them in their expedition against Hungarie'.

But after the Elizabethans no one seems to have shown any interest in, or indeed known anything about, the Tartars' Englishman.

The shaft of light from the candle of the St Albans monk has helped to bring to life the 'Englishman', as he was known to his contemporaries, seven and a half centuries later by giving me a starting point for the quest to uncover his identity and piece together his extraordinary career.

The freshly turned-up documents, with their nuggets of information about his painful peregrinations and amazing adventures, make fascinating reading, even in the cumbrous medieval script, and a critical reconstruction of the life and times of this scholarly English adventurer makes up this book.

He was seen by his contemporaries as a callous representative of the awesome Tartar power. My impression is that he was more a victim of circumstances than a conscious shaper of history. His actions, stripped of the motive force of free will, offer a sobering sight of a remarkable individual caught up in the blind forces of destiny.

In following in the footsteps of the Tartar Khan's Englishman across continents and civilisations, I hope I have rescued a part of our common heritage from oblivion.

Highgate, March 1978

PART I

Strife in England

ONE

A full confession

THE YEAR OF GRACE 1241 was not a good year for Europe. Western Christendom was divided, the kings of England and France engrossed in their interminable squabbles, and Pope Gregory and the Holy Roman Emperor Frederick II were locked in a bloody and shaming war to decide by the sword 'the spiritual leadership' of our continent.

Christendom, having tired of the crusades, was rapidly losing interest in rolling back conquering Islam from the Holy Land. With its religious fervour now mainly directed against its own heretics, like the Albigenses and Waldenses, Western Christendom was content to contain, rather than confront the Arabs, who were still fired by a surfeit of aggressive zeal.

The portents for the year, as every single chronicler worth his salt earnestly recorded, were bad indeed. An eclipse of the sun was taken as an omen of wholesale calamities, and several learned monks construed the blood-red colour of the sun as a heavenly sign that Christendom would be drowned in a sea of blood before the year was out.

Others feared worse. The cleric Thomas of Spalato, writing in his Adriatic city port, gave a most graphic account of the superstitious terrors that seized his fellow Europeans.

There has been a most wondrous and awful eclipse of the sun; the day became murky and the air filled with darkness, and in the sky there appeared all the stars as if it were night, and a biggish star shone brightly west of the sun. Everyone was seized by such terror that people were running hither and thither, as if demented, thinking that the end of the world was nigh . . .

Although it was seen throughout Europe, it is said that in

Asia and Africa there was no eclipse of the sun. The same year a comet appeared in the north and seemed to be suspended for several days just above the Kingdom of Hungary; and it was being taken for a portent of great and wondrous events.

The events betokened by these and other heavenly signs eventually surpassed the worst expectations and have become deeply etched in the collective memory of Europe. Admittedly, it was not so difficult for these chroniclers to predict great calamities for 1241, having learnt from eye-witnesses that the eastern half of the continent was already in ruins, and its population put to the sword or enslaved by terrifying horsemen from Asia.

Matthew Paris, the well-informed monk of St Albans, had already recorded in his annals for the previous year that 'the detestable people of Satan, to wit, an infinite numbers of Tartars brake forth from their Mountayne-compassed home, and piercing the solid rocks [of the Caucasus], poured forth like Devils loosed out of Hell, or the Tartarus, so that they are rightly called Tartari or Tartarians. Swarming like locusts over the face of the Earth, they have brought terrible devastation to the Eastern Confines [of Europe] laying it waste with fire and sword'.

All the same, the princes and kings of Europe feigned surprise and, in their ignorance, preferred to equate the threat from Genghis Khan's empire, which then stretched from the China Sea to the Dniestr, with the periodic incursions of marauding bands of nomadic horsemen easily dealt with by the armoured knights of Christendom.

There was also the hope that, satiated by the rich spoils from the lands of the Russian princes, the Tartars, or as they should correctly be called the Mongols, would, if ignored, go back from where they came.

In the meantime the 'Tartar threat', like similar deadly threats to the very existence of Europe in the ensuing centuries, was seized upon by the warring factions of Europe and exploited to serve their petty ends.

Pope Gregory's side began to spread the rumour that the Holy Roman Emperor Frederick, 'that well-known friend and supporter of Arabs, Jews and heretics', had actually called in the Tartars and that the so-called 'Tartar threat' was nothing more than a shabby stratagem to 'unite Christendom against the Lord Pope'.

Others preferred to get on with their domestic squabbles and local wars, seeing even a certain advantage in the Tartar devastations. When a deputation of Ismaelites and Eastern-rite Christians from the Levant came to the court of King Henry III of England to seek help against the Tartars, Peter, Bishop of Winchester, warned the King against aiding them: 'Let those dogs devour each other and be utterly wiped out; and we shall see then, founded on the ruins, the universal Catholic Church, and there shall truly be one shepherd and one flock'.

But in the spring of that fateful year, when the Mongols suddenly appeared in the very centre of Europe butchering in their millions the Catholic faithful—not eastern 'dogs'—of Hungary, Bohemia, Silesia and Poland, some of the Western rulers began to see the immensity of the danger threatening the continent.

A few even realised that unless they could unite Christendom against the Mongols, they, their crusades, petty wars and the interminable bickering between the Pope and the Holy Roman Emperor would be swept away in the sea of blood spilt by the invading Asiatic horsemen.

The Landgrave of Thüringia addressed the following urgent call to arms to the Duke of Boulogne and his English vassals:

Hear, ye islands, and all ye people of Christianity, who profess our Lord's Cross, howl in ashes and sackcloth, in fasting and tears and mourning; let your tears flow in streams.

For the day of the Lord is come, is just come, that great and bitter day. An unheard-of persecution of the Cross of Christ has come from the North and from the sea, and it is with trouble of mind and affliction of heart, with a fearful look, and groaning of the spirit, and taking breath every now and then, that I endeavour to tell you the tale as well as I am able.

How innumerable nations, hateful to other men, and of unbounded wickedness, treading the Earth in disdain, from the east even to the frontiers of our dominion, have utterly destroyed the whole earth. They have destroyed cities, castles and even market towns, and spared neither Christians, pagans, nor Jews, putting to death all alike without mercy. They do not eat men, they devour them . . .

But to sum up all in a few words, the Tartars aforesaid have wholly destroyed all Russia and Poland as far as the confines of the Kingdom of Bohemia, and the middle part of Hungary, and have suddenly entered the cities, and hanged their chiefs in the midst of them . . .

We propose to dwell in the heavenly kingdom, to seize arms and grasp the shield. For we would rather die in war than see the evils [destroy] our nation. And if our shield shall be broken under the first discharge of javelins, when our house is on fire, and our land devastated, the neighbouring houses and neighbouring provinces will be alarmed. Farewell!

As the Mongol horsemen battered their way westward the alarm bells began to ring throughout Christendom. Emperor Frederick wrote to the kings of England and France, urging them to arm themselves and prepare for a holy war.

The Pope too eventually realized that the Tartars were not exactly the figment of his adversary's imagination, and as Batu Khan's troops built hecatombs from the bodies of slain Europeans he called for a crusade and sent preachers to carry the cross. But his call fell on deaf ears, and the crusade never materialized.

The Holy See, still regarding Islam as Christendom's sole enemy, sent some financial aid to the hard-pressed King of Hungary to keep up the fight against the Mongols, while simultaneously it embarked on a policy of appeasement to win over the shamanist—and therefore from the religious point of view, uncommitted—Tartars to his great design: to destroy Arab power and recover the Holy Land.

It was put about that, while Europe burned, the Pope preferred to fight the Tartars with spiritual weapons and convert them to Christianity.

The Tartars, oblivious of the schemes and stratagems of Europe, proceeded with their plan to conquer the world. In a despatch to his suzerain which survived in the *Secret History of the Mongols,* written in 1242, Batu Khan reported: 'Through the power of the Eternal Heaven and the blessing of the Imperial Kin, we have made the people of Russia our slaves. Eleven other states have been forced into our yoke, and the golden bit has been placed into their mouths.'

Our trembling continent suddenly saw the Tartar hordes as 'the sword of the Lord's anger for the sins of the Christian people', and Batu Khan, their prince, who was leading the drive to the Atlantic, was spoken of as 'the punishing Rod of God' and likened to Attila the Hun.'

As the year drew to its close the extent of the Tartar holocaust became clear. Fear, panic and confusion spread across the continent as reports of the Tartars' unheard-of cruelty and their cold-blooded destruction of innocent millions were being passed from community to community, monastery to monastery, king to king.

Philippe Mousket van Doornik, a Flemish chronicler, wrote:

Et li Tartare fort et rice
Gueroiierent viers Osterrice
Et viers Hungrie derement . . .
Et s'ierent encor li Tataire
Dieu anemi, Dieu aviersaire
En la grant tiere de Roussie
Et voloient destuire Austriie.

('The powerful and strong Tartars/Have fought against Austria/ And against Hungary terribly . . . /And the Tartars/God's enemy, God's adversaries/Moved against the great land of Russia/And wanted to destroy Austria.')

In the New Year the gateway to Western Europe lay wide open, the Tartars having crossed to Austria on the ice of the frozen Danube. Soon they were probing the defences of the well-fortified town of Wiener Neustadt. A heretic French priest called Yvo de Narbonne, who was taking refuge in the Austrian town from the attentions of the papal inquisitor, recorded in a letter to his bishop, Mgr Malemort of Bordeaux, the town's siege and the subsequent remarkable events:

This present Summer, the foresaid Nation, being called Tartars, departing out of Hungarie, which they had surprised by Treason, layd siege unto the very same Towne, wherein I myselfe abode, with many thousands of Soldiers.

Neither were there in the said Towne on our part above 50 men of warre whom, together with 20 Crosse-bowes, the Captaine had left in Garrison. All these, out of certaine high places, beholding the enemies vaste Armie, and abhorring the beastly cruelty of Anti-Christ his accomplices, signified forthwith unto their Governor.

The hideous lamentations of his Christian subjects, who suddenly being surprised in all the Provinces adioyning, without any difference or respect of condition, Fortune, Sexe or Age, were by manifold cruelties, all of them destroyed; with whose carkasses, the Tartarian chieftaines, and their brutish and savage followers, glutting themselves as with delicious cakes, left nothing for vultures but the bare bones. And a strange thing it is to consider that the greedy and ravenous vultures disdained to prey upon any of the reliques which remained.

Old and deformed Women they gave, as it were for daylie sustenance unto their Dog-headed Cannibals; the beautifull devoured they not, but smothered them, lamenting and scritching, with forced and unnatural ravishments. Like barbarous miscreants, they deflowered Virgins until they died of exhaustion, and cutting off their tender Paps to present for dainties unto their chiefs, they engorged themselves with their Bodies.

As suddenly as they came, the Tartars evacuated Central Europe and the heretic French priest lived to tell his tale. Their withdrawal was due to the death of the Great Khan Ogodai in Mongolia, and the ensuing problems of succession, rather than the armed might of a handful of West European princelings, as the monastic chroniclers would have us believe.

In any event, the emboldened Christian forces captured eight Tartar officers near Wiener Neustadt. One of them was recognized by Prince Frederick the Warlike of Austria and identified as an Englishman.

It was an astonishing and staggering discovery, bordering on the unbelievable. Englishmen from the westernmost fringes of Europe were about as likely to be found riding into the heart of our continent with the Asiatic hordes as Moonmen. It was not just that this Englishman came, as it were, from the wrong direction; he was in the most unlikely company. England was a devoutly Christian country and the mainstay of the Holy Roman Church in the time of Henry III. Furthermore, Englishmen were, in the minds of most Europeans, more readily associated with fair service to church, king and country than the cold-blooded destruction of innocent millions. Yet there he was, this native of England, not just dressed like the rest of the bloodthirsty horsemen but one of them.

Prince Frederick's father, Leopold, who was one of the prime movers and central figures of the fifth crusade, knew him from the Holy Land some twenty-four years earlier. But Frederick himself also knew of 'the Englishman', as he became known to those he had negotiated with, as the Tartar Khan's envoy plenipotentiary, personal interpreter and rumoured spy chief in Europe

The Englishman's harsh method of negotiation and his consummate double-dealings lent a sinister ring to his appellation. Neither the princes and kings with whom he had negotiated, nor the chancelleries of Europe, knew his actual name; to his contemporaries he was simply 'the Englishman' who betrayed Christendom, a war criminal.

The first clue as to the identity of this mysterious figure, and how he came to aid with his diplomatic skill the alien hordes bent on the annihilation of Europe, can be found in his crusader background and presence in the Holy Land around 1218, the time of the fifth crusade.

Another pointer is that he must have moved in the highest circles of crusader leadership if his meeting with the Austrian ruler was remembered by the latter's son after twenty-odd years, for princes would hardly have taken much notice of a simple pilgrim.

Although he had every reason to try to protect his anonymity while serving as Batu Khan's all-powerful ambassador, something of his station in England must have been known to the Duke of Austria. Unfortunately, the heretic French priest omitted to record it for posterity.

But he found him interesting enough to devote a whole letter to him, and thus Father Yvo has helped to bring the Englishman to life again over seven centuries later.

That Father Yvo included certain facts related by the Englishman in his letter, while omitting others, seems to be due to his determination to use the Englishman's case to resume communications with his old bishop and to show that he had purged himself of his heresies. In an impassioned plea he urged Bishop Malemort 'to persuade the kings of France, England and Spain, between whom you hold a middle place, by every means in your power, to lay aside all their private quarrels, for ever, or at least for a time, and hold wise and speedy counsel among themselves, how they may be able safely to encounter so many thousands of such savages. For I call to witness the faith of Christ, in which I hope to be saved, that if all are united, they would crush those Tartar monsters or, singly, will be crushed by them.'

The information included in Father Yvo's letter, incomplete, distorted and in part even contradictory, has nevertheless provided a starting point in the quest to piece together the jigsaw of the Englishman's extraordinary career.

After many dead ends and red herring leads in the archives of a dozen European and Asian nations, sufficient original contemporary material could be found to identify the irresistible forces behind his adventures and establish the circumstances that enabled him to bridge the gap between the 'Army of God' and the Mongol hordes, and to serve them both.

These new facts, coupled with the sobering sight of a remarkable individual caught up in the blind forces of destiny, now assure the Englishman a fairer hearing than he received at Wiener Neustadt in 1242.

The Englishman must have realized that his luck had run out at that Austrian town and that his life was not worth a beggar's farthing, as even a full confession could only save a miscreant's soul, not his life, in war-torn thirteenth century Europe.

In making a full confession, supported by 'such oaths and protestations as the Devil himself would have been trusted for', the Englishman must have hoped to achieve something beyond a sporting chance of talking himself out of a very tight spot. Even through the blurred rendering of Father Yvo's tendentious letter, it seems quite clear that what the Englishman was trying to do was to justify his motives and actions in Tartar service and rebut the charges of 'traitor to Christendom'.

Although he must have been eager and willing to talk he was, in accordance with the custom of the time, 'being allured [tortured is a more appropriate word] by the princes to confess the truth about the Tartars. And he, without hesitation, made his statement'.

He began his confession, witnessed by Father Yvo, by admitting that he had been 'perpetually banished from the Realm of England in regard of certain notorious crimes by him committed'.

The Englishman further reported of himself that 'presently after the time of his banishment, namely when he was about 30 years of age', he went to the city of Acre in the Holy Land.

The nature of 'the certain notorious crimes by him committed' was either too complicated or, more likely, seemingly irrelevant to the charges facing the Englishman at Wiener Neustadt, for Father Yvo to bother to write it down. But since perpetual banishment was a favourite method of the kings of England of ridding themselves of dangerous political offenders or high-ranking rebels whose execution would have created more problems than it would have solved, it is reasonably safe to assume that the Englishman belonged to this category. This is corroborated by the instant and harsh justice meted out to ordinary criminals in thirteenth century England.

But the fact that 'presently after the time of his banishment' he went to the city of Acre in the Holy Land provides an even firmer proof of the political nature of his exile, for his arrival in Acre in 1218 coincided with that of the English contingent of the fifth crusade.

A detailed and careful checking of the list of English crusader-pilgrims reveals in their ranks several leaders of the baronial faction which had fought King John and, after his death, his infant son Henry, for a charter of rights, the Magna Carta, and had been excommunicated or perpetually banished after the crushing of the rebellion in 1217.

The only way out for the highest-ranking outlaws and political clerics excommunicated by an implacable papal legate in Henry's camp was a pilgrimage to the Holy Land, which held the promise of a fresh start and the lifting of the excommunication. And this would fully explain the Englishman's presence in Acre in 1218.

After relating a curious incident in the city of Acre and his subsequent expulsion from the ranks of the crusaders, the doubly banished Englishman spoke volubly of his tribulations in the neighbouring Middle Eastern countries.

His saving grace, it appears, was his extraordinary gift for languages. Even Father Yvo admitted, however grudgingly, that the Englishman was 'somewhat acquainted with letters', a rare attribute among the roistering barons of England.

Father Yvo quoted the Englishman as stating that 'in Chaldea he began to commend to writing those words which he heard spoken, and within a short space of time so aptly to pronounce and utter them himself that he was reputed for a native of that country; and by the same dexterity he attained to many languages'.

As it transpires from the Englishman's confession, this gift for mastering foreign tongues and speaking them like a native attracted the attention of Tartar spies gathering intelligence on the weaknesses and rivalries of Christendom. The Tartar agents appear to have been on the look-out for well-educated people that their nomadic civilization could not produce. The Englishman, with his flair for languages and knowledge of the political intricacies of Western Europe, would have been just the sort of person the Tartar Khan's chancellery needed most.

'The Tartars, having intelligence of him by their spies, drew him perforce into their society . . . They allured him by many rewards to their faithful service, by reason that they wanted interpreters,' recalled Father Yvo.

This new phase in the bizarre life of the Englishman was justified to his interrogators with the claim that the 'Tartars drew him perforce into their society' and, having had little choice, he 'served them faithfully' due in no small part to the 'many rewards' of his new masters.

His dramatic break with Christendom resulted in a long and arduous journey to Karakorum, the seat of Mongol power, where no European had been before. He preceded Marco Polo by over half a century, yet the account of the Venetian's travel to the court of the Great Khan alone has assured him a fine place in Europe's hall of fame, while the Englishman has been completely forgotten.

During his interrogation he must have been told not to waste time on irrelevant details of his journey, or possibly Father Yvo could see no advantage in including them in his letter. After all, the heretic French priest was concerned with weightier issues. Furthermore, at a time when, crusaders apart, most Europeans hardly ventured beyond the confines of their parishes there was not much interest in travels literally beyond the ends of the world. So it was left to this present inquiry to follow in the Englishman's footsteps and, on the strength of freshly unearthed documentary evidence, fill in the missing details.

Father Yvo's account of the confession contains a vital pointer to the Englishman's rapid rise in Mongol service and the devastating use he made of his power during his diplomatic missions nearly two decades later:

This fellow, on the behalf of the most tyrannical King of the Tartars, had been twice, as an Envoy and Interpreter, with the King of Hungary, menacing and plainly foretelling those mischiefs which happened afterwards, unless the King would submit himself and his kingdom unto the Tartar yoke.

Extant contemporary documents confirm that between 1238 and 1240 King Béla IV of Hungary had repeatedly been visited by a Tartar ambassador who had threatened and cajoled him, demanding his unconditional surrender. Béla, the proud ruler of a then powerful Christian kingdom imbued with a strong proselytising zeal, simply ignored the communications of the heathen Tartars and lived to regret it.

But more significantly, the Englishman admitted in his confession to have headed those embassies. Apart from the surprising intelligence that he also spoke Hungarian, this reveals more about his position in Tartar service than the rest of his confession put together.

It shows that the Englishman was not a mere interpreter, as he had started off at the time of his recruitment, but a fully fledged envoy plenipotentiary. An examination of the names of sixty Mongol ambassadors* who respresented the will of the khans in Eastern Europe between the middle of the thirteenth and four-teenth centuries reveals that this post was reserved—with only two exceptions—for Mongols and other ethnic Central Asians, emphasizing the honour and trust bestowed on the Englishman by Batu Khan.

Who then was this mysterious Englishman who lived by his wits in an alien world, managed to overcome with surprising ease great adversities, and used his position so callously to deceive and destroy dozens of unwary nations? For as he himself admitted of the Tartar negotiating ploys, 'by these fictions, they [the Mongols] prevailed upon some simple kings to make a treaty with them, and those princes perished all the same'.

To identify him and unmask his self-imposed incognito after 736 years of protecting anonymity, it was necessary to look more closely into the causes and circumstances of his banishment from England.

A critical look at the barons' fight against King John's despotic rule has helped to place in the right social and political context the Englishman's 'crime'. And by delving into the original materials amassed by chroniclers, 'who all lived when the King reigned, and

* See pages 141–3.

wrote for that time what they saw, or heard credibly reported', as one of them put if, it became possible to retrace his steps and establish the truth about the Englishman.

TWO

King John's tyranny

ENGLAND in the second decade of the thirteenth century—the formative years of the Englishman's early manhood, when he took his first political steps—was a country rent by the intense passions aroused by the controversy between King John and the barons over their rights.

It was a country of startling contrasts: there were mighty lords and impoverished serfs, disaffected barons and reformist clerics, influential Templars and orthodox scholastic monks; and on the throne one of the worst kings in English history.

Apart from the barons seeking the restoration of their ancient rights, there were also other stresses and new ideas at work in English society, challenging the very framework of medieval life and hastening the show-down between King and barons. Although overlaid by contemporary cant, the chief source of these new ideas were the burghers of London and other trade centres, and the reformist clerics harbouring a new brand of national consciousness in their attitude to Rome.

These reformist clerics held that the Pope, Innocent III, had no right to meddle in the lay affairs of kings or the government of nations like England, and insisted that 'the Lord had conferred on St Peter nothing except the power over the church and church property'.

Since parallel with the King's battle against his barons there was an interlinking conflict between the King and Pope Innocent III, who was trying to reduce the English monarch to a mere vassal of Rome, the ideas of the clerics espousing the separation of the Rome-led church from the English state fell on fertile ground.

Early notions of royal absolutism had been propounded,

centuries ahead of other states in Europe. Thanks to the meticulous notes of Roger of Wendover, the monastic chronicler of the time, the 'iniquitous preachings' on the subject of one reformist cleric called Master* Alexander, surnamed Mason, have survived.

As a privileged counsel of King John in the years of papal interdict, this 'pseudo-theologist', as Wendover calls him, suggested to King John that 'a king was the rod of God, and has been made a prince in order to rule his people and others subject to him with a rod of iron, and to break them all "like a potter's vessel", to bind those in power with shackles, and his nobles with manacles of iron . . . By these and other fallacies he so gained the King's favour that he obtained several benefices which had been taken from religious men by the said King's violence'.

Theories on separating church and state and absolute monarchs were one thing, the actual exercise of power another. After thirteen years on the throne of Englard King John's rule was arousing growing anger and resentment throughout the country.

With his despotic rule, crushing taxes, corrupt administration and employment of foreign officers he had alienated all estates, and the exactions and usurpations of the Crown and ill-treatment of peasantry had broadened the opposition.

As the year 1212 was drawing to its end John was embroiled in a three-cornered fight—with the Pope and the highest echelons of the English church which remained true to Rome; with the French king; and with the powerful barons of the realm. Having made common cause with Otto, the Holy Roman Emperor, to crush France, the Pope's faithful ally, the fortunes of war in Germany and France shattered his hopes of destroying both the Pope and Philip Augustus at once.

Yet the loss of his continental dominions was the least of his troubles. The papal interdict, in effect, had freed the barons of England from their allegiance to him and, in January 1213, Pope Innocent ordered King Philip of France to embark on a crusade 'for the benefit of his soul' and expel John from England and assume the English crown for ever.

A poor tactician and strategist, John had hopelessly under-

---

* The title 'Master', or 'Magister', was used in medieval times to denote exceptional learning.

estimated the powers arrayed against him. In his hour of need he tried to conciliate the oppressed population by a series of measures which he hoped would at least regain the allegiance of the ordinary people and isolate the barons.

He checked the harshness of the forest courts, forbade the extortions practised by his officials on merchants and pilgrims, and even began 'showing mercy on widows'.

King John, being in great straits [wrote the contemporary chronicler Matthew of Westminster] wished to turn the miseries which he had incurred by his own guilt on those who had sought to restrain his madness.

And he began to accuse first one, and then the other, of his nobles of treason, calling them jealous, miserable wittols, whose wives—as he used to boast—he had raped and whose daughters he had deflowered.

Among others, he began to insult beyond measure Robert FitzWalter with reproaches and threats, and he endeavoured to destroy his London castle, namely Baynards Castle, on the Monday which was the feast of St Hilary, by stirring up enemies against him in London.

He certainly had a penchant for violating the wives, marriageable daughters and sisters of his barons, as at least three contemporary monastic scribes greatly concerned with the sexual activities of the royal couple recorded. His second wife, Isabella of Angoulême, 'an incestuous, evilly disposed adulterous woman who was hateful to him and who hated him', appears to have carried on in the same manner.

'Of these crimes', Roger of Wendover wrote, 'she had been often found guilty, on which the King ordered her lovers to be seized and strangled with a rope on her marital bed.'

The King's sexual excesses, however infuriating, could hardly have goaded the barons of the realm into open revolt as suggested by the celibate chroniclers, with an understandable tendency to place undue emphasis on the evils of the flesh.

The rapes could just conceivably have acted as the proverbial straw that broke the camel's back if there had not been other, more weighty reasons for the barons' disaffection, such as John's habit of dispossessing his barons to satisfy his own greed and fill the perennially empty exchequer.* Many barons would, no doubt, have put up with dishonour, but hardly any would have been prepared to contemplate with equanimity the 'unjust exactions which reduced them to extreme poverty', as Roger of Wendover wrote. 'Other nobles again, whose parents and kindred he had exiled, turned against him because he converted their inheritances to his own uses; thus the King's enemies were as numerous as his nobles.'

In any event, his disastrous quarrel with the Pope was, after his continental defeats, beginning to rally all his enemies at home in a united front, playing into the hands of the barons who had merely awaited a suitable opportunity to rise against the unrestrained despot on the throne.

The King's two harsh nicknames give the measure of the man as seen by his contemporaries. Behind his back he was called 'John Soft-Sword', as a judgement of his achievements on the battle field, and 'John Lackland', as a pitiable ruler, because 'by his cruelties and oppressions, and various fornications and injuries, he lost the following territories: first of all, the Duchy of Normandy, the county of Blois, the counties of Maine, Anjou, Poitou, Limousin, Auvergne and Angoulême.'

While moving with his army against the rebellious Welsh, he learnt that, abetted by the Pope's absolution from allegiance to him, his barons were plotting to seize him. Fearing for his life he quickly disbanded his troops and moved back with his foreign mercenaries to London.

---

* King John was not squeamish in his sources of revenue and he extorted money without prejudice from nobles, commoners and peasants. Roger of Wendover describes how on one occasion, when the King needed money urgently, he compelled the Jews to pay a heavy ransom. 'By the King's order, all the Jews throughout England, of both sexes, were seized, imprisoned and severely tortured in order to do the King's will with their money.

'Some of them then after being tortured gave up all they had and promised more, that they might thus escape; one of this sect at Bristol, even after being dreadfully tortured, still refused to ransom himself out or to put an end to his sufferings, on which the King ordered his officers to knock out one of his cheek-teeth daily until he paid 10,000 marks of silver to him. After they had for seven days knocked out a tooth each day with great agony to the Jew, and had begun the same operation on the eighth day, the said Jew, reluctant as he was to provide the King with the required money, gave the said sum to save his eighth tooth, although he had already lost seven.'

He then demanded hostages from his barons in order to establish who would and who would not obey him, and thus find out the names of those involved in the conspiracy. Virtually all the nobles of England sent sons, daughters or other relations as hostages; but Robert FitzWalter and Eustace de Vesci apparently thought it safer to flee the country. King John condemned the two to perpetual exile and, as the monk Ralph of Coggeshall* recorded, he 'demolished the castles and seized the estates' of the outlaws.

The baron Robert FitzWalter thus became the central figure in the country's fight against the despotic King, although there were many barons involved in the conspiracy.

Roger of Wendover indicates the wide ramifications of this first plot against King John. When FitzWalter fled to France, the barons sent with him 'a paper, sealed with the seals of each of the aforesaid nobles, to the King of France, telling him that he might safely come to England, take possession of the kingdom—as suggested by the Pope—and be crowned with all the honour and dignity.'

Seeing a marvellous opportunity to invade England with papal blessing, the French king ordered his nobles to assemble with their retainers at Rouen at Easter 1213, fully armed and their horses well shod for battle.

He also ordered huge stores of corn, meat, wine and other supplies to be loaded into his ships, and requisitioned all other available vessels to carry provisions for the invasion army.

Because some of his barons and knights were rather slow in taking up arms to fight in England, he announced that those who failed to join his army should be publicly branded as cowards and be persecuted on a charge of treason. These threats produced the desired effect and soon Philip had a large army awaiting his signal to sail for England.

The Pope, meanwhile, wrote to knights, nobles and other men-at-arms in Western Europe to take the cross and follow King Philip 'and thus revenge the insult which had been cast on the universal church. He also ordered that all those who afforded money or personal assistance in overthrowing the contumacious English King should, like those who went to the Holy Land to visit

* *Chronicon Anglicarum*

the Lord's Sepulchre, remain secure under the protection of the Church, as regards their property, persons and spiritual interests.'

In the face of his total isolation in the country and the impending French invasion, John had no option but to go down on his bended knees and humbly beg for Pope Innocent's forgiveness. Defeat and ignominy were staring him in the face, but he was very lucky.

Pope Innocent was not interested in having England crushed, like his tool, King Philip of France, but to force it back into the Rome-led European spiritual community. And so Pandulf, the ironfisted Papal Legate, was despatched to England with a secret peace formula.

John met Pandulf in May 1213 at the Templars' Ewell House, near Dover, and accepted unconditionally all Pope Innocent's demands. He promised to make full reparations to the church for the confiscated property, and receive in full honour all the pro-Rome bishops he had banished. But what appears to have galled him most was that the Pope had made, as a supplementary condition, the restoration of all the rights and estates of Robert FitzWalter and Eustace de Vesci, who had succeeded in convincing the Pope that all their tribulations were due to their unflinching loyalty to Rome.

Having become absolutely obsessed by his desire to crush his rebellious barons, and FitzWalter first and foremost, he accepted with seeming good grace this extra condition.

But the bitterest pill was yet to come. Pandulf, determined to exact his pound of flesh, ordered John to resign the crowns of England and Ireland and to receive them back from his hands as the Pope's fiefs, and the King accepted even this exorbitant price to win the Pope's support for his fight against the hated barons. John 'granted and freely surrendered to God and his Apostles Peter and Paul, to the Holy Mother Church of Rome, and to Pope Innocent and his successors the whole realm of England and the whole realm of Ireland, with all rights thereunto appertaining, to receive them back and hold them thenceforth as a feudatory of God and the Roman Church.'

He then swore fealty to the Pope for both realms and pledged *all his successors* to a like engagement. He also undertook, most humiliatingly, to pay the Holy See a yearly tribute of 1,000 marks.

But his ignominious submission to Rome brought him only a

brief respite, for things had gone too far for a reconciliation with his barons.

With the French invasion stopped by the Pope, King John began to plan his revenge on his enemies, but this time he appeared determined to take them on singly. In 1214 he planned to launch an attack in Poitou to recover some of his lands and he demanded feudal service from his barons. But the northern barons refused to serve, and when he issued writs for the collection of scutage of three marks per fee, the northern barons also refused to pay.

The ill-timed demand for scutage provided his barons with the long-awaited opportunity to challenge John openly. This latest infringement of their rights was so blatant in their eyes as to justify, if need be, a resort to arms.

For the barons claimed that in the days of Richard the Lion Heart, and of King Henry I, there was the accepted and commonly observed notion that the obligation to foreign service—and therefore the payment of scutage for war—did not form part of the regular obligations of barons. In short, they insisted that they were not bound legally to serve in, or pay for, any war apart from the defence of the realm.

John, however, demanded that they pay scutage for war 'because it always used to be done' in his father's and brother's days.

The barons' fight against the unwarranted increase in feudal obligations was, in its intention, a fight for class privileges and feudal immunities. But luckily for them, and England, their struggle for the restoration of their lapsed rights coincided in part with the legal interests of the commons, and by rising against a thoroughly rotten despotic ruler they served the common good of the country.

Yet the barons of England were, to a man, descendants of the Normans who helped William to conquer the country. But in the intervening century and a half they had lost all interest in Normandy; they had become English landowners and their interests were in some respects closer to the burgeoning new class of commons than to their feudal lord, the king, with estates on both sides of the Channel.

So when John demanded of them to perform their feudal service to help recover his lands from the clutches of the French king, they were not prepared either to fight or to pay for John's continental

war. Stupidly, he carried on with his Poitou campaign despite his
barons' desertion, and on 27 July 1214, the French king inflicted a
humiliating defeat on John's rag-tag mercenary army at Bouvines.

A document, drawn up by the barons as the clash of interest
with the King was drifting towards an open civil war, shows a
strong nationalistic streak in the justification of their stand and
their condemnation of John's surrender of England to the Pope:

> Woe to you, John, last of the kings, detested one of the chiefs of
> England, disgrace to the English nobility! Alas! England,
> England, till now chief of provinces in all kinds of wealth, thou
> art laid under tribute [to Rome]; subject not only to fire, famine
> and the sword, but to the rule of ignoble slaves and foreigners,
> something which no slavery can be worse.
>
> We read that many other kings, yea, and princes, have
> contended even to the death for the liberty of their land which
> was in subjection; but you, John, of sad memory to future ages,
> have designed and made it your business to enslave your
> country, which has been free from times of old and, that you
> might drag others with you into slavery, like the serpent who
> dragged down half the host of Heaven, have in the first place
> oppressed yourself.
>
> You have, from a free king, become a tributary, a steward
> and a vassal of slavery; you have bound by a perpetual slavery
> this noble land, which will never be freed from the servile
> shackles unless through the compassion of Him who may at
> some time deign to free us and the whole world, whom the old
> servitude retains under the yoke of sin.

This passionate plea for the freedom of England did not,
however, prevent the barons from making common cause with the
King of France and from offering the crown of England to his son,
Louis.

If the Khan's Englishman was one of these idealistic but not too
scrupulous barons—as his exalted acquaintances in the Holy Land
after his banishment would allow one to surmise—his subsequent
actions were prompted by these strongly held views of his noble
faction. But even if he was one of the political clerics or prominent
burghers of London who came to back the barons' fight, he must
have shared their strong ideological motivation.

And this helps to establish a clear cause-and-effect relationship between the struggle for England's charter of rights and the perpetual banishment of the Englishman.

Since all the threads of the barons' rebellion lead to Robert FitzWalter and he was throughout in the vanguard of the fight, the fate of FitzWalter and the Englishman became, as it will be shown, closely linked in the crucial years of the civil war and the ensuing period of retribution.

THREE

John's hare-brained scheme

KING JOHN, having submitted his crown and country to Rome in the hope of unstinted papal support for his fight against the barons, became quickly disillusioned with the Pope and gave clear indications that he regretted his action.

To be a tribute-paying vassal of Rome was not a position for the King of England. He began to cast about and seek 'to release himself from the fetters of the peace in which he had involved himself. He was truly sorry that he had been led to give his consent to the aforesaid peace.' But there seemed to be no way out.

Pope Innocent, who found on his accession Christendom divided and its states revolving around different orbits, soon made the Holy See the sole centre towards which all states of Western and south Central Europe gravitated. There seemed to be nothing outside the confines of the Rome-led community but ignominy and defeat.

In his desperation, John embarked on an ominous gamble, which could have had more dramatic effects on the course of English history than the loss of the wars against Napoleon and Hitler put together: he decided to embrace Islam and turn England into a Muslim country.

This virtually forgotten episode of English history was dutifully recorded by Matthew Paris in his Latin *Chronica Major*, and there is little reason to question its veracity because he heard it, as it were, straight from the horse's mouth—from the confidants of one of the envoys entrusted by John to put his hare-brained scheme into effect.

Paris was probably one of the greatest historians of the Middle Ages, well informed, full of curiosity and with a keen eye for the significant and picturesque.

Although a monk of St Albans monastery, he was a courtier and a man of the world; he was also a notable scholar, with strong likes and political biases. But his independent judgement was sound and his integrity unquestionable. He took great pains, like any good newspaper reporter, to get his facts from eye-witnesses.

King John's son, Henry III, is known to have contributed many items of invaluable information to him, and the close link between St Albans and the court enabled him to get as much first-hand news from envoys' reports and royal despatches about continental affairs as of home events.

His strong disapproval of the King's misgovernment and the Pope's greed, two of the constantly recurring themes in his chronicles, come out very clearly in the report on John's attempt to convert England, lock, stock and barrel, to Islam.

According to Matthew Paris, in 1213* the desperate John sent a secret mission to Mohammed al-Nassir, the very powerful Emir of Morocco (he uses the emir's name in its Latin form of Murmelius) with an offer of homage and tribute.

His envoys were the knights Thomas Hardington and Ralph FitzNicholas, and a very surprising third member of this secret embassy was Master Robert, a cleric of London. There is no explanation in Paris's chronicle for the inclusion of a Catholic priest in the delicate mission of turning England into a Muslim country, and the only likely reason is that he was charged by the King, on the strength of his diplomatic acumen, to ensure that the envoys carried out his instructions faithfully and did not double-cross him. It is a conjecture that has been borne out by the King's attitude to Master Robert after the failure of the embassy, and also by other circumstantial evidence gathered in the painstaking work of identifying Batu Khan's English diplomat.

The envoys were instructed by John to tell 'the great king of Africa, Morocco and Spain that he would voluntarily give up to him himself and his kingdom, and if he pleased would hold it as

---

* Matthew Paris in his *Chronica Major* puts this mission after John's attempt at reconciliation with Pope Innocent and his subsequent disenchantment with Rome. But Thomas Walsingham, the fourteenth century compiler of the *Gesta Abbatum S. Albani*, which is based in part on the 'supplementary' material Paris decided not to include in his *Chronica Major* for fear of overloading it, gives the date of the embassy as some time during the Interdict, that is in 1212. But the whole drift of events and logic of action would confirm the correctness of the dating of the contemporary *Chronica Major*—1213.

tributary from him; and that he would also abandon the Christian faith, which he considered false, and would faithfully adhere to the law of Mohammed.'

With characteristic improvidence he also pledged his support for the Moorish king's planned final assault to wrest the whole of Spain from the King of Aragon.

These messengers on behalf of their lord, the King of England, saluted the [Moorish] king with reverence, and fully explained the reason of their coming, at the same time handing him their king's letter, which an interpreter, who came at a summons from the [Moorish] king, explained to him.

When he understood its purport, the king . . . closed the book he had been looking at, for he was seated at his desk studying. At length, after deliberating as it were for a time with himself, he modestly replied: 'I was just now looking at the book of a wise Greek and a Christian named Paul, which is written in Greek, and his deeds and words please me much; one thing, however, concerning him displeases me, and that is that he did not stand firm to the faith in which he was born, but turned to another like a deserter and a waverer.

'And I say this with regard to your lord, the king of the English, who abandons the most pious and pure law of the Christians under which he was born, and desires, fickle and unstable that he is, to come over to our faith'.

After this somewhat surprising soliloquy in the defence of Christian religion and against religious inconstancy, the Moorish king began to probe for a motive behind John's desire to opt out of the Christian community. He asked searching questions about conditions in England, the state of the realm and the disposition of its people.

Thomas Hardington, described as the most eloquent of the envoys and the nominal head of the embassy, sketched with oratorial skill the richness of its soil, the fertility of its fields and the skills of its people. Englishmen, he told the Emir proudly, were handsome, ingenious and experts in every liberal and mechanical pursuit.

They all spoke three languages—Latin, French and English— and could produce by smelting all kinds of metals from ore found in the land.

He gave brief but succinct summary of the traditional role of anointed kings in governing England and spoke at some length about the freedom-loving people of the country who acknowledge the domination of no one but God.

Carried away perhaps by his own eloquence, he launched into a long discourse emphasizing his countrymen's devotion to Christianity and the great store they set by their religion. 'Our church and the services of our religion are more venerated there than in any part of the world, and it is peacefully governed by the laws of the Pope and the King.'*

It was an oration that ran directly counter to the purpose of the embassy, and the level-headed reply of the Moorish ruler duly reflected the doubts aroused by Thomas Hardington over the feasibility of converting such a deeply religious Christian country to Islam.

After a typically Muslim appraisal of John's manliness and wordly chances, the Emir refused the King's offer to convert England to Islam and bring it into the Arab orbit.

Your king, he told the ambassadors, was a petty monarch, senseless and growing old. He was a man of no consequence quite unworthy of any alliance with a Muslim ruler like himself.

He justified his decision by pointing out the weakest link in John's foolish plan:

I never read or heard that any king possessing such a prosperous kingdom subject and obedient to him, would voluntarily ruin his sovereignty by making tributary a country that is free, by giving to a stranger that which is his own, by turning happiness to misery, and thus giving himself up to the will of another, conquered, as it were, without a wound.

I have rather read and heard from many that they would procure liberty for themselves at the expense of streams of blood, which is a praiseworthy action; but now I hear that your wretched lord, a sloth and a coward, who is even worse than nothing, wishes from a free man to become a slave, who is the most wretched of all human beings.

---

* The remark that England was jointly ruled by the laws of the Pope and King John reaffirms the assumption that the embassy took place after John's surrender to Rome and the lifting of the papal interdict.

With these words he dismissed King John's envoys, telling Thomas Hardington and Ralph FitzNicholas never to let him set eyes on them again, 'for the infamy of that foolish apostate, your master, breathes forth a most foul stench to my nostrils'.

As King John's humiliated ambassadors were leaving, the Emir noticed Master Robert, the London cleric, the third member of the embassy who never uttered throughout the audience and stood at a distance from the other two envoys.

He was, in the words of the patently biased St Albans chronicler of the episode, a small dark man, with one arm longer than the other and misshapen fingers, 'and with a face like a Jew'. His cowl and tonsure revealed, however, that he was a Catholic priest and this made the Emir wonder why he should have been chosen to conduct such a delicate negotiation. Since Master Robert was 'a contemptible looking person', the Emir felt that he must be very clever indeed to have been included in the embassy, and ordered the guards to bring him back.

The details of his long, private conversation with the Emir he related to his St Albans friends after the embassy's return to England, and Matthew Paris recorded them for posterity.

At the start of their conversation the Emir cautioned him to answer all his questions truthfully, for if he were to tell just one lie, he would never believe a Christian priest again.

What the Emir wanted to know most of all was whether King John was a man of moral integrity and a ruler worthy of the title.

The London priest, mindful that the reputation of his faith and vocation depended upon the truthfulness of his reply, told the Emir the unvarnished truth about John's reign. John was a tyrant rather than a king, and a destroyer rather than a governor, who oppressed his own people and 'acted as a trusted friend to aliens'.

In Master Robert's words, John was 'a lion to his own subjects and a lamb to foreigners and those who fought against him'. But worse still, he was an insatiable extorter of money, a ruler who would invade the lands and take away the possessions of his subjects on the flimsiest of pretexts.

In his religion he was wavering and unreliable, and as a warlord he was slothful and acted as if 'he was eager to lose the kingdom of England or destroy it'.

The Emir was appalled. On learning that John had not even sired many sons and that he had no redeeming features, he wondered aloud why the wretched English allowed such a man to lord over them. They must be very servile and soft, he concluded.

But Master Robert disagreed most vehemently and firmly defended his countrymen. 'The English are the most patient of men until they are offended and injured beyond endurance', he told the Emir. 'But now, like a lion or an elephant, when he feels himself hurt or sees his own blood, they are enraged and are proposing and endeavouring, although late, to shake the yoke of the oppressor from their necks.'

After his passionate defence of the English, the private audience came to an end. The Emir gave the London priest costly presents of gold, silver and silks and parted with him on friendly terms. But the Moroccan ruler gave no gifts to John's two other envoys and even refused to say farewell to them.

Upon the embassy's return to England, King John 'wept with bitterness at being balked in his purpose'. Yet instead of punishing his candid Master Robert, whose inopportune frankness had sealed the fate of the mission, he heaped presents and honours on him, greatly in excess of the rewards he grudgingly gave his two other envoys.

'By way of reward, this wicked extortioner bestowed on Master Robert the charge of the abbacy of St Albans, although it was not vacant, so that this transgressor of faith remunerated his own clerk with the property of another', the St Albans chronicler bewailed.

Robert's harsh stewardship at St Albans and alleged turning to his own use 'everything which was then in the church and convent', earned him the undying enmity of the monks, including the chronicler's.

This hostility against the stranger who 'cheated the house of more than a thousand marks' is reflected in Paris's biased physical description of Master Robert. Yet the Emir's quoted surprise at why such 'a contemptible looking person' should be sent to manage such a difficult diplomatic business shows Paris's own bafflement about Robert's actual role in the attempted conversion of England, and his true political colours.

What is clear is that Robert was John's 'own clerk' and that the king must have been certain that he would serve his political purpose faithfully and without compunction, something he could not be certain of in the case of the other two envoys of knightly rank.

In the event, the two knights acted mostly according to their brief, while Master Robert did the opposite and, in the course of his secret talk with the Moorish king, assured the failure of the King's hare-brained scheme.

It is, of course, perfectly possible that this change of heart occurred when the Emir charged him to tell the truth about John as befitting a Christian and a priest, but it is rather unlikely, particularly in view of John's generous gifts to Robert upon the failed embassy's return to England.

As even Paris felt obliged to note, Master Robert was 'a wise and clever man' and an accomplished diplomat who 'well understood that business'. His sensitive antennae could not have missed the tidal wave of anti-John sentiment in 1214 and it must have dawned on him that he was, with the King, on a losing wicket.

A judicious 'revelation' that it was he who, during his secret talks with the Arab ruler, thwarted John's plan to convert England to Islam, would, he must have felt, help him to build bridges to the barons' camp led by Robert FitzWalter, who had close ties and a festering feud with St Albans.

This would perfectly explain his sudden frankness with 'some of the chief servants of the abbot, and a monk at St Albans, namely Laurence, knight and seneschal, and Master Walter, a monk and a painter. And them he kept as familiars, to whom he showed his jewels and other secret presents from the emir, and related what had passed between them, in the hearing of Matthew, who has written and related these events.'

But what was of even greater significance to Master Robert was that the barons and their high-ranking priestly backers came to hear about his embassy and of his role in the sinking of John's planned Arab alliance.

So when John de Cell, the temporary abbot, bribed the King with 700 silver marks to have Master Robert of London and his minions at the monastery removed from St Albans, the King's former cleric crossed over to the barons' side expecting a friendly welcome and a suitable position in the entourage of their leader, Robert FitzWalter.

Master Robert's proven diplomatic skills, his untroubled switching of allegiance and political unscrupulousness, and his actions in the Magna Carta rebellion make him a plausible candidate for the Englishman.

FOUR

FitzWalter's fight for a charter

ON 25 AUGUST 1213, groups of richly dressed nobles rode through the hot and dusty streets of London. The jangling of their retainers' arms and the clatter of their great horses on the rough paving stones roused the dogs and scattered the scratching hens.

Bishops in their fine habits, accoutred with red sashes, rich abbots in expensive garb followed the barons. Priors and deacons made their way across London without the ostentation of their superiors' cavalcades. Both the barons and the churchmen of the kingdom were assembling at St Paul's at the invitation of Archbishop Stephen Langton of Canterbury, the bane of King John's life.

The King hated the stern archbishop for his meddling in lay affairs, acting as it were as a self-appointed conscience of the country, and because his opposition to Stephen's appointment, instead of his own nominee, to Canterbury had brought upon England, and himself, the papal excommunication.

'The king hated like viper's poison all the men of noble birth in the kingdom', according to Wendover, 'and especially Robert FitzWalter, Sayer de Quency and Stephen Archbishop of Canterbury'. It was an all-consuming hatred of paranoid proportions.

The ostensible reason for the St Paul's gathering was to ease the ban on church services, in view of John's reconciliation with Pope Innocent, before the formal lifting of the interdict. It was a meeting that the King could hardly construe as yet another plot against his person, the more so as Archbishop Langton duly granted permission for the priests of England 'to chant services of the church in a low voice, in the hearing of their parishioners'.

However, the King was suspicious, and for once not without foundation. The Archbishop's true purpose in calling the meeting was to hearten the baronial opposition and to reassure them that, in fact, King John's absolution was conditional on a promise of good government.

Wendover, quoting 'reports' from what today would be described as 'conference sources', recorded that the Archbishop 'called some of the nobles aside to him and conversed privately with them'. In these conversations, it seems, he tried to channel the barons' grievances and seething rebelliousness into a legal framework. Since the kings of England customarily made their solemn pledges to their subjects by charters, the Archbishop naturally enough turned to an earlier charter as a constitutional safeguard against King John's abuses.

'A charter of Henry, the first king of England [made at his coronation in 1100], has just been found', he told the barons. 'On the basis of this you may, if you wish, recall your long-lost rights and your former condition.

'And placing a paper in the midst of them, he ordered it to be read aloud for all to hear:

'Henry by the grace of God king of England, to Hugh de Boclande justiciary of England, and all his faithful subjects, as well French as English, in Hertfordshire, greeting. Know that I by the Lord's mercy, have been crowned king by common consent of the barons of the kingdom of England; and because the kingdom has been oppressed by unjust exactions, I, out of respect to God, and the love which I feel towards you, in the first place constitute the holy church of God a free church, so that I will not sell it, nor farm it out, nor will I, on the death of any archbishop, bishop, or abbat, take anything from the domain of the church or its people, until his successor takes his place. And I from this time do away with all the evil practices, by which the kingdom of England is now unjustly oppressed, and these evil practices I here in part mention. If any baron, earl, or other subject of mine, who holds possession from me, shall die, his heir shall not redeem his land, as was the custom in my father's time, but shall pay a just and lawful relief for the same; and in like manner, too, the dependants of my barons shall pay a like relief for their land to their lords. And if any baron or other subject of mine shall wish to give his daughter, his sister, his niece, or other female relative, in marriage, let him ask my permission on the matter; but I will not take any of his property for granting my permission, nor will I forbid his giving her in marriage except he wishes to give her to an enemy of mine; and if on the death of a baron or other subject of mine, the daughter is left heiress, I, by the advice of my barons, will give her in marriage together with her land; and if on the death of a husband the wife is surviving and is childless, she shall have her dowry for a marriage portion, and I will not give her away to another husband unless with her consent; but if a wife survives, having children, she shall have her dowry as a marriage portion, as long as she shall keep herself according to law, and I will not give her to a husband unless with her consent; and the guardian of the children's land shall be either the wife, or some other nearer relation, who ought more rightly to be so; and I enjoin on my barons to act in the same way towards the sons and daughters and wives of their dependants. Moreover the common monetage, as taken throughout the cities and counties, such as was not in use in king Edward's time, is hereby forbidden; and if any one, whether a coiner or any other person, be taken with false money, let strict justice be done to him for it. All pleas and all debts, which were due to the king my brother, I forgive, except my farms, and those debts which were contracted for the inheritances of others, or for those things which more justly belong to others. And if any one shall have covenanted anything for his inheritance, I forgive it, and all reliefs which were contracted for just inheritances. And if any baron or subject of mine shall be ill, I hereby ratify all such disposition as he shall have made of his money; but if through service in war or sickness he shall have made no disposition of his money, his wife, or children, or parents, and legitimate dependants, shall distribute it for the good of his soul, as shall seem best to them. If any baron or other subject of mine shall have made forfeiture, he shall not give bail to save his money, as was done in the time of my father and my brother, but according to the degree of forfeiture; nor shall he make amends for his fault as he did in the time of my father or of my other ancestors; and if any one shall be convicted of treason or other crime, his punishment shall be according to his fault. I forgive all murders committed previous to the day on which I was crowned king; but those which have been since committed, shall be justly punished, according to the law of king Edward. By the common advice of my barons, I have retained the forests in my possession as my father held them. All knights, moreover, who hold their lands by service, are hereby allowed to have their domains free from all amercements and from all peculiar service, that as they are thus relieved from a great burden, they may provide themselves properly with horses and arms, so that they may be fit and ready for my service and for the defence of my kingdom. I bestow confirmed peace in all my kingdom, and I order it to be preserved from henceforth. I restore to you the law of king Edward, with the amendments which my father, by the advice of his barons, made in it. If any one has taken anything of mine, or of any one else's property, since the death of my brother king William, let it all be soon restored without alteration; and if any one shall retain anything of it, he shall, on being discovered, atone to me for it heavily. Witness Maurice bishop of London, William elect of Winchester, Gerard of Hereford, earl Henry, earl Simon, earl Walter Gifford, Robert de Montfort, Roger Bigod, and many others.'

When the barons grasped the drift of the Archbishop's thoughts and the purport of the ancient charter, they swore to seize the first opportunity 'to fight for their rights and, if necessary, die for them'. On his part, Archbishop Langton promised them his assistance 'as far as it lay in his power'.

When King John returned to England after his disastrous defeat in the Poitou campaign in the autumn of 1214, he found that all classes and every opponent of his cruel despotic rule had made common cause in his absence and formulated their grievances. The barons' challenge was rapidly becoming a national cause.

A final meeting between the barons and King, engineered to avoid civil war, turned out to be a waste of time. A resort to arms now seemed inevitable.

On 4 November 1214, the leading barons and Archbishop Langton met in great secrecy at (Bury) St Edmund. By common acclaim they agreed to withdraw their fealty from John.

'All, therefore, assembled in the church of St Edmund', writes Wendover, 'and commencing from those of the highest rank, they all swore on the great altar that, if the king refused to grant their liberties and laws, they themselves would . . . make war on him, till he should by a charter under his own seal, confirm to them everything they required'.

One of the first to take the oath was Robert FitzWalter and his newly appointed chaplain, Master Robert.

The barons gave the King till after Christmas to comply with their demands. In the intervening period they prudently armed themselves and their followers to secure their rights by might if, as they suspected, the King should break his solemn oath.

John too prepared for war. But apart from recruiting an army, he worked out a clever stratagem based, according to the St Albans chronicler, on Pope Innocent's greed. For 'he knew, and had learnt by manifold experience, that the Pope was beyond all men ambitious and proud, and an insatiable thirster after money, and ready and apt to perform any sin for a reward or the promise of one'.

He therefore sent envoys to Rome with a large sum of money and verbal assurances that he would always be a humble subject and tributary of the Holy See. The envoys then promised further sums of money on condition that, if and when a suitable opportunity arose, the Holy Father should excommunicate the barons of England and humiliate the Archbishop of Canterbury.

It was a *quid pro quo* offer, perhaps not too subtle, but one that promised good results. John then sat back and waited for the moment when, with the Pope's help, he could 'glut his evil disposition by disinheriting, imprisoning and murdering his barons when excommunicated. And these plans, which he wickedly raked up, he more wickedly carried into execution.'

John's appeal for help to the Pope in his hour of need was perhaps the shrewdest political move of his reign. Even without the unashamed attempt at bribery, the Pope would have had no option but to come to John's aid and, due to the changed political circumstances, turn on his erstwhile allies.

John's submission to Rome made it as much a matter of honour as political necessity for the Pope to support his client. Indeed, the Pope would have lost his credibility as the protector of nations if he failed to succour a penitent. He would also have lost his authority as the political leader and overlord of the frontierless Community of Christendom.

The principal consideration for Pope Innocent, therefore, was not the justness of John's cause but the realization that if another king were to take the throne of England in defiance of papal authority—who was not bound by an oath of fealty as a tributary of Rome—he could hardly keep as tributary the other rulers of Christendom.

Thus it was the requirements of the Pope's power politics that decided the issue and helped the Plantagenets to hang on to the throne of England. The Pope's authority was worth many divisions, to use the measuring rod of later generations. He was traditionally looked upon in Western Europe, both by the laity and the clergy, as the sole impartial dispenser of justice on earth and the champion of the people against royal tyranny and feudal oppression.

This belief, coupled with the notion that the care of the world was entrusted to the popes and that all who refused to acknowledge the primacy of the heir of St Peter and submit to him were in direct opposition to the behest of the Lord, played straight into King John's hands.

He also decided, his recent flirtation with Islam notwithstanding, to take up the cross as a crusader, securing for his person and his possessions the Church's absolute protection.

There was, however, no holding back the malcontent barons. Their challenge to the despot on the throne, due as much to the magnitude of their grievances as to their belief in the justness of their cause, was generating its own momentum.*

While John was staying at New Temple, the Templars' London seat, in January 1215, a group of barons headed by Robert FitzWalter called on him in full armour. They formally demanded that he should confirm in a charter the rights of the kingdom.

'The king, hearing the bold tone of the barons in making this

---

* A French view of the quarrel between John and his barons lends an extra dimension to the civil war in England and the French intervention. The contemporary chronicler, known as 'L' Anonyme de Béthune', wrote: 'Que voz en diroie je plus? Apres cete bataille de Bovines [1214], dont je voz ai conte, mut une descorde en Angleterre entre le roi Jehan et ses barons, ki torna à grant mal . . .

'Quant li barons d'Angleterre qu'il n'auroierent nul pooir vers le roi, il se mistrent dedens la cité de Londres, et pristrent conseil entre'els et trovèrent à lor conseil qu'il envoieroient en France à Looys, le fil le roi Phelippe, et li manderoient que, s'il voloit venir à els, il le recevroient al roi, et li mettroient le règne en sa main se il venoit jus sa chape trossée; car li rois Jehans avoit tant fait qu'il n'i avoit mais nul droit, ne si oir autresi, et forjugiés en estoit per sa desert. Dui conte alerent en cel message.'

demand, much feared an attack from them, as he saw that they were prepared for battle'. So he played for time and replied that, since the demands were a matter of great importance, he needed a truce till after Easter. Then, after due deliberation, he would be able to satisfy both their demands and the dignity of the crown.

In Easter week, 1215, the earls and barons assembled at Stamford, Lincolnshire, followed 'by almost all the nobility of the kingdom', according to Wendover, and a very large army. King John, however, did not appear to give his promised reply and the barons then put in writing their detailed demands, asking the King's representatives to present them to John without delay.

The King rejected the barons' demands as amounting to a surrender of his kingdom, while the Pope enjoined both parties to show moderation, eschew the use of force and negotiate.

But the barons had had enough. They formally renounced their allegiance to John and elected Robert FitzWalter as their leader. He took on the telling title of 'Marshal of the Army of God and of the Holy Church'.

The well-to-do burghers and merchants of London and many other towns also sided with the barons, and on 17 May 'the rich citizens let the barons' army into London, while the poor were afraid to murmur against them'. Significantly, FitzWalter, the lord of Baynards Castle, led the 'Army of God' into the city.

Wendover named the principal figures of the baronial faction trying to force John to grant the kingdom its charter of liberties in the following order: 'Robert FitzWalter, Eustace de Vesci, Richard de Percy, Robert de Roos, Peter de Bruis, Nicholas de Stuteville, Saer earl of Winchester, R. earl of Clare, H. earl of Clare, earl Roger Bigod, William de Munbray, Roger de Creissi, Ranulph FitzRobert, Robert de Vere, Fulk FitzWarine, William Mallet, William de Montacute, William de Beauchamp, S. de Kime, William Marshall junior, William Maudut, Roger de Mont-Begon, John FitzRobert, John FitzAlan, G. de Laval, O. FitzAlan, W. de Hobregge, O. de Vaux, G. de Gant, Maurice de Grant, R. de Brachele, R. de Muntfichet, W. de Lanvalei, G. de Mandeville, earl of Essex, William his brother, William de Huntingefeld, Robert de Greslei, G. constable of Meautun, Alexander de Puinter, Peter FitzJohn, Alexander de Sutune, Osbert de Bobi, John constable of Chester and Thomas de Mulutune.'

At the beginnning of June 1215, with the barons' army camped at Staines, John's situation became desperate. On 15 June he agreed to meet the barons at Runnymede, where he formally accepted the barons' demands, prefaced 'These are the articles that the barons seek and the King concedes'. Its forty-nine points form the basis of the Magna Carta. The final clause provides for the setting up of a council of twenty-five barons to supervise the charter's enforcement, taking the final vestiges of authority from John. Robert FitzWalter was one of the twenty-five executors.

No sooner had the barons left Runnymede than John sent envoys to the Pope in Rome, claiming that the barons had 'extorted laws and liberties' and occupied London without the Pope's consent, 'although England, by right of dominion, belonged to the Church of Rome'.

This revealed that John had not intended to keep his solemn undertaking made at Runnymede and reinforced with his seal, because the brief given to his messengers was in defiance of his promise, under §61, that he would not seek to have the charter set aside by any outside authority.

The Pope reacted swiftly. His bulls dated 24 and 25 August made it clear that the barons were up against the awesome authority of papal power. 'Are the barons of England endeavouring to drive from the throne a King who has taken the Cross and who is under the protection of the Apostolic See, and to transfer to another the dominion of the Roman Church? By St Peter, we cannot pass over this insult without punishing it', Pope Innocent raged.

His next thunderbolt struck home, for he declared the Runnymede accord null and void. The charter itself was 'as unlawful and unjust as it is base and shameful . . . whereby the Apostolic See is brought into contempt, the royal prerogative diminished, the English outraged, and the whole enterprise of the [fifth] Crusade gravely imperilled'.

The Pope also suspended and kept in Rome Archbishop Langton of Canterbury in a further act of blatant interference in England's temporal affairs.

As the civil war flared up once again, the barons and the rest of the opposition were no longer interested in an agreement but sought the destruction of the King.

Early in 1216 Robert FitzWalter and the Earl of Winchester

went to Philip Augustus, the ruler of France, inviting his son, Louis, to come over to England and join their side as a pretender to the throne of England to replace John.

The French king at first hesitated, 'but when the barons sent him four and twenty pledges of the best men's sons in the kingdom, he sent them aid.'

The Pope countered this by sending his legate, Cardinal Gualo, post-haste to France to forbid the sailing of Louis and his host for England. When he failed to prevail upon Louis, he excommunicated him.

The Pope also excommunicated the thirty-one leading English barons* and placed London, for its support for the rebels, under interdict. The excommunications and the interdict were published and sent to all the cathedrals of the country, except in London. For the clergy of St Paul's, like the burghers of London, rejected the papal bull and appealed against it.

They asserted, with unexpected political consciousness, that it had been obtained by 'false suggestions, and was therefore of no account, more especially as the ordering of lay affairs pertained not to the Pope.'

Pope Innocent's reaction was uncompromising: he instructed the clergy of England to have the excommunications enforced 'against the barons of England, together with all their aiders and abetters, who are persecuting their lord, King John of England, and all those who have lent their assistance or money to seize or attack the said kingdom, or to obstruct those who go to the assistance of the said king, and to make public that the lands of the said barons are laid under the ecclesiastical interdict.'

Among the new names† added to those excommunicated for

* Robert FitzWalter, S. earl of Winchester, R. his son, G. de Mandeville, and William his brother, R. earl of Clare, and G. his son, H. earl of Hereford, R. de Percy, E. de Vesci, J. constable of Chéster, William de Mowbray, William d'Albincy, W. his son, R. de Roos, and William his son, P. de Cressy, John his son, Ralph FitzRobert, R. earl of Bigod, H. his son, Robert de Vere, Fulk FitzWarren, W. Mallet, W. de Montacute, W. FitzMarshal, W. de Beauchamp, S. de Kime, R. de Mont Begon and Nicholas de Stuteville'.

† 'Walter de Norton, Osbert FitzAlan, Oliver de Vaux, H. de Brailbrock, R. de Ropele, W. de Hobregge, W. de Mauduit, Maurice de Gant, R. de Berkley, Adam of Lincoln, R. de Mandeville, W. de Lanvaley, Philip FitzJohn, William de Tuituna, W. de Huntingfield, Alexander de Puintune, R. de Muntfichet, R. de

their signal contribution to the fight against the tyrant John there are at least two which can be included among the candidates for the 'Englishman'. The first is 'R[obert], chaplain of Robert FitzWalter', who was with his lord in the vanguard of the Magna Carta struggle and who had defied his spiritual father by celebrating Mass, and causing other excommunicated priests to celebrate Mass for the excommunicated baronial host; the second is 'W[illiam] archdeacon of Hereford', guilty of the same crime although on a much smaller scale. A third possible candidate, Master Gervase, the Chancellor of London, 'a most open persecutor of the said king' threatened with 'more severe punishment unless he make a meek reparation for his offences', must, however, be eliminated due to his declining years—the 'Englishman' was about twenty-eight in 1216.

The arrival of Louis with an army enabled the barons to recover much of the territory lost during the early successes of John, but the contemptuous French attitude towards the barons soon showed that they were pursuing completely different aims.

The French attempt to conquer and take over England distressed the barons, who now found themselves between the devil and the deep blue sea.

They knew they were in trouble on every side; for Louis had, notwithstanding their protests, given their lands and castles, which he had subdued, to the French and, what hurt them most, had branded them with treachery. Their alarm was increased by being excommunicated day after day, and deprived of all earthly honour, and they consequently fell into great trouble of both body and mind. Many of them thought of switching alliance back to John but dared not.

The plight of the population was even greater. While Louis' army pillaged and burnt the country in the south King John's troops burnt and ravaged the north and east, and the people were ill-treated by both sides.

Then, in October 1216, King John died unexpectedly, aged fifty,

Continued from previous page.

Gresley, Geoffrey constable of Meantune, W. archdeacon of Hereford, J. de Fereby, R. chaplain of Robert FitzWalter, Alexander de Suttune, W. de Coleville, R. his son, Osbert de Bobi, Osbert Giffard, Thomas de Muletune, and G. chancellor of London.'

from dysentery brought on by a surfeit of peaches and new cider. Before the year was out Pope Innocent too was dead and his seat taken by Pope Honorius III, creating a new situation in the English civil war.

John's death certainly helped to save the crown for the Plantagenet line, but it was Cardinal Gualo, the Papal Legate, who with his diplomatic skill averted the disaster facing the royalist side. At a time when one false step could have lost all, he got his priorities absolutely right.

He had John's nine-year-old son Henry (III) crowned king and appealed to the barons to pledge their allegiance to the young monarch, 'whose age proves him innocent, it being utterly unjust that the son should pay the penalty for the father's crime'.

In a brilliant move he and Henry's regent re-issued the Magna Carta, converting the barons' instrument against royal tyranny into a manifesto capable of rallying men of moderate views to the royal cause. The re-issue of the charter was a triumph for Robert FitzWalter's cause, in spite of his personal failure.

By linking the throne with the charter, Cardinal Gualo skilfully reversed the false step which Pope Innocent had taken at the beginning of the barons' rebellion.

The papal legate also converted the civil war into a crusade and placed the formidable moral armoury of the Church at the disposal of the King's army. To show the just nature of the royalist cause, Gualo gave permission for Henry's army to wear the crusaders' white cross on their garment and assured them of certain salvation. King Henry, who was made to swear fealty to Rome at his coronation and to promise to be a dutiful tributary of the Holy See, owed his crown to the Pope, and he knew it.*

After a succession of military reverses in 1217, a host of

---

* Looking back in his old age on his moral debt to Rome, Henry III wrote: 'To the Holy Roman Church we will firmly adhere, both in prosperity and in adversity; on the day when we do not do this, we consent to lose an eye or even our head. God forbid that anything separate us from devotion to our spiritual father and mother. For besides all the reasons which affect us in common with the other Christian princes, we are above all others bound to the church by an especial reason: for just after our father's death, while still of tender age, our kingdom being not only alienated from us, but even in arms against us, our mother, the Roman Church, through the agency of Cardinal Gualo, the legate in England, recovered this kingdom to be at peace with us, consecrated and crowned us king, and raised us to the throne of the kingdom'.

waverers left Louis and joined the King's side. The first to desert the sinking ship were the great magnates of the country, but the French king, too, began showing more prudence and stopped his aid for his son's army.

On taking Lincoln, the King's forces captured Robert Fitz-Walter, his son Robert, his chaplain Robert, and most of the 'commanding barons', and the plight of the 'Army of God' became acute.

> At this time there was a great deal of wavering among the barons, to which ruler they should entrust themselves [wrote Wendover]. For they were treated so contemptuously by the French that many of them rejected their assistance . . .
>
> On the other hand, it seemed to them a disgrace to return their allegiance to a king whom they had renounced, lest they should be like dogs returning to their vomit; and, being thus in difficulty in every way, they could not mend the broken reed.

Louis, realizing the hopelessness of the situation sued for peace in June 1217, but insisted on a complete amnesty for both his lay and ecclesiastical supporters. Cardinal Gualo, however, absolutely refused to pardon the rebellious priests who had continued to minister to the spiritual needs of the barons' army in spite of the papal interdict.

Louis honourably stood by his church friends but, after a decisive naval defeat, he signed a treaty of peace at Lambeth Palace, surrendered his strongholds, released his supporters from their oath of allegiance, donned the white garb of penitents and appeared barefoot, together with his French knights, before the papal legate to show repentance. A few days after his reconciliation with the Holy Roman Church he sailed for France.

In a gesture of magnanimity, King Henry promised that no layman should lose his inheritance for having sided with the barons and agreed that the baronial prisoners should be freed without the customary payment of ransom.

The King also sought reconciliation with the burghers of London, despite their signal and open support for the rebels, and allowed them to retain their ancient liberties and trade privileges.

But at the insistence of Cardinal Gualo, who was determined to punish most savagely the priests who had sided with the rebels, 'bishops, abbots, priors, secular canons and many other clerics, who had advised or shown favour to Louis, were excluded from the absolution [from excommunication] and the peace, even though they were just and eminent men. They were made paupers by the papal legate who swallowed everything they owned'. *

Cardinal Gualo showed no mercy. He turned the canons of St Paul's out in a body and insisted that the priestly 'ring-leaders' of the rebellion be perpetually banished from England.

This was the Englishman's 'notorious crime' and this is how he came to be banished for ever from England. It was an unexpected and unforeseeable side-effect of King John's cash arrangement with the Pope to have his opponents anathemized.

A process of elimination, imposed by the logic of events and the conditions of the peace, has helped to eliminate all the excommunicated barons and commoners from the list of suspects and narrow down the candidates for the Englishman to the political priests.

The date of the Englishman's banishment and his subsequent pilgrimage to the Holy Land in 1218 further reinforce the assumption that he was one of the politically committed priests especially victimized by Cardinal Gualo.

Since the highest ranking and the very rich among the political clerics could purchase a papal absolution at a price, the Englishman was clearly not one of them. Hugh, Bishop of Lincoln, for instance, paid 1,000 silver marks to the Pope and 100 marks to his legate,† and many others followed his example.

Even Master Simon Langton, the Archbishop's brother, and Master Gervase of Hobregge, excluded by name from the papal absolution 'for having gone so far in their obstinacy as to cause divine services to be performed for Louis and the excommunicated barons by excommunicated priests', were pardoned after considerable payments and allowed to return from their Rome exile after a mere eighteen months.

But the poorer political clerics, who had shown similar obstinacy in celebrating Mass and causing other excommunicated priests to

---

* *Annales de Dunstaplia*

† Cardinal Gualo fleeced the higher echelons of clergy and leading barons so mercilessly in the course of his 'peace-making' that, according to Paris, he amassed a vast amount of treasures before his departure from England. With a part of this extorted gold he built the church of St Andrea at Verceli in northern Italy.

say Mass for the excommunicated barons, found themselves the real victims of the Magna Carta rebellion. The Englishman was one of them.

For these perpetually banished priests, and a handful of gravely compromised barons, there was nothing left but to set off on the long road to Jerusalem.

PART II

The Long Road
to Jerusalem

FIVE

Innocent's crusade

TO BE CAST OUT from the bosom of the Holy Roman Church, the focal point of medieval life, and to be banished for ever from one's own country was an ordeal beyond the ken of most thirteenth-century Europeans, whose horizons were limited to their parishes.

In the warm Indian summer of 1217 the Englishman found himself beyond the pale of well ordered life. There was no refuge for him in the monasteries or quiet country parishes from the hounding of Cardinal Gualo's zealous minions; no one dared to shelter him and risk excommunication. The barons and the magnates who used to be his confederates were even less inclined to help the victims of the rebellion, fearing expropriation of their property more than excommunication.

He was now on his own, an outcast in a hostile world, without the supporting links of kinship, class, country or culture. Although he had certainly been an influential figure of the Magna Carta rebellion, he was not rich and the fleecing cardinal made sure that the worldly goods and chattels of the banished political clerics were confiscated before their expulsion.

He was, of course, a literate man and a priest, and that meant that as he sailed into his exile he was not without some resources and connections, although to be sure it was not much of a recommendation to be an excommunicated priest.

It is not easy to gauge whether he left his native land with his illusions shattered or with a cynical shrug. What can, however, be established is that, before the Pope's abrupt switching of sides in response to John's bribes, there seemed to be no clash between his political convictions as an Englishman fighting for his rights and his duties as a priest of Rome.

The papal intervention on the side of the tyrant changed all that, and the Englishman's subsequent conduct shows that once the two became incompatible, he acted as an English priest and not as a tool of Rome. The spiritual needs of his excommunicated fellow-countrymen took absolute precedence over his vow of obedience to the Vicar of Rome.

In any case, the Papal Legate's crude political intervention in the internal affairs of England and his sweeping acts of repression brought home to the Englishman the duality of the Holy See's policies. No amount of pious cant or inquisitorial argument could hide the fact that, under the guise of spiritual guidance, St Peter's heir was seeking to extend his earthly power.

The Englishman's hatred of Rome, an indirect proof of his emotional involvement in the fight for a charter of rights, manifested itself clearly during his career as a Mongol ambassador.

This hatred certainly limited somewhat his options, although his later actions indicate that he was not so scrupulous as to allow convictions, emotions or principles to interfere with his determined climb to power and success.

Nevertheless, at the start of his banishment the only road open to him that held the promise of redemption, both political and spiritual, was the pilgrim's road to Jerusalem.

He could, of course, also have joined the crusade against the heretic Albigenses in France, or the Patarens and Waldenses in Central Europe or, if he had no stomach for this, he could have sought his luck as a knight errant in the Latin Empire of Constantinople, the true haven of all adventurers. But since these options did not hold out the chance of an eventual return to a position of power in England, he seems to have fixed his eyes on Jerusalem.

He was lucky. In 1217 Western and south Central Europe were in the grip of the fifth crusade. Stores were being amassed, ships were being rigged out and the ports of the North Sea and the Mediterranean were a hive of activity as crusaders and pilgrims set off for the Holy Land.

Pope Innocent's crusade had had an inauspicious start. Although the spiritual interest of the Middle Ages was firmly riveted to the recovery of the Holy Land from Islam, the fiery zeal of the early crusades of the eleventh and twelfth centuries was by now largely spent.

The defence of the Holy Sepulchre did not attract the masses under crusader flags as it did in the previous century, and the fifth crusade owed its inception to Pope Innocent's fervent desire to recover Jerusalem from the Arabs, rather than any pressing military need of Outremer, the crusader kingdom.

In fact, the first two decades of the thirteenth century had been extremely peaceful for the crusader kingdom due to the truces—1198-1203; 1204-1210; 1211-1217—granted by Sultan Malik al-Adil, the younger brother who took over from Saladin. The military situation notwithstanding, preachers had been tramping the length and breadth of Christendom throughout the early years of the century urging a crusade against Islam both in the East and in Spain, but without success.

Where religious appeal had failed the fanaticism whipped up by Stephen, a twelve-year-old shepherd boy, and the resultant children's crusade* had succeeded in giving a fresh impetus to Innocent's campaign to recover Jerusalem.

Some of the shrewder contemporaries had seen through this hysterical boy from Cloyes, France, who, in May 1212, appeared at the court of King Philip of France with a letter which, he claimed, had been given to him by Christ in person, who had bidden him to preach the crusade. King Philip had not been impressed and had told him to go home, but the boy had other ideas.

As Wendover noted:

> This youth, who was a boy in age, but of vile habits, at the instigation of the Devil, went about amongst the cities and castles of France, chanting in French these words: 'O Lord Jesus Christ, restore to us the holy cross!', with many other additions.
>
> And when the rest of the boys of his own age saw and heard him, they followed him in endless numbers and, being infatuated by the wiles of the Devil, they left their fathers and mothers, nurses and all their friends, singing in the same way as their teacher; and what was astonishing, no lock could detain them, nor could the persuasion of their parents recall them, but they followed their master towards the Mediterranean Sea.

Stephen promised his followers that the sea would dry up before them and they would pass like Moses through the Red Sea, and

* Father Donovan in his *Pelagius and the Fifth Crusade* described it as 'a mass movement of child delinquency'.

they would pass without as much as a drop of water on their shoes to the Holy Land. The army of children travelled on foot, but Stephen rode on a pretty cart with a canopy to protect the youthful preacher from the hot sun. Many of the children died on the way of thirst and exhaustion.

In Marseilles, bitter disappointment at the sea not parting before them made many disciples turn on Stephen, but the rest of the children's crusade camped on the seashore in the hope that God would relent and the promised miracle would occur.

Instead of the expected miracle-workers, two shady merchants of Marseilles, Hugh the Iron and William the Pig, appeared eventually before the youthful crusaders offering to take them to the Holy Land. The children, singing hymns of praise in gratitude for the Lord fulfilling his promise to Stephen, put to sea in seven ships, but they were landed on the Algerian coast and sold unceremoniously into Moorish slavery. None returned or saw the Holy Land.

Meanwhile, news of Stephen's crusade inspired a similar children's movement in Germany. A boy called Nicholas began preaching the cross in the Rhineland and soon attracted a following of tens of thousands of children, among them many girls and boys of noble descent, and the inevitable camp-followers of vagabonds and prostitutes.

Nicholas set out from Cologne for the port of Genoa with some 20,000 followers, expecting the Mediterranean to part before him. When this did not happen Nicholas moved on to Pisa. There, two ships offered passage to some of the more impatient children to Palestine, but nothing was ever heard of them thereafter.

Nicholas, still awaiting the miracle, made his way to Rome, where the Pope told him that he and his followers must go back home and take on the cross when they grew up. Only a few made the arduous journey back to the Rhineland.

After the disaster of the children's crusade, the Pope used the Lateran Council of 1215 to put his crusade on a spiritually sounder footing. 'The very children put us to shame', he was recorded as saying. 'While we sleep they go forth gladly to conquer the Holy Land.'

The council reaffirmed the privileges and indulgences to be accorded to the crusaders, which were tailor-made for the Englishman. It also arranged for the financing of the transportation and the war, and set 1 June 1217 as the date when the crusader fleets must sail for Palestine.

Although preachers urged the people of Europe from Ireland to Hungary throughout 1216 to take the cross, only popular visions of crosses floating in the air and other significant omens in the sky helped to get the fifth crusade off the ground.

Oliver of Paderborn, a pious scholarly cleric with unwavering faith, who preached the cross in his native province of Cologne, described these heavenly signs with childlike simplicity in his eye-witness account of the events and actions of the fifth crusade.*

The province of Cologne was stirred up to the service of the Saviour of the World through the signs which appeared in heaven.

For in the diocese of Cologne and in the diocese of Munster in a village of Friesia, namely Bedum, in the month of May on the 16th day before Pentecost [May 16], when the cross was preached there, a triple form appeared in the sky. One white appeared towards the north, another white towards the south of the same shape, and a third in the middle, tinted with colour, having the fork of a cross and a figure of a man suspended upon it, with arms raised and extended, with the mark of nails in hand and feet, and with bowed head. This middle one was between two others on which there was no likeness of a human body.

At another time, in a village of Friesia, at the time of the preaching of the cross, there appeared alongside the Sun a cross of a blue colour; more saw this than the former.

A third apparition was in the diocese of Utrecht in the village of Dokkum, where St Boniface was martyred. When on the feast of the same martyr [June 5] many thousands had assembled there, there appeared a large white cross as if one beam had been artificially placed over another. This sign we all saw. But we believe that the two apparitions were manifested so that all the ambiguity of the first visions might be removed.

To the list of heavenly signs favouring his purposed crusade, Pope Innocent added the ultimate authority of the Lord's own sanction. In a letter to the faithful of Europe he stated that Sultan al-Adil was the incarnate of the Beast of the Apocalypse and the 666 years

---

* *Historia Damiatana*

allotted to the Beast in the Book of Revelations was now almost up, for about six and a half centuries had passed since the birth of Mohammed. The time for its destruction, the Pope hinted, was nigh.

Innocent did not see his fondest dream come true. He died in 1216 and his successor, Pope Honorius III, took over the grand design. In response to his personal letters to the crowned heads of Christendom, Frederick II, the Holy Roman Emperor, took the cross personally in 1217 to give an inspiring personal example. However, he cautiously delayed his own departure to make certain that he would not find someone else on his throne upon his return from the Holy Land.

But Duke Leopold VI of Austria sailed with his army for the crusader city of Acre in September of that year from the Adriatic port of Spalato (Split), and was followed by King Andrew II of Hungary and a part of his army a fortnight later. The rest of the Hungarian pilgrim army had to stay behind because Venice failed to provide transport.

The Friesian contingent, too, got bogged down in Lisbon on the first leg of its journey, and French pilgrims found themselves stranded in the ports of Italy after Venice, Pisa and Genoa— which had landed the fat contracts to transport and feed the pilgrims— found it difficult to provide ships in sufficient numbers.

There were even graver problems hindering the crusade. The scions of France's great families simply refused to head for the Holy Land in the company of the 'pilgrim riff-raff'. While the poor of France took the cross with enthusiasm, the rich barons whose families had provided the vanguard of earlier crusades and the backbone of the Frankish empire of Outremer, kept delaying their departure in order to avoid having to rub shoulders with the ordinary pilgrims. In their haughtiness they also objected to having to fight the Infidels in the company of Central European knights.

The Outremer chronicler Eracles wrote with bitterness in his French-language chronicle: 'But from the land beyond the mountains [Alps] there came but a few crusaders, for the rich barons of France did not deign to keep company with either the Germans or Hungarians'.*

* *L'Estoire de Eracles.*

Because of the Magna Carta struggle and the ensuing civil war, the English contingent was small and its ranks only began to swell towards the end of 1217, when the prisoners of the defeated baronial army were freed by King Henry, and the banished and excommunicated seized on the crusade to salve their souls.

Extant documents show* that the baron Robert FitzWalter, his son Robert, and presumably his chaplain Robert too, were freed from captivity on 8 October 1217. Within three months the king granted FitzWalter his scutage and soon afterwards the former Marshal of the 'Army of God', together with other leading exponents of the barons' rights, set out on their involuntary pilgrimage.

Not even the unifying gloss of the crusade could hide the fact that the English contingent was not exactly an army of knights in shining armour. It was probably the strangest and most ill-assorted band of men to have ever set out to further their own ends under the protection of the crusader cross.

Oliver, the son of King John, lent lustre to the English force and underlined its royal patronage, but his retinue of mercenaries and adventurers put the enterprise in truer perspective.

Then there were the illustrious earls of Chester and Arundel, both staunch royalists who had fought on John's side in the civil war. They had taken the cross with pious intention and pure heart, but they were in the company of Robert FitzWalter and his son, their excommunicated chaplain, John, Constable of Chester, the Earl Sayer of Winchester, William de Harcourt and their large retinue of political outcasts, who were anything but zealous crusaders.

They were followed by a motley crowd, described by the chroniclers of the crusade as 'impious men, committers of sacrilege, rogues, perjurers and adulterers', who streamed to the Holy Land in search of plunder and adventure.

---

* *Rotuli patentium.*

SIX

Sojourn in 'Sin City'

As THE MASS of pilgrims and crusaders from North-West Europe was making its way across France early in the spring of 1218, the traditional pilgrim routes, with their network of hostelry, became clogged. The travellers spilled across the French countryside, fending for themselves as best they could. But most of those in serious trouble with the powers spiritual and temporal, like the Englishman, headed straight for Paris to seek succour from the influential military order of the Templars, which had its continental operational centre there.

A throw-away line in Matthew Paris's great chronicle discussing the fate of a Tartar dispatch shortly before the onslaught of Batu Khan's hordes on Central Europe in 1241, asserts that it was delivered by 'the English Templar'.* And since there was no other Briton in the Mongol diplomatic service, this provides an invaluable clue to the way the Englishman had tried to extricate himself from his desperate situation right after his banishment from England: he accepted the helping hand of the Templars and joined their ranks.

It was a clever and logical step to take because the Templar rules enjoined the order especially to seek out excommunicated knights and clerics and to admit them, after absolution, to their order.

Even if, in the Englishman's case,† the Templars could not

---

* Cahun, the learned scholar of the Mongol period also noted, as a baffling curiosity, the role of 'an English Templar' in the Tartar diplomatic service on p. 353 of his capital work *Introduction a l'Histoire de l'Asie*.

† The order could secure immunity from sentences of excommunication pronounced by bishops and parish priests but not the Pope or his legate.

secure an absolution, the order at the time was at the zenith of its political influence and military power and thus held out the hope of a judicious intercession, in the fullness of time, with the powers in Rome and in England on the Englishman's behalf.

The influence of the Templars in England was as great as elsewhere in Europe and the tentacles of the order reached into every sphere of life, from the huts of poor villeins to the royal palaces.

The privileges of Templars in England were indeed so formidable that King Henry III was forced, soon after ascending the throne, to complain of the usurpation of the Templars on the royal domains. But after the papal bull *De insolentia Templariorum Reprimenda* put them in their place, King Henry granted them free warren in all their demesne lands and confirmed in a special charter all the donations of his predecessors. This included the power to hold courts; impose and levy fines and amerciaments upon their tenants; to buy and sell or hold market; to judge and punish their villeins and vassals; to try thieves and malefactors belonging to their manors; to judge foreign thieves taken within their manors. The charter also exempted them from the royal and sheriff's aids, and from hidage, carucage, danegeld and hornegeld; from military and wapentake services, scutages, tollages, lastages, stallages; from shires and hundreds, pleas and quarrels; from ward and ward penny, averpeny and hundredespeny, borethalpeny, thethingepeny; from the works of parks, castles, bridges, royal houses and other works; from toll in all markets and fairs, highways and bridges throughout the kingdom. Henry's charter also gave them the chattels of felons and fugitives, and all waifs within their fee.

In addition to the various immunities, including excommunication, the privilege of sanctuary was thrown around their houses, and papal bulls enjoined that no person should lay violent hands upon the persons or the property of those flying for refuge to the Templar houses.

Richard the Lion Heart was a Templar and lodged in the order's chief house in Acre during his crusade; King John resided for months on end in the Templar's House in London and Templars mediated in his quarrel with Pope Innocent and arranged a meeting at their Ewell House, near Dover, between the King and the Papal Legate in 1213; John also deposited vast sums with the Templars, and the almoner of King Henry III was a Templar. The rich and the famous, though not members of the order, sought a spiritual link with the 'holy warriors of the Temple' and asked to be buried in the Temple Church in London.

The military valour of the order in checking Arab expansionism secured the Templars a special place in the councils of Christendom, and at the Lateran Council the Templar Grand Master was received with the pomp and circumstance befitting a crowned head. But above all, the Templars were fabulously rich and acted as international bankers, with their Paris House serving as the centre of the world's money market. To be invited to join this magnificent, if strictly ruled, order must have been the first hopeful sign of better things to come for the Englishman.

The Templars, also known as the Poor Knights of Christ and of the Temple of Solomon, were divided into four categories as befitting a strictly regimented military order: at the top were the knights, who were eligible to this station by birth; then came the chaplains, the order's own clergy who were exempt from the jurisdiction of bishops and owed obedience to the Grand Master alone; the third category was the serjeants, who were originally the esquires of knights; and finally the brothers, recruited from among men of simple birth.

The rights and duties of each class of Templars were clearly defined and strictly observed. The knights were entitled to three horses and had to wear white garments with a cross on their surcoats; the chaplains were spared the most humiliating punishments and were allowed a separate drinking cup; serjeants were entitled to two horses and had to wear black garments; the brothers too had their own uniform but they were not allowed to wear animal skins or cloaks.

St Bernard, the Abbot of Clairvaux, who framed the code of statutes governing the order, had obtained papal sanction from the Council of Troyes (in 1128) for the central purpose of Templars: 'Under Divine Providence, as we do believe, this new kind of religion was introduced in the holy places, that is to say, the union of warfare with religion, so that religion, being armed, maketh her way by the sword, and smiteth the enemy without sin.'

His description of a typical knight* is most revealing and makes one flinch from the physical reality of Templar life:

---

* *De laude novae militiae,* Chapter V.

The military knights never dress gaily and wash but seldom. Shaggy by reason of their uncombed hair, they are begrimed with dust, and swarthy from the weight of their armour and the heat of the sun.

They do their utmost to possess swift and strong horses, without ornaments, nor decked with trappings, for they think of battle and victory, not pomp and circumstance. Such hath God chosen for his own, who vigorously and faithfully guard the Holy Sepulchre, all armed with sword and most learned in the art of war.

But they were enjoined in particular not to gaze too much on the countenance of women. 'Therefore no brother shall presume to kiss neither widow, nor virgin, nor mother, not sister, nor aunt, nor any other woman. Let the knighthood of Christ shun feminine kisses, through which men have very often been drawn into danger.'

If all this did not appeal to the Englishman, there were other regulations which were tailor-made for him. The most important among these was the binding rule of silence on matters that had brought a member into the order. 'We forbid therefore all tales related by any brother of follies and irregularities of which he hath been guilty in the world', the rules state, making the order a spiritual forerunner of the Foreign Legion.

No manuscript of the original French-language *Règle du Temple* survived, but a later Latin copy— *Regula Pauperum Commilitonum Christi et Templi Salamonis*— show that to the end the order was submitted to the same draconian discipline as láid down by St Bernard.

The rules of the Temple were jealously guarded by the order and this gave rise to wild legends of terrifying secret rituals of initiation, which played no mean part in the eventual suppression of the order a century later.

In fact, the researches of generations of students of Templar life have failed to turn up any proof that there had been any secret rules, and paragraph LVIII of the Latin-language copy of the rules shows that a candidate, far from being plunged blindly into an initiation ordeal, was made to listen carefully as the rules were being read out aloud to him.

And if he shall have undertaken diligently to obey the precepts thereof, then, if it please the Master of the Order [in 1217 it was William of Chartres] and the brothers to receive him, let the brothers be called together, and let him make known with sincerity of mind his desire and petition unto all. Then, indeed, the term of probation should altogether rest in the consideration and forethought of the Master, according to the honesty of life of the petitioner.

After listening to the seventy-one paragraphs of the Rules of the Temple, the Englishman became a probationary Templar in the spring of 1218 and spent the few months until his ship sailed for the Holy Land at the end of August, in Paris, the 'sin city' of Christendom.

No other city in Europe boasted of such well-earned reputation and it will come as a shock to those despairing of the crime-waves, vice-rings and corruption sweeping the cities of Europe today that virtually nothing has changed in the intervening seven and a half centuries.

Since London was just as beset by crime as any metropolis in those days, the thing that must have struck the Englishman was the openness and blatancy with which the inhabitants of Paris pursued their vices.

According to Jacques de Vitry, the French preacher who observed Paris with the fresh eye of a country boy before leaving for the Holy Land to become the Bishop of Acre in 1218, the most awful thing to admit was that the clergy of Paris was more dissolute than the rest of the population.*

Like a scabby goat or a sickly sheep, Paris corrupts by her mischievous examples the multitudes who flock to her from every part; she devours her own inhabitants and drags them down with her to the depths of the abyss.

Mere fornication had never there been considered a sin; the prostitutes, spread out on every side in the roads and on the squares, almost physically dragged into their house of debauchery the clerics who were walking by. If by some chance these men refused to go in, immediately the prostitutes shouted after them, calling them Sodomites.

This shameful and abominable vice had overcome the city to

---

* Jacques de Vitry (Jacobus de Vitriaco), *Histoire des Croisades*, Livre II.

such an extent that, like an incurable leprosy or an intractable poison, men deemed it a matter of honour to support publicly one or several catamites.

In one and the same house, schools were on the upper floor and the places of prostitution down below. On the upper floor masters gave lessons to children, while downstairs bad women carried on their infamous business.

On one side, the courtesans squabbled among themselves or with their pimps, on the other side the clerics argued and shouted loudly in their animated disputes. The more wanton one became and shamefully lavish in one's spending, the more enthusiastically one was praised and proclaimed by almost everyone as an honest and noble man.

If anyone wanted to live amongst these according to the Apostle 'in temperance, justice and piety', he was immediately denounced as mean, miserable hypocritical and superstitious, by the lewd and effete men.

Nearly all the students in Paris, both foreign and homegrown, were completely involved in learning or researching something new. There were those who learned only to know, which is but curiosity, and those who studied to become known, which is vanity; others still did so to make money, which is greed or the vice of simony. Only a very few of them learnt in order to improve themselves or to enlighten others.

They challenged each other, contradicted each other, not only on the subject of different [religious] sects, nor in connection with some discussion, but rather the diversity of the countries provoked dissension, hatred and virulent animosity between them and they shamelessly affronted and insulted each other.

They declared that the English were drinkers and ridiculous; the offspring of France proud, soft and artistically dressed like women; they said that the Germans were brutish and obscene in their carousing; the Normans were vain and conceited; the inhabitants of Poitou traitors and always flatterers of fortune. Those hailing from Burgundy they considered coarse and insane; the Bretons were reportedly wanton and unstable, and they were frequently reproached for the death of Arthur [actually murdered by King John personally]. The Lombards were called mean, mischievous and no good in fighting; the Romans were thought seditious, violent and slanderous; the

Sicilians cruel and tyrannical; the inhabitants of Brabant were men of blood, fire-raisers, brigands and ravishers; those from Flanders fickle, wasteful, given to gluttony, soft like butter and cowardly. After such insults words were often substituted by blows . . .

The Englishman could hardly have missed these conspicuous facets of cosmopolitan Paris, even if he had been less peceptive than Jacques de Vitry, and there is no reason to surmise this. Regrettably he was enjoined by the Rules of Temple not to write letters or receive letters, or communicate even with his own parents, thus, unlike Vitry, he could not impart his impressions.

But while he was sampling Parisian life, Pope Honorius's fleet, equipped at the cost of 20,000 silver marks, set sail from Brindisi with the main body of crusaders who had waited a year to be transported to the Holy Land.

Meanwhile, two French noblemen—Hervé de Donzy, Count of Nevers, and Hugh de Lusignan, Count of La Marche—concluded an agreement with the Genoese to transport a select company of French and English crusaders* to Acre. The Genoese fleet sailed for the Holy Land at the end of August, under the spiritual guidance of Robert Cardinal Courcon, an Englishman by birth.

On board were the spiritual leaders of Western Europe: the Archbishop of Bordeaux, the Bishops of Paris, Lyon, and Angers, and the Bishop-Elect of Beauvais. The Earls of Chester, Arundel, Derby and Winchester were also on one of the Genoese ships, together with Robert FitzWalter. And since the Englishman had belonged to the closest entourage of the Marshal of the 'Army of God', it is safe to assume that he sailed with his lord from Genoa to the Holy Land.

It is no wonder that, having arrived at Acre in such august company, the Austrian ruler took notice of him and remembered him even after twenty years.

---

* Ogerius Panis, *Annales Januenses*, 1218, in *Fonti per la Storia d'Italia*.

PART III

In Search of Prester John

SEVEN

The Englishman in Acre

ACRE, where the Englishman landed together with the rest of the Anglo-French crusader force in September 1218, was a rich and bustling city with a population of between 30,000 and 40,000 people. Although the seat of government of the Frankish kingdom and the residence of the Patriarch of Jerusalem, the city nevertheless reflected the powerful influence of the Muslim East.

Under a thin veneer of West European culture imported by the Frankish colonists, a diverse cosmopolitan population coexisted and prospered in the city, which was washed by the Mediterranean on two sides and backed by fertile coastal lands and orchards.

The defences and fortifications of the town, built mainly by Italian military masons, were formidable, providing a sense of security for the population singularly lacking in the other cities of Outremer. A thirteenth century plan of Acre drawn by Mario Sanudo reflects its well thought-out defences.

However, it had a weak point. Although it was the general practice of West European fortress builders to place a town's citadel at a corner of the town walls, with direct access to the country, in Acre it was enclosed within the fortifications as a result of somewhat haphazard extension of its walls. This meant that if the town fell, as it did at the end of the century, the citadel could not continue the fight as a self-contained unit as it had no links with the outside world.

From the writings of the chroniclers of the crusader kingdom—William of Tyre, Jacques de Vitry, Oliver of Paderborn and the Arab writer Usamah ibn-Munquidh—there emerges a picture of extraordinary cultural and commercial vitality.

Acre's nobility was purely Frankish, but their vassals, the

land-hungry lesser nobles and peasants of France and the Low Countries, had intermarried with the indigenous Arab-speaking Christians who followed the Orthodox Church. The new generation born of mixed parentage, known as the Poulani, established a life-style closer to the Muslim East than Western Europe, and their accommodation and practical coexistence with the Muslims shocked the new arrivals from Western Europe, fired by the crusading ideal of liberating by force the holy sites of Christendom.

Although the population of Acre was predominantly Christian, as the thirty-eight Christian churches of the city clearly indicated, it also had a sizeable Muslim section. The Muslims had their own mosque for worshipping, were employed as tax collectors and in other government posts, could plead in Arabic and swear on the Koran in court and had a host of other rights and privileges. There was also a small Jewish community of artisans but their influence, reduced during the crusader massacres in the previous century, was moderate compared to the Muslim merchants'.

The tolerance of the indigenous Christian population towards their Muslim neighbours was dictated by their commercial and financial activities. Indeed, as the crusaders arriving from Europe so often noted with bitterness and censure, business interest not only took precedence over religious dogma but simply did not allow a straightforward identification with the crusader aims against Islam. Theirs was a way of life that pioneered what today would be called 'peaceful coexistence' in a harsh climate, leading to ceaseless clashes with the intolerant new-comers from Western Europe.

Jacques de Vitry, the recently appointed Bishop of Acre, was dismayed to find that the Christians of Outremer had no yearning for a crusade and he bitterly criticised the corruption and religious indifference of the Poulani.

They were, he reported to the Pope, a mendacious, godless, treacherous lot, and their priests were no better. They mercilessly exploited the pilgrims and corrupted them body and soul.

The native Arab-speaking Christians, particularly the Nestorians and Maronites of Syria and the Georgians and Armenians, blindly hated the West Europeans and the Roman Church and preferred Muslim rule. These native Christians spoke the same tongue, wore the same garments and led the same life-style as the

Muslims and, Vitry alleged, readily agreed to spy for the Sultan al-Adil, acting as a kind of fifth column.*

The Poulani were brought up in luxury, soft and effeminate, more used to baths than battles, addicted to unclean and riotous living, clad like women in soft robes. How slow and slothful, how timid and cowardly they proved themselves against the enemies of Christ, is doubted by no one who knows how greatly they are despised by the Saracens . . . They make treaties with the Saracens, and are glad to be at peace with the enemies of Christ; they are quick to quarrel with one another and they often call upon the enemies of the faith to help them against Christians, and are not ashamed to waste the forces and treasures which they ought to use against the Infidels for the greater glory of God, instead of fighting against one another to the injury of Christendom . . .

They are suspicious and jealous of their wives, whom they lock up in close prison, and guard in such strict and careful custody that even their brethren and nearest relatives can scarce come at them; while they forbid them so utterly to attend churches, processions, the wholesome preaching of God's Word, and other matters appertaining to their salvation, that they scarce suffer them to go to church once a year. Howbeit some husbands allow their wives to go out to the bath three times a week under strict guard. The richest and most powerful of them, to show that they are Christians, and to some extent excuse their conduct, cause altars to be set up near their wives' beds and get Masses performed by starving chaplains and half-fledged priests. But the more strictly the Poulani lock up their wives, the more do they by a thousand arts and endless contrivances struggle and try to find their way out. They are wondrously and beyond belief learned in witchcraft, and wickednesses innumerable, which they are taught by the Syrian women.

---

* 'The Syrians are for the most part untrustworthy, double-dealers, cunning foxes even as the Greeks, liars and turncoats, lovers of success, traitors, easily won over by bribes, men who say one thing and mean another, who think nothing of theft and robbery. For a small sum of money they become spies and tell the secrets of the Christians to the Saracens, among whom they are brought up, whose language they speak rather than any other, and whose crooked ways they for the most part imitate. They have mingled among the heathen, and learned their works.'

Now, the pilgrims who come, with great toil and at ruinous expense, from far away, are not only treated with ingratitude by the Poulani, but make themselves offensive to them in divers ways . . .

The Poulani used to let lodgings to pilgrims at immoderate rent, and cheated innocent strangers in every way they could, worming money out of them for debts which they never incurred, and so made a wretched living by plundering their guests. They also harboured assassins and robbers, gamblers and common harlots, in hopes of thereby obtaining greater gain, and they paid a yearly tribute to rich and powerful men that they might be their patrons, and back them up in their aforesaid iniquities, to the greater wickedness and damnation of both parties; for they who had for a great sum gained the privilege of keeping whores and gamblers, wrung all the more money out of those whores and gamblers.

The regular clergy, after they had become infected by the poison of riches, and had gotten very great possessions, set at naught their superiors, broke their bonds asunder, and cast away their yoke from them; they became an offence not only to the churches and the people of the churches, but envying and belittling one another, to the grave scandal of Christendom, they proceeded to open insults, manifest hatred, and to battle with one another, not only with words but with blows . . . So greatly did the impiety and unrighteousness of wicked men abound, that they often did not fear to administer the Holy Sacrament to men who were put under an interdict by their prelates, and specially anathemized by name . . . Wherefore it came to pass that the strictness of church discipline was relaxed, and worldly and pestilent men set at nought the sentences passed upon them by their prelates, and cared not for the terrible sword of spiritual justice.

Abbots and priors, with their hireling monks and pitiful chaplains, cast aside the fear of the Lord, and feared not to put their sickle into other men's corn, joining together outlawed or renegade persons in holy matrimony, visiting the sick out of covetousness, not out of piety, and administering the Sacraments to them against the will of their own proper pastors. They used to admit the dead freely to burial, against the will of the prelates, thus illegally taking upon themselves the rights of parish priests. The duty of monks is to mourn and pray, not to administer the Sacraments to laity.

Not only monks, but even nuns, disobeying their superiors, shook off the yoke of discipline, and came out of their cloisters and they irreligiously frequented the public baths in the company of secular persons.

Vitry added to this indictment, however, that the situation had improved and he did not wish his present subordinates to be blamed for past crimes.

The Italian colonists, although they were not leading indolent, luxury-seeking lives like the Poulani, were consumed by mutual jealousies, and they were more interested in cutting the throat of their fellow-Italian business competitors than fighting the infidels. Furious armed clashes between the Venetian, Pisan and Genoese merchants were frequent and Bishop Vitry found them, too, a dead loss for the purposes of the crusade.

His judgement was sound, for after two decades of peace and prosperity, the hard-headed merchants of the Italian city republics saw greater advantage in expanding their vital eastern trade links than in taking the cross.

However, they also needed the cooperation of the crusaders to conquer the coastal cities of the Eastern Mediterranean so necessary to expand their trade monopolies.

The crusades, as the Venetians and Genoese so well appreciated, drew a steady flow of soldiers, settlers and pilgrims to the Holy Land, and the high cost of their transportation and keep on board their ships provided cash to purchase eastern wares, mainly silks, china, spices and sugar, for the return journey, doubling their profits.

The Italian merchants and the diplomats of their city republics were attuned to the needs and sensitivities of both sides and succeeded in sustaining their precarious balancing act even in the difficult closing months of 1217. But their task was rapidly becoming impossible in the face of the zeal of the crusader princes determined to fight the Infidels and spill their blood in the defence of the cross.

The military situation at the end of 1217 and beginning of 1218 was chaotic. There was no one in overall charge and the crusader armies were little better than an unruly mob bent on plunder. On

the arrival of King Andrew of Hungary, Prince Leopold of Austria
and King Hugh of Cyprus,* John of Brienne, King of Jerusalem,
wanted to launch a campaign immediately, considering himself the
natural leader of the crusade. But the Austrian and Hungarian
troops looked to King Andrew and the Cypriots to King Hugh for
leadership, and the Templars, Teutonic Knights and Hospitallers
were obeying their leaders only.

After the taking of the fort of Beisan, the crusaders reverted to
their main interest, the search for holy relics, and in aimless sallies
crossed the River Jordan, traipsed along the eastern shore of the
Sea of Galilee and returned through Galilee to Acre, laden with
what the Hungarian chronicler János Thurocz† described as
important relics.

But Vitry saw it as a systematic campaign of pillage of the
churches of the Holy Land: 'Woe to him who pillages from others',
he thundered.

When you, who had obtained the power to govern others, have
finished plundering, you in turn will be plundered . . .

And not only did they pillage themselves, they devastated
whole areas with fire and spared neither the fruits of the Earth,
nor the contents of the monasteries, snatching up the chancels
with their sacrilegious hands and snatching away by sheer force,
from the bosom of the Lord, those consecrated objects for the
spiritual ministry. Moreover, while they quarrelled among
themselves on the flimsiest of pretexts, they handed over to their
impious henchmen the possessions of the poor.

The Austrian and Hungarian rulers, the only ones to come out
of this with their honour not too tarnished, tried in vain to check
the plundering. King Andrew, in fact, decided to return home
forthwith with his own collection of relics. In spite of the entreaties

---

* Apart from the Prince of Austria and the King of Hungary, the constellation of
temporal and spiritual leaders gathered in Acre included Otto the VII, Duke of
Meran; Walter, Lord of Avesnes of Flanders; Eustorgius of Montague, Archbishop
of Nicosia; Robert of Ableiges, Bishop of Bayeux; Egbert of Meran, Bishop of
Bamberg; Peter, Bishop of Györ; Tamás, Bishop of Eger; Berthold of Meran,
Archbishop of Kalocsa; Engelbert, Bishop of Zeitz (Naumburg); Otto of
Aldenburg, Bishop of Munster; and Otto VI, Bishop of Utrecht.

† In his chronicle, Thurocz listed the water jug used at the marriage feast; a part of
Aaron's rod, and the right hands of St Thomas and St Bartholomew.

of the Patriarch of Jerusalem, he pulled out most of his 15,000 troops and pilgrims and set out for his country even before the arrival of the main crusader force from Western Europe. His crusade, which had plunged his country into heavy debt, had achieved nothing, and the Patriarch of Jerusalem excommunicated him for injuring the cause of the cross with his precipitate withdrawal. Leopold of Austria stayed on, but, having run out of money, was forced to borrow 50,000 besants, a vast sum in those days.

A considerable section of the crusader army, 'composed of the lazy and the timid and the wealthy', never bothered to leave Acre, quite content with the diversions and entertainments of the city.

As crusaders and pilgrims kept pouring into Acre in their tens of thousands in 1218, adding to the multitudes already there, they destroyed the delicate inter-communal balances and created—through shortages and epidemics—a desperate situation. The city was floundering under the weight of the crusader armies.

William of Chartres, the Templar Grand Master, wrote openly to Pope Honorius about the problems created by the Holy See's lack of foresight in providing sufficient food and housing for the crusaders flocking to the Holy Land in response to the call of crusade preachers.

By these our letters we hasten to inform Your Paternity of the state of that Holy Land which the Lord hath consecrated with his own blood. Know that, at the period of the departure of these letters, an immense number of pilgrims, both knights and foot soldiers, marked with the emblem of the life-giving Cross, arrived from Germany and other parts of Europe . . .

Never do we recollect the power of the Pagans so low as at the present time; and may the omnipotent God, O Holy Father, make it grow weaker and weaker day by day.

But we must inform you that in these parts corn and barley, and all necessities of life, have become extraordinarily dear. This year the harvest has utterly disappointed the expectations of our husbandmen, and has almost totally failed.

Indeed, the natives now depend for support altogether upon the corn imported from the West, but as yet very little foreign grain has been received. And to increase our uneasiness, nearly all our knights are dismounted, and we cannot procure horses to supply the places of those that have perished. It is therefore of the utmost importance, O Holy Father, to advertise all who design to assume the Cross of the above scarcity, that they may furnish themselves with plentiful supplies of grain and horses.

But nothing was done to mitigate the calamity. Food was so scarce in the summer of 1218 that even with gold it was difficult to secure basic supplies. According to the *Annales Ceccan*, some sixty-six ships carrying poor crusaders to the Holy Land were simply sent back home, 'and over 100,000 of the same kind had died of hunger'.

The food shortages had led to riots and 'all manner of other troubles and lawlessness' in Acre. The worst offenders, according to Oliver of Paderborn, were the Bavarians. Their brutality in the streets of the city created tensions not only with the inhabitants but also with the more sober crusader elements, led by Prince Leopold of Austria. When the Bavarians' 'acts of violence against everyone, including nuns, monks and abbots, whom they cast out of their hospices', grew into indiscriminate murder of native Christians, the Austrian ruler fought and disarmed the Bavarian rabble 'as befitting a Catholic prince'.

Vitry blamed the troubles on the great number of criminals, excommunicants and other outlaws among the West European pilgrims who were drawn to the Holy Land by the promise of adventure and the absolution of their sins.

But the crude excesses of the Western princes and dukes provided, if any was needed, a bad example for the crusader armies.

Armed with swords they besieged the public highways and spared neither pilgrims nor monks . . . Even on the seas, turning themselves into pirates and privateers, not only did they rob merchants and pilgrims, but more often they burnt their ships and tossed them into the depths.

Princes and men of position became apostates and associates of thieves. Those who were supposed to safeguard peace, defend their subjects, keep away from them corrupt men, as one keeps wolves from the sheep, accepted presents from blasphemous and profane men, gave them succour and assistance. If they saw a thief, they hurried to join him, as if to say: 'Share with us, let's share the money between ourselves'.

Thus they supported the thieves, robbers, the sacrilegious, the usurers, Jews, hired assassins, murderers and mutineers—whom it was their duty to punish severely, extirpate and obliterate from their midst—and allowed them to carry out with impunity their evil doings . . .

And it happened even more often that the nobles, having succumbed to extravagance and luxury, wasted a lot of money on their tournaments and their grand and worldly vanities, and got into debts with money-lenders, while clowns and buffoons, vagrant parasites and actors, dogs of the court and flatterers plundered them of their inheritances.

It seemed as if they said to their prince or tyrant: 'Demolish, demolish right down to the foundations; crucify, crucify, kill and eat'.

Then to crown their damnation, the princes themselves allowed to mushroom everywhere wicked women, houses of debauchery, gamblers, publicans, vulgar taverns, which resemble the dens of robbers.

That Vitry was not exaggerating is borne out by the accounts of all the contemporary chroniclers. The Templars, disgusted with the 'sinful city, full of impurities', withdrew from Acre, and fortified Castle Pilgrim, just outside the city, on a rocky promontory washed by the Mediterranean on every side except the east.

The chief advantage of this formidable fortress was that it lay in a key position, where the Arabs did not hold a single fortified town right up to Jerusalem. It also allowed the Templars to remain in garrison, while not being subjected to the miasma of Acre, until the crusade would begin in earnest.

On 24 May 1218, with the galleys of the Templars in the van, the crusader fleet set out for Damietta in Egypt, which had been designated as the main target before the 'Army of the Lord' could liberate Jerusalem. Jacques de Vitry, Oliver of Paderborn, Prince Leopold of Austria and the grand masters of the military orders accompanied the expeditionary force to the mouth of the Nile.

When Robert FitzWalter and the Englishman, together with the rest of the Anglo-French crusaders, arrived in Acre four months later the situation had eased somewhat, and there were again all sorts of diversions and entertainment to amuse the town folk and those canny crusaders who had stayed behind.

Whatever his moral shortcomings, the Englishman was a political animal and a truly devout Christian, and inescapably the general picture he conceived of crusader life must have been of a discredited bunch of sinners passing through a fallen and doomed city. Furthermore, despite the hopes he had pinned on returning from the Holy Land purged and with the past behind him, it must have become increasingly clear to him that basically his was a one-way journey.

In the scant biographical data furnished by the Englishman's confession, the city of Acre features as one of the few firm points by which one can plot his peregrinations. But there is a missing connection: the Austrian prince whose son recognised him twenty-odd years later was not in Acre at the time of the Englishman's arrival, having joined the crusader forces besieging Damietta in the spring. Yet the encounter must have taken place amid suitably impressive circumstances to stick so indelibly in the Austrian prince's mind.

There is persuasive evidence that it took place towards the end of October, when the Englishman, together with the rest of the English and French crusader army, arrived in Damietta. The illustrious English and French nobles were received in style by Cardinal Pelagius, the Papal Legate in charge of the crusade, and the rest of the European princes and dukes.

EIGHT

War crusader-fashion
at Damietta

THE EARLY SUCCESSES of the crusader armies at Damietta, due to
a clever war machine devised by the preacher Oliver of Paderborn,
had created a mood of great expectancy in the Christian camp.
With the aid of Oliver's floating tower, built on two ships lashed
together, the crusaders stormed the fort outside Damietta on 24
August 1218, and, after fierce fighting, took it. They also broke the
huge chain slung across the sole navigable channel of the Nile and
destroyed the protecting bridge of boats, allowing the Christian
fleets to sail right up to the walls of the city and lay siege to it.

The news of the disaster at Damietta greatly affected the ageing
Sultan al-Adil, and he died within days. The head of the Ayubite
Empire was succeeded in Syria by his younger son, al-Muazzam,
and in Egypt by his elder son, al-Kamil.

The crusaders took a vast amount of fabulous booty from the
fort of Damietta and promptly fell out over it. 'We all swore',
wrote Oliver with bitterness, 'that the spoils carried off from
Damietta should be given up to be divided among the victors; this
was also enjoined under terrible anathema by the Papal Legate
[Pelagius]. Truly the concupiscence of the eyes made many men
thieves'.

Between the taking of the fort and the arrival of the English and
French contingents late in October, there was a perfunctory siege
of the town, while the main body of crusaders 'was so given over to
dissipation that the knights devoted themselves to leisure, while
the common people turned to the taverns and to fraudulent
dealings'.

Thanks to the great interest aroused by the first great feat of
arms against Islam in the Holy Land in two decades, most
European chroniclers recorded the names of the English and

French crusaders who arrived at Damietta, allowing one to pinpoint the Englishman's landing there.

Both Paris and Wendover, as well as Walter of Coventry, are agreed that after the taking of the fort of Damietta 'a great number of pilgrims came from various quarters to assist the crusade . . . At the same time too there arrived from the kingdom of England, the illustrious Ralph earl of Chester, with the earls Sayer of Winchester and William of Arundel; the barons Robert Fitz-Walter, John, Constable of Chester and William de Harcourt, with large retinues, and Oliver, the son of the King of England.'*

Their arrival, witnessed by the whole Christian camp awaiting reinforcement, must have provided the occasion for the acquaintance of Prince Leopold and the Englishman, who stepped ashore in the company of the son of the late English king and Robert FitzWalter, the former Marshal of the 'Army of God'. The link, both in time and space, between the still youthful crusader and the ageing Tartar envoy captured and recognized at Wiener Neustadt, is thus established.

Neither his conduct nor his feats of arms, if any, attracted the attention of the 'resident' chroniclers of the siege, thus his presence there passed unrecorded. But facts culled from his adventures in Mongol service suggest that, instead of whiling away the tedium of inaction in the pursuit of pleasures, like the other crusaders besieging Damietta, he learnt Hungarian. And this quaint intellectual pursuit reveals a new facet of the Englishman, making him a more rounded, less shadowy figure.

His tutor must have been one of the crusaders headed by Bishop Tamás of Eger, who stayed behind after King Andrew's return home and fought under the leadership of Prince Leopold of Austria. What is even more astonishing is the speed with which he learnt this notoriously difficult language. Since Prince Leopold and the mixed Austro-Hungarian force returned home in the spring of 1219, he had at his disposal no more than six months.

The assumption that the Englishman learnt Hungarian at Damietta is based on the reports of two Dominican friars who, on encountering Batu Khan's envoy in 1236, noted with admiration that among the string of languages he spoke was Hungarian. Since

* However, Eracles, in *Recueil des Historiens des Croisades,* puts the arrival of FitzWalter and the rest of the English contingent in September 1219.

his chances of learning this language during his peregrinations in the Middle East and in Mongolia were very slim indeed, the only real opportunity he had was at Damietta.

Dramatic confirmation of the friendship between the Englishman and influential Hungarian barons and clerics, based apparently as much on shared political views as linguistic interests, can be found in the sudden clamouring of Hungarian magnates, after the return of the crusaders, for a charter of rights. In 1222, that is barely over two years after the return of Bishop Tamás's crusader force from the Holy Land, the hard-pressed King Andrew issued his 'Golden Bull' (*Arany Bulla*), which shows a striking similarity both in scope and conception to the Magna Carta.*

This similarity could hardly have been coincidental, considering the distances separating the two countries and that the barons of no other continental country between these states had shown similar interests in a charter of rights. However, the close physical proximity of the architects of Magna Carta to Hungarian barons struggling against a system of government hardly less corrupt and arbitrary than King John's, would inevitably result in their conversation in Latin, the lingua franca of the period, veering towards their mutual problem. The seed planted by the Englishman in the minds of his language teachers at Damietta grew into the great charter of freedoms which became the basis of Hungary's constitution.

The military developments of the siege of Damietta would have held out little prospect of uncovering the trail of the Englishman but for a seemingly contradictory, yet crucial piece of news recorded in a couple of English chronicles. One was in the *History of England* by the Elizabethan antiquarian Stow, drawing apparently on sources which must now be presumed lost, and the other in the *Gesta Abbatum S. Albani*. The scribes of the latter would have had particular interest in this piece of news since it concerned Robert FitzWalter, their 'great adversary'.

Stow asserts that Robert FitzWalter became gravely ill and died at Damietta in 1220. More vaguely, but in the same vein, the St

* Lawrence Lowell in his authoritative *Governments and Parties in Continental Europe* (1896) said of the 'Golden Bull': 'This venerable law was made in 1222, and was therefore nearly contemporary with Magna Carta, to which it bears a notable resemblance'.

Alban's chronicle states that after the accession of Henry III, the lord of Dunmow became infirm, 'his future declined' and within a short time he died. Yet Matthew Paris, who could hardly have erred on such a vital issue as the date of the death of one of the most forceful personalities of his own life time, states that Robert FitzWalter died, reconciled with his sovereign, in 1235 in England.

The equally authoritative *Annales de Dunstaplia* confirms Paris's report by stating that FitzWalter returned home 'sick' from the Holy Land and the date of his return, it indicates, was before 1221.

The solution to this mix-up in the English annals is that in all probability it was Robert FitzWalter junior who died of scurvy at Damietta, since there is no trace of him afterwards, and the heir to the FitzWalter title in 1235 was Walter, his son, who was at the time still under age. Robert FitzWalter senior returned to England, gravely ill, in August 1220 together with the Earl of Chester, as stated by the Dunstable chronicle. He could do so safely, since the dust stirred up by the barons' rebellion had settled and the exclusion clause from the peace and papal absolution applied only to the political clerics, the scape-goats of the civil war.

Since the Englishman belonged to FitzWalter's closest entourage from the early days of the Magna Carta struggle, the old baron's departure from the Holy Land removed the Englishman's sole friend and protector. And when he was to run into serious trouble with his new masters, the Templars, there was no one to stand up for him.

The ups and downs of the Damietta campaign were written down in considerable detail by both Vitry and Oliver, but their close involvement in the politics of the campaign precluded an unbiased and balanced account.

Peter Montaigu, a Spaniard, who became the Templar Grand Master upon the death of William of Chartres in the scurvy epidemic that decimated the crusader army at Damietta, gave a fair summary of the criminal incompetence of the crusader leaders in a letter to Brother Alan Marcel, the preceptor of the English Templars in London.*

Hitherto we have had favourable information to communicate

---

* The letter was included by Matthew Paris in his collection of Addenda to his *Chronica Majora*.

unto you touching our exertions in the cause of Jesus Christ. Now, alas, such have been the reverses and disasters which our sins have brought upon us in the land of Egypt, that we have nothing but ill news to announce.

After the capture of the town of Damietta, our army remained for some time in a state of inaction, which brought upon us frequent complaints and reproaches from both the Eastern and the Western Christians. At length, after the Feast of the Apostles, the Legate of the Holy Pontiff, and all our soldiers of the Cross, put themselves in march by land and by the Nile, and arrived in good order at the spot where the sultan was encamped, at the head of an immense number of the enemies of the Cross.

The river Taphneos, an arm of the great Nile, flowed between the camp of the sultan and our forces, and being unable to ford this river, we pitched our tents on its banks, and prepared bridges to enable us to force the passage. In the meantime, the annual inundation rapidly increased, and the sultan, passing his galleys and armed boats through an ancient canal, floated them into the Nile below our positions, and cut off our communications with Damietta . . .

Nothing now was to be done but to retrace our steps. The sultans of Aleppo and Damascus, the two brothers of the sultan [al-Kamil], and many chieftains and kings of the pagans, with an immense multitude of Infidels who had come to their assistance, attempted to cut off our retreat. At night we commenced our march, but the Infidels cut through the embankments of the Nile, the water rushed along several unknown passages of ancient canals, and encompassed us on all sides.

We lost all our provisions, many of our men were swept into the stream, and the further progress of our Christian warriors was forthwith arrested. The waters continued to rise, and in the terrible inundation we lost all our horses and saddles, our carriages, baggage, furniture and moveables, and everything we had. We ourselves could neither advance nor retreat, and knew not whither to turn. We could not attack the Egyptians on account of the great lake which extended itself between them and us; we were without food, and being caught and pent up like fish in a net, there was nothing left for us but to treat with the sultan.

ed to surrender Damietta, with all the prisoners
had in Tyre and at Acre, on condition that the sultan
us the wood of the true Cross and the prisoners that
ed at Cairo and Damascus. We, with some others,
uted by the whole army to announce to the people of
Damietta the terms that had been imposed on us.

These were very displeasing to the Bishop of Acre [Jacques de
Vitry], to the Chancellor, and some others, who wished to
defend the town, a measure which we should indeed have
greatly approved of, had there been any reasonable chance of
success; for we would rather have been thrust into perpetual
imprisonment than have surrendered—to the shame of
Christendom—this conquest to the Infidels. But after having
made a strict investigation into the means of defence, and
finding neither men nor money wherewith to protect the place,
we were obliged to submit to the conditions of the sultan who,
after having exacted from us an oath and hostages, accorded to
us a truce of 8 days.

During the negotiations the sultan faithfully kept his word, and
for the space of 15 days furnished our soldiers with the bread
and corn necessary for their subsistence. Do, therefore pitying
our misfortunes, hasten to relieve them to the utmost of your
ability. Farewell.

This unmitigated disaster could however, have been avoided
had Pelagius, the Papal Legate, not been so inflexible. For
al-Kamil had, just before the capture of Damietta, made a very
advantageous peace offer: if the crusaders evacuated Egypt, he
would return them the True Cross, hand over Jerusalem,
Bethlehem, Nazareth and the whole of Galilee.

The King of Jerusalem, the Frankish barons and the noble
crusaders of England, France and Germany were all in favour of
it, but Pelagius thought any deal with the Infidels would be a slight
on the sufferings of Christ and rejected the peace offer. The
military orders supported him for strategic reasons, fearing that
they could not hold Jerusalem without Outrejourdain.

After the misfortunes at Damietta, the crusader army and the
Englishman with them, fell back on Acre. There, in the words of
Oliver they grew sluggish through idleness and riotous living, and
'provoked the wrath of the Almighty against themselves'.

In the case of the Englishman this would be a fair comment. For as he admitted in his confession, shortly after his banishment from England 'he lost all that he had at dice in the city of Acre' and was expelled in the winter 1221-1222 from the crusader army as a punishment for his behaviour.

Now his expulsion on account of a bit of gambling in a city so addicted to gambling and other vices would seem extraordinarily severe even though there was a scarcely used decree, passed by Richard the Lion Heart, that no crusader below the rank of knight must indulge in gambling.

With the crusader army being in disarray, no one but the Templars would have bothered to punish so excessively such a minor transgression. And as it has been shown, the Englishman had become a probationary Templar in Paris.

Since the Templars were well aware that religious zeal cannot be kept up, particularly in times of defeat, without strict discipline, the impression that the Englishman was being made an example of to stem the tide of loose living is almost inescapable. 'These wise men', wrote Vitry of the Templar fathers,

> from the beginning safeguarded themselves and provided for the good government of their successors by determining in nowise to disregard or to leave unpunished the negligences and trespasses of their delinquent brethren, but they weighed carefully and exactly measured the heinousness of the crime and the circumstances of the sinner.
>
> From some they took away their red cross, and cast them out for ever, lest one scabby goat should infect the whole flock of sheep; others they condemned to eat scanty meals on the floor without table-linen, until they had made atonement for their faults, that by this public disgrace they might be made to blush, and the rest to fear. For their greater penance and confusion they were not allowed to drive away the dogs that ate with them.
>
> Others they used to chain and imprison either for a time or for life, according to their deserts and as they saw fit, so that they might set them free from the prison of Hell; and in many other ways, according to the precepts of their wholesome rules, they constrained such as were rebellious and stiffnecked to walk in ways of regular discipline and honourable conversation.

The circumstances of the Englishman's expulsion from Acre

show clearly the disciplinarian intent and deterrent value of public humiliation.

The Templars shaved his head 'as if he were a fool', stripped him of his habit, and although it was winter-time, they sent him forth clad in a penant's sackcloth shirt, cow-hide sandals and a cape of horsehair. He was, as he attested in his confession, also made 'to utter inarticulate cries like a dumb man', perhaps crying out his sins in public, as he took his journey over many countries to nowhere.

Here he was, at the age of thirty, down and out, with the final links to his own world and way of life severed. The die was cast for him, as the old Latin saying — 'alea jacta est' — goes.

NINE

Down and out in the Near East

THE PREDICAMENT the Englishman found himself in upon his expulsion from the crusader kingdom put to the test the concept of man as the constructor of his own destiny. His was a terrible freedom, the freedom of an outcast from human society, but in practical terms his options were very limited. As he wandered from village to village in neighbouring countries, uttering his cries of penance, his freedom of choice amounted to no more than whether to carry on at all or to opt out of this world. But he was a religious man and a priest—as the process of elimination in the search for the Englishman's identity has shown—who could not commit the mortal sin of suicide, however tempting.

He therefore had to concentrate on survival, and his wretched physical state precluded in any case any thoughts of giving his life some direction or planning for the future.

An easy way out, taken by many a crusader, would have been to cross over to the Muslim side and embrace Islam, but the life of a renegade apparently did not appeal to him. Being a man of letters, as Father Yvo's report of him noted, would certainly have opened the gates of Sultan al-Kamil's palace, for the Sultan was known to be greatly interested in European languages and culture. In fact he bought up all the literate Christian prisoners his agents could find, and they were employed as interpreters, teachers and secretaries of the Cairo ruler's chancellery. But for his conscience, the Englishman could also have ignored the Templars' punishment and sought to establish himself in one of the Venetian or Genoese colonies in the Middle East, but to do so he would have needed quite a lot of money, clothes, arms, connections and friends, and he had none.

All he could do, therefore, in the winter of 1221 and in the new Year of Grace 1222, stretching endlessly ahead of him, was to carry on walking and begging 'in this shameful state of want and in an enfeebled state of body'.

At first, as he stated in his confession, he met with great kindness from the Muslims who took him in, 'wearing out his life somehow or other, though daily, in the levity of his tongue and the foolishness of his heart, had wished himself at the Devil'.

Eventually, however, he became very ill 'from the excessive toil and the continual change of air and diet' in the land of the Chaldees (southern Iraq), and he thought his last hour had come.

'Not being able to go further, or to turn back, he stopped where he was, breathing with difficulty', Father Yvo quoted the Englishman as stating in his confession.* 'And being somewhat acquainted with letters, he began to put down in writing the words which were spoken, and afterwards pronounced them so correctly that he was taken for a native, and he learnt several languages with the same dexterity'.

The Englishman's extraordinary gift to learn languages at the age of thirty and speak them so well as to be taken for a native provides proof of his outstanding intelligence. Not many people would have busied themselves with learning at what then amounted to middle age and in such appalling circumstances, but the Englishman's intellectual entertainment stood him in good stead and proved his saving grace.

During his brief crusader career and throughout his subsequent ordeal, the talk of the Middle East was a mysterious Christian king of the East, known by the cryptic name of Prester or Presbyter John. The Christian armies fervently believed, and the Muslims greatly feared, that this Eastern ruler was on his way to help liberate Jerusalem from Islam. Although nobody seemed to know who exactly this Prester John was and whence he came, the sudden appearance of Genghis Khan's Tartar horsemen in 1220 on the periphery of the Middle East lent credence to the existence of this legendary ruler.

The very fact that he came from Asia, a land of mystery, and that he was an enemy of Islam who had destroyed Muslim power in Central Asia, stirred the imagination of Christians. They invested Genghis Khan with the attributes of this Eastern 'saviour' and when news came of the destruction of the powerful

* See Appendix I.

Khwarismian empire (Turkestan) by the horsemen of 'Prester John', Pelagius, expecting his 'impending aid', refused al-Kamil's advantageous peace offer at Damietta.

As the Mongol hordes poured into the Middle East in 1221 and ravaged Transcaucasia, the belief in the Christian camp that Genghis Khan had gone to war to aid the crusaders became an article of faith, not a challengeable assumption. That the Eastern horsemen actually destroyed the Christian kingdoms of Georgia and Armenia, instead of galloping across the desert sands to the aid of the crusaders, was simply overlooked, since it did not fit into what was expected of Prester John.

After the taking of Damietta in 1221 an Arab prophecy, fore-telling that Islam would be abolished when Easter fell on 3 April, gave a tremendous boost to crusader morale, and the Englishman must also have heard of it. When this happened the following Easter, a fresh rumour spread like wildfire, asserting that a nephew of Prester John, a King David, had set out with three powerful armies to vanquish the Muslims. The expectation of these armies and the almost deliberate mixing up of fact and fiction led to the hopeless crusader break-out and defeat in 1222.

Oliver of Paderborn also mentions in his Damietta chronicle another prophecy, that 'a certain king of the Christian Nubians was to destroy the city of Mecca and cast out the scattered bones of the false prophet Mohammed, and certain other things which have not yet come to pass. If they are brought about, however, they will lead to the exaltation of Christianity and the suppression of the Saracens'.

How widespread the expectation of Prester John's intervention on the Christian side was is shown by Coggeshall's chronicle.* In his 1220-1221 entry, the English monk mentioned the 'rumours sweeping right across Christendom of the coming of King David of India, whose other name is Priester John, to the aid of the crusaders'.

Vitry, in his endeavour to boost the sagging spirit of the crusaders, had an Arabic book translated which bore the telling title of *Excerpta de Historia David regis Indiorum qui Presbyter Johannes a vulgo appellatur*. The book contained the prophecy

---

* *Radulphi Coggeshale Abbatis Chronico.*

that Muslim power would be destroyed by two rulers—an Eastern and a Western—which was construed as the meeting up of Frederick II, the Holy Roman Emperor, and Prester John on the ruins of Islam.

At his vantage point in Acre, Vitry also gathered together the reports of merchants following the caravan routes across Central Asia who carried news of the growing number of Christians in the East, and the kindly act of their ruler who had freed a multitude of Christian prisoners from captivity. The Christian rulers of the Caucasus sent him similar reports, building up hopes of Prester John striking a blow for Christendom.

Jacques de Vitry's report of Prester John was confirmed in the consciousness of Europe by an independent account emanating apparently from Hungary. In 1223, Richard of Saint-Germain wrote that 'the king of Hungary informed the Pope that a certain King David, or Prester John as he is being called, has entered Russia with a great multitude of people. He had left India seven years before, taking with him the body of the blessed apostle; and during his [westward] journey his army killed 200,000 Russians and Cumanians'.

This information, with its basic kernel of truth presented to suit the climate of religious expectation, differed from Vitry's account and could only have come from the Hungarian crusaders who must have heard it from some Muslim merchant or other traveller from the East.

With the mirage of Prester John keeping the world in thrall, even the learned men of letters in Europe failed to notice how old and enduring the legend of the Eastern priest-king was. The first authentic mention of him was made by Otto, Bishop of Freising, in his chronicle of 1145. He recounted that the first news of 'Johannes rex et sacerdos' was brought to the Holy See by the Bishop of Gabala.

According to this, after destroying the armies of Media, Persia and Assyria, Prester John was heading for the Holy Land to defend Jerusalem against the Muslims, but was prevented from getting there by adverse conditions.* Thus the second crusade had

---

* *Ottonis Freisingensis Chronica*: '. . . Narrabet etiam, quod ante non multos annos Joannes quidam, qui ultra Persidem et Armeniam, in extremo oriente habitans, rex et sacerdos cum gente sua Christianus est, sed Nestorianus, Persarum et Medorum reges fratres, Samiardos dictos, bello potierit, atque Ecbatanam cuius supra mentio

ended without this new saviour actually materializing, but in 1165 his legend was given a powerful fillip by a letter allegedly written by the great king himself to Pope Alexander III ('Presbyter Joannes potentia dei et virtute domini Jesu Christi Rex regum et dominus dominantium amico suo Emanueli Rome gubernatori') in which he recounted his great power and fabulous wealth.

Although the Pope's reply remained unanswered, the legend of Prester John retained its magic and reached its peak half a century later during the siege of Damietta. If popes, princes, crusaders and the chroniclers of thirteenth century Europe all pinned their hopes on Prester John, it is hardly surprising that in his hour of need the Englishman also turned to him. The court of this distant Eastern ruler must have seemed to him like a genteel Shangri-la, where he could start afresh and forget all about perpetual banishment, expulsion and the rest of his tormenting experiences.

And, according to his confession, he did not even have to go in search of Prester John, his agents came to seek him out and invite him to his faraway court.

'The Tartars heard of him through their spies, and drew him over to their interests: when they had got an answer about their claim of subjugating the whole world, they bound him to be of loyal service, by bestowing on him many gifts; for they were much in need of persons to be their interpreters'. The Englishman's flair for languages acted as *deus ex machina*.

In 1222, Genghis Khan's empire stretched from the China Sea to Transcaucasia, but the Tartars were still unfamiliar with the ways of urban civilisation. Their enormous and constantly growing empire imposed new responsibilities and created new needs with which this warrior race could not yet cope.

They began to adopt the habit of a settled way of life but, as Genghis Khan realised, the process took much longer than conquering the continent of Asia. For the needs of administration,

---

facta est, sedem regni eorum expugnaverit. Cui dum praefati reges cum Persarum, Medorum et Assyriorum copiis occuerent, triduo utrisque mori magis, quam fugere volentibus, dimicatum est; Presbyter Joannes, sic enim eum nominare solent, tandem versis in fugam Persis, cruentissima caede victor extitit. Post hanc victoriam dicebat, praedicta Joannem ad auxilium Hierosolymitanae ecclesiae procinctum movisse, sed dum ad Tigrim venisset, ibique nullo vehiculo traducere exercitum potuisset, ad septemtrionalem plagam ubi eundem amnem hyemali glacie congelari didicerat, iter flexisse'.

diplomacy, finances, taxes and the manifold problems of running and welding together an inchoate empire of gigantic proportions, the Mongols looked to the urban civilisations of China and Europe.

Venice and Genoa were quick to offer help to the Mongols, whose conquests changed the main trade routes from the Far East. The safety of their new overland route to China made the hazardous sea-route a bad risk, and lent the Italian colonies on the Black Sea a new vital role. In the 1220s, as the armies of Genghis Khan sliced through the Caucasus and ranged as far south as Chaldea, the Black Sea became the focal point of East-West trade. Colonies of Venice and Genoa suddenly found themselves acting as the gateway to the vast Tartar hinterland, and the attempts of the Italian merchants to exclude each other from the lucrative markets being opened up by Genghis Khan's host led to a murderous rivalry between the Italian city republics.

An essential role in Genghis's campaigns was allotted to intelligence. Preparatory intelligence was carried out well before the outbreak of hostilities, and the secret scouting continued throughout the fighting. In this, 'merchants' who worked on the enemy side played a vital role. They would be infiltrated with supplies of merchandise and goods in order to establish links with the local population.

In the course of Genghis's Transcaucasus campaign, Tartar agents penetrated every corner of the Middle East, and provided the Mongol army command with a comprehensive picture of the weaknesses and rivalries of the kingdoms and their rulers.

Although Mongol spies operated throughout Asia and in northern Africa, they found it more difficult to operate in the crusader kingdom and in Western Europe. But with the help of the Venetians, Mongol intelligence easily overcame this obstacle. Venice was quite willing to sacrifice the interests of Christian Europe in return for Mongol help in ousting the Genoese from the Crimea and the destruction of their trade centres. The Venetians began to act as part of the Mongol intelligence system, and this was no mean help.

With the aid of Venice, the Mongols soon extended their tentacles to Western Europe and penetrated the highest echelons of European society, including the Holy See and the crusader leadership.

Frederick, the Holy Roman Emperor, in a letter to Henry III drew the English king's attention to the danger posed by the ubiquitous agents of Tartar intelligence: 'By their spies which everywhere they have sent before, the Tartars know the public discord and the unfortified and weaker parts of the lands, and hearing of the heartburning of kings, and the strife of kingdoms, are much encouraged and animated.'

It was from Venice's point of view a worthwhile *quid pro quo,* even if not exactly in keeping with the crusader spirit, but then the Italian city republics had made enormous financial gains and extorted territorial and political advantages from earlier crusades too.

The helping hand of the Venetians' world-wide intelligence network must have been invaluable to the Mongols. Apart from its diplomatic service, Venice employed women and monks with great effect, because they could penetrate places no ordinary spy could reach.

Venice also made use of an army of local 'friends' of the 'Pearl of the Adriatic', who gathered intelligence and served as couriers. People living in border areas were much sought after by the Venetians because they could slip into the neighbouring country and return without attracting undue attention. For more delicate missions Venetian agents disguised themselves as mendicant monks or pilgrims because, in the static world of the Middle Ages, these classes of people did not arouse suspicion in any community. Now this facility and accumulated experience in intelligence gathering was put at the disposal of the Mongols.

It is impossible to establish whether the Englishman was approached by Tartar spies or Venetians recruiting for Genghis Khan's empire. If Tartar agents sought him out, then he would most likely have travelled to the Italian Black Sea colony of Soldaya, which had excellent connections with Genghis Khan's empire and led the exploration and opening-up of markets under Mongol rule. It also served as an entry and exit point for envoys travelling to and from the Mongol ruler.

If, however, the Englishman was 'discovered' by Venetians then he would have crossed over at Tana, in Azov, where the Venetians had a forward trading post doing brisk business with Far Eastern merchants and Tartar representatives in the early period of Venetian-Mongol links.

In practical terms it made little difference whether a Venetian Christian or a shamanist Tartar enlisted the Englishman. But the ability to spot the talent under the rough exterior of a sick vagrant, clad in sackcloth, whom most people would have shunned instinctively, reveals a lot about the range and scope of contemporary intelligence activities. It was in a way a recruitment stranger than fiction.

TEN

The struggle between Venice and Genoa

THE MERCANTILE IMPERATIVES that drove the Italian city republics to seek fresh spheres of influence in South-East Europe also helped to cement Venetian-Mongol cooperation. The scope of this cooperation extended to many fields and its strategic needs greatly influenced Mongol military considerations in the years when the Englishman acted as the personal envoy of the warlord Batu Khan, preparing the invasion of Europe.

The dynamism with which Venice, and up to a point Genoa, pursued its expansionist policies to the detriment of the rest of Europe deserves closer examination, because it sheds some light on the economic and political factors that must have had a strong bearing on the Englishman's diplomacy.

Throughout the thirteenth century, the twin pillars of Venetian policy were the acquisition of trade concessions and the exclusion of Italian rivals from these markets. The doges were not particularly scrupulous in the means of attaining their ends.

In the fourth crusade, for instance, Venice· undertook to transport to the Holy Land and feed for a year 9,000 knights and 2,000 foot soldiers for 85,000 silver marks and half the conquests. When the cash was not forthcoming the Venetian fleet refused to sail. Doge Dandolo, however, offered a deal: the payment could be postponed if the crusader army would storm and take for Venice Hungary's Adriatic port of Zara.

After the taking of Zara, Doge Dandolo also managed to convince the crusader leaders that it would be worth their while to occupy Constantinople, the richest city of Christendom, rather than proceed to the Holy Land and fight the Infidels. In 1204, the crusader armies stormed and sacked Constantinople and dealt a death-blow to the Byzantine empire, the last barrier against the rising power of the Seljuk Turks in Asia Minor.

Under Venetian guidance, the Frankish crusaders set up the Latin Kingdom, which soon became the linchpin of Venice's growing colonial empire. Under the new doge, Ziani, Venice entered the most glorious period of its colonial history. Although Ziani could not bend an entire crusade to serve Venice's imperial purposes, like his predecessor, he nevertheless won sufficient backing from the Franks to complete the conquest of Byzantium's eastern empire.

The secret of Venice's success was that it handed the trappings of power to the Frankish knights of the crusader empire, while it retained the real economic levers of power. This moderation dazzled the Franks, who were still somewhat inexperienced in the art of diplomatic deals.

However, what the Venetians were in effect saying to the Franks was: 'You look after the defences of Constantinople and we provide you with food and other provisions. We leave the mainland to you and we only claim the worthless islands as our share.

'You attend to the glorious business of war-making and support yourselves by means of compulsory taxes from the unreliable Greeks. We, for our part, will work for you, sail the seas on your behalf and face all the hazards of trading.' This magnanimity, so appreciated by the Frankish knights, who understood little outside warfare, allowed the Venetians to amass vast fortunes and make the apparent rulers of the Latin Kingdom entirely dependent on them.

But the Genoese and the Pisans were not taken in by this display of Venetian unselfishness, particularly as a Venetian naval squadron prevented them from landing or trading in Constantinople. The Venetian galleys also blocked all the ports of the Black Sea and patrolled the Levant. In their anger the other Italian merchants turned to open piracy, and schemed with the Greeks, who were also bitterly resentful of the usurpation of their empire.

The Genoese, deprived of all their trade routes, attacked the Venetian navy on the high seas but were so soundly beaten that half a century of truce was only just enough to repair their navy.

The Venetians held all the trump cards, and the ace was the Tartar link. Egypt, tired of the endless trouble with Europe, closed its ports to Western merchant ships, and trade in eastern spices, hand goods and precious stones became both difficult and unprofitable.

But the Tartars who now controlled the East knew that, by going up the Don, ships could approach the Volga, which flowed into the Caspian Sea. And with the Venetian galleys sailing up to Tana, in Azov, all that remained to connect East and West in one, continuous and in part navigable trade route was to bridge the little distance between the Volga and the northernmost tip of the Sea of Azov. This was no problem for the Tartars, and soon oriental merchandise from Samarkand was beginning to flow to Europe via the Caspian Sea, the Volga and the Venetian trading post of Tana.

There the Venetians took over the goods brought by Central Asian Muslim merchants, who then loaded up Venetian crystal, coloured glass, silver jewels from Thessaly and cloth from Western Europe, which were in great demand in the bazaars of Asia.

The only threat to Venice's complete trade monopoly came from the centuries-old north-south trade route to the Baltic controlled by the Russian city of Kiev. The merchants of Kiev and the Greek traders of Constantinople, with their contacts throughout Europe and the Levant, were rivals and Venice could not tolerate any competition endangering its new trade route. The city of Kiev, prosperous and powerful, had to be neutralised and eliminated.

There is persuasive evidence that Venice used the Mongol army to achieve this. In the spring of 1238, after the extraordinary successes of Batu Khan's westward drive in Russia, in the course of which he took the towns of Gorodets, Pereyaslav, Rostov, Yaroslav, Volokalamsk and Tver, there was an inexplicable switch in the direction of his campaign. Instead of continuing to exploit his victory in the west, Batu Khan veered south.

In the course of this his personal envoy had some mysterious negotiations with the Venetian consul in the Crimea. It resulted in the militarily startling transfer of the Tartar base of operations from the mid-Volga to the Don, securing the Volga-Don link and threatening Kiev. Within eighteen months Kiev was completely destroyed. The ferocity of the Tartars was such that virtually nothing was left standing in the city, and it ceased to exist as a trade and cultural centre. No other town in Russia was so mercilessly extirpated and its entire population put to the sword.

Seven years later, the papal envoy Carpine, on his return

journey from the Karakorum, stopped over in the ruins of Kiev. He recorded that in the few houses still standing there were a handful of Italian merchants who had transferred from Constantinople. Three of them—Manuel Veneticus, Jacobus Venerius and Nicholas Pisanus—were Venetians.

Venice now held the trade monopoly for the East-West route, the Black Sea trade and the Mediterranean commerce, and the Kievan rival was but a heap of blackened ruins.

It is both significant and revealing that the Italian colony of Soldaya in the Crimea, which had come under Mongol occupation about the same time as Kiev, suffered no damage at all and was required merely to pay a small annual tribute.

The most sinister, and certainly the most lucrative, feature of the Venetian-Mongol cooperation was the revival of the ancient slave trade between Europe and the Middle East. Venetian galleys began the mass shipment of young Kipchak slaves, bought from the Tartars who captured them in the plains between the Volga and the Don. The Venetians sold them to Egypt as army recruits, fuelling the war against the crusaders with fresh supplies of soldiers for the Muslim side.

These erstwhile slaves, who were known as the Mamelukes, eventually formed the backbone of the Egyptian army and one of them—Baibar—became the sultan of the country.

The first shipments began during the early 1220s, when Génghis Khan's hordes overran the Caucasus and Transoxania, but after the vast invasion of Eastern Europe in the 1230s, the number of slaves sold by the Venetians in the slave market of Cairo more than doubled.

The Mongols used their tax system to assure ample stocks of slaves. In occupied Russia, for instance, Batu Khan's tax-collectors at first took, according to the eye-witness friar, Piano de Carpine, from each household one child out of every three, and all the men who had no wives. Spinsters and 'all paupers' were similarly taken without more ado and sold into slavery.

Those left behind were counted and the following per capita annual tribute was exacted: a skin of a white bear or black sable, or one black beaver; one polecat pelt or one black fox skin. Since this tax was levied regardless of age, availability of pelts or financial position, a great many people simply could not pay it. And those who failed to pay these taxes on the due date were immediately taken by the tax-collectors to the Tartars who made them slaves and sold them off to the Venetians or Genoese.

With the help of new power alignments in the Middle East in the second half of the century, the Genoese successfully challenged Venice and their long-simmering hostility erupted in open warfare. One of the results of this was a redistribution of markets and Genoa's successful insistence on a fair share of the slave trade.

The deeds of the notaries of Caffa, in the Crimea,* offer a glimpse of the men behind this heinous trade. Among the leading traders were the Venetian brothers Giacomo and Michele Rainero, and Pasquale Venier.

Contemporary Arab sources offer a broader view of the scope and extent of the slave trade, because the outcome of Egypt's internal power struggles and the fight against the crusaders depended on the quality of Mongol slaves.

The Sultan Kalaun, for instance, is recorded as having bought 12,000 East European and Caucasian slaves from Batu Khan's horde, while his son, an-Nassir, purchased an equal number. According to the Arab writer Ibn Hadzhar, an-Nassir paid to Venetian merchants 47,000 silver dinars for their human cargoes in the space of a couple of years.

The chronicler Ibn Iyas noted that 'when the Mameluke Saragatmüsh became emir, he alone bought 800 slaves, while the emir Yalbek 3,000.'

Apart from young males destined for the army, there was also lively trade in female Christian slaves. According to Al-Makrizi[†] there were hundreds of East European women slaves in the households of Egyptian officials who were not even related to the ruling Mameluke élite. The Sultan Kalaun alone owned 1,200 European female slaves.

In a faraway corner of Upper Egypt, a fairly insignificant nomadic shaikh, al-Mikdam ibn Shammas, owned, according to Ibn Hadzhar, 400 slaves, indicating the wide diffusion of the Mongol prisoners shipped into Egypt by the Italian slave merchants.

Both the Venetian and Genoese merchants, particularly those of Soldaya which had become the central slave market for Mongol prisoners, grew exceedingly rich on the proceeds of their gruesome

* *Actes Pera-Caffa* No 1 (CCLXXI and CCCVIII).

† *As-Suluk*, Volume II.

business. In recognition of their contribution to the building up of
the Mameluke army, the sultans of Egypt exempted them from
paying taxes and custom dues not only on their human cargoes but
also on the goods purchased for the return journeys of their
galleys.

To encourage the trade, the Mongols also granted similar
exemptions in the ports controlled by them, according to the Arab
writer Ibn Tagribardi.

With their coffers filled to overflowing, the Venetians began to
act as bankers both for the Mongol khans and the Egyptian
sultans, further strengthening the Volga-Nile trade link.

Just how rich these thirteenth century slave traders were can be
gauged from an isolated incident in which, in a fit of pique, a
high-ranking Mongol official stabbed to death a Genoese called
Sacran in the Crimea. The murdered merchant was found to be
carrying on him 60,000 silver dinars—a sum well in excess of a
king's annual expenditure—and in the holds of his ships he had
sugar and spices worth 40,000 dinars to buy slaves from the
Mongols for the return journey to Egypt.

Although this incident resulted in the 'writing off' of 100,000
dinars, the slave trade continued to flourish.

The Venetians' use of the Mongol army to eliminate trade
rivals, their slave trade and collaboration in the field of intelligence
with the Asiatic conquerors bent on occupying Europe, raise the
question whether the charge of 'traitor to Christendom' levelled
against the Englishman would not have been more justified in the
case of Doge Ziani or Doge Sanudo, who have gone down in
Italian history as honourable empire builders.

PART IV

Genghis Khan's World

ELEVEN

Journey into the unknown

IN 1223, the Englishman was on his way to the seat of Mongol power in the Gobi Desert, where no European had penetrated before.

His journey into the heart of Asia took him along the same route that was followed by the monks Piano de Carpine, William Rubruquis, D'Ascelin, and a couple of other Western envoys who, some twenty years later, travelled overland to Karakorum in the forlorn hope of winning over the Mongol ruler to the fight against Islam.

To keep in touch with his armies Genghis Khan had forged together the ancient caravan routes into a unified communication system. The chain of post stations girthing his immense empire provided a route service unrivalled anywhere in the civilised world.

Since the system remained basically unchanged between the Englishman's pioneering passage and the Western envoys' travel, it allows a fairly accurate reconstruction of what the Englishman's journey must have been like. It also enables us to follow in his footsteps.

The papal envoys' Latin travelogues, which survive in the Vatican Library, provide a moving account of the hardships suffered by these devout and dedicated men venturing into the unknown interior of the Mongol empire. Even the behaviour of the Tartar driver-guides, called *yams,* who accompanied and controlled the Western travellers, could hardly have changed in the intervening few years. Thus the Englishman's experiences must have been equally harrowing, but at least he had the hope of meeting the legendary Prester John at the end of the journey.

The Minorite friar Rubruquis,* entrusted with an embassy by the French crusader King Louis, entered the Tartar empire at Soldaya in the Crimea after having convinced the local authorities that his credentials were in order.

The advantages of travelling as an envoy entitled to help and protection were explained to him by some Christian merchants, who had heard him give a different version of the purpose of his journey during a sermon in the St Sophia cathedral in Constantinople. They impressed upon him not to repeat again that he was first and foremost not an ambassador but a proselytiser going among the unbelievers in accordance with the rules of his order.

'These said merchants cautioned me to speak guardedly, for they said [to the Tartars] that I was an envoy, and if I said I was not an envoy I would not be allowed to pass.'

Once the purpose of his journey was clarified and the credentials checked, he had to settle on a suitable means of transport. The Tartar officials offered Rubruquis and his embassy a choice between two-wheeled carts, drawn by teams of oxen, or pack-horses.

But the merchants, obviously seasoned travellers in the Mongol empire, advised him against travelling on horseback for two reasons. One was that if he were to buy *kibitkas,* covered carts used by Russian traders, he could put inside them all the goods his embassy did not wish to unload every day, whereas if he were to use pack-horses everything would have to be unloaded at every post station and reloaded onto fresh horses. But another equally important consideration in the opinion of the merchants was that his embassy could not be hurried along by the guides and he could ride more slowly to suit the ambling of the oxen.

'Unfortunately, I accepted their advice, for I was two months on the way to Sartach (the first major stop), which I might have reached in one had I gone with horses,' Rubruquis remarked.

Rubruquis eventually set out for Karakorum with four covered carts, two extra carts lent to him to carry the bedding, and a horse each for the five-man embassy. The Mongols also provided two *yams* to drive the carts and look after the oxen and horses. The Mongol word survives to this day in Russian as *yamshchik*, and denotes the same occupation.

---

* Rubruquis, or Rubruck as his name is sometimes spelt, was a Fleming. He set out from Soldaya in mid-June, 1253.

The friar Carpine, entrusted with an embassy by the Pope,* received better advice from a Mongol official who had checked his credentials. Although he entered the Tartar empire from the north via Kiev, because of his Polish-born fellow envoy and interpreter Benedict, and rejoined the main route to Karakorum just north-east of the Black Sea, he made better speed due to having decided to use pack-horses.

The Mongol official also gave him some excellent advice when he told him not to take Western horses on such an arduous journey. 'They would all die', he was told,

> for the snows are deep, and these horses do not know how to dig out the grass from under the snow like the Tartar horses, nor could anything else be found on the way for them to eat, because the Tartars have neither straw, nor hay, nor fodder. So on the Mongols' advice, we decided to leave our horses there with two servants to keep them.
>
> And we had to give the Mongol officials presents that he might be pleased to give us pack-horses and an escort.

Presents played a very important role in any dealings with Tartars, who not only expected them but demanded them, and sometimes with menaces. It reveals their insistence on the observance of the traditional Eastern proprieties of encounter with another fellow human being; however, they applied the social niceties, evolved among nomads in the vast and sparsely populated plains of Central Asia, to the changed circumstances of administering a huge empire which necessitated regular contact with aliens ignorant of these customs.

A station master (*daroga* in Mongol, which is still used as the Russian word for road), for instance, made himself deliberately disagreeable to Friar Carpine and hindered his journey until he was promised some presents. 'But when we gave him what appeared to us suitable, he refused to receive them unless we gave more; and so we had to add to them according to his will, and something else he extorted from us deceitfully and maliciously.'

Rubruquis, on the other hand, well advised by his merchant

---

* Carpine, an Italian, set off from Lyons on 16 April 1245, and returned with a reply from the Tartar Khan in the summer of 1247, the round trip having taken just over two years.

friends, carried in one of his carts quantities of dainty biscuits, fruits and muscadel wine, much favoured by the Tartars, to make his journey easier. For as the merchants had told him, 'among the Tartars no one is looked upon in a proper way who comes empty handed.'

But in spite of the occasional difficulties over the size or suitability of presents, fresh horses were provided at each station and the system functioned well. There were long stretches where travellers could change horses many times a day, enabling them to cover vast distances.

'We had to rise at dawn and travel till night without a stop', Carpine complained. 'Often we arrived so late that we did not eat at night, but the food which we should have eaten at night was given to us in the morning; and we went as fast as the horses could trot, for there was no lack of horses, having usually fresh horses during the day, those which we left being sent back to the previous station. And in this fashion we rode rapidly without interruption.'

In fact, while riding across the vast plains of the Cumans (more frequently referred to as Kipchaks), whose land stretched from southern Moldavia to the Caspian Sea, travellers were provided with fresh horses up to seven times a day.

However, along the desert tracts in the land of the Cangitae, east of Cumania, the going became slow and the lack of water caused great hardship to both men and beasts. The heads of missions were provided with stronger horses capable of covering long stretches without stops.

Many travellers appear to have died of thirst or in ambushes along the desert tracts of Cangitae, and also in parts of Cumania, 'where human bones and skulls were scattered about the ground like cattle-dung'.

The attackers were roving bands of Christian Hungarians and Russians and shamanist Alans who, upon their escape from Tartar slavery, apparently waged a desperate partisan war against the Mongol lines of communications. According to Rubruquis, they were mounted, well armed, and attacked exclusively at night, 'killing whomsoever they could find'. Because of their lightning attacks and their skill in using bows and arrows at night, they were greatly feared by the Tartars, as the guides repeatedly told the friar.

'We travelled eastward, seeing nothing but the sky and the Earth', wrote Rubruquis of his journey across the desert, and his

unpretentious, simple description has lost none of its evocative
power. .

We trudged along for another three days without seeing anyone.
Just when both we and the oxen were well worn out and could
not find any Tartars, suddenly two horsemen came cantering
towards us; we met them with great delight . . . Finally, on the
fourth day we found some people, and we were as happy as
shipwrecked mariners on reaching port. Then we got horses and
oxen and travelled along from stage to stage.

But the pleasure of renewed human contact was apparently a
short-lived one, for soon the misery of the desert began to seem
preferable to the importune attentions of the natives.

For one thing, the Tartar guides wanted to stop over at every
chieftain's camp and honour them with presents. But the travellers
just did not have sufficient supplies of food and presents for such
socialising, and there was nothing they could buy with money.

Rubruquis, for instance, had to feed daily eight people — the
five members of his embassy, the two Tartar drivers and a
guide — and in addition there were 'those who came by hazard and
all wanted to eat with us'.

The food provided by the frugal Tartars for official travellers
was not suited to European stomachs: strips of dried horse-flesh,
cakes of evil-smelling dried milk, butter stored in sheep's gut, and
kumiss, fermented mare's milk. Water too was a problem, because
the watering holes were made so muddy by horses and cattle that
the travellers could not bring themselves to drink it. 'Had it not
been for the biscuits and wine we had, and God's mercy, we
should probably have perished', the friar believed.

The Pope's envoy was faced with similar problems. 'No matter
whence the ambassadors come from, they are, on arriving among
the Mongols, in dire straits as to victuals and clothing', he reported
to the Holy See. 'For their allowances are poor and small,
especially when they reach the camp of any of the princes and are
forced to wait there, because then they give so little to ten men that
two could barely live on it. Nor while at the courts of the princes,
nor on the road do they give to eat but once a day, and little
enough then'.

The inquisitiveness of the people was equally trying. To
Rubruquis the deprivations of the desert journey seemed like a

flea-bite compared to difficulties he had to face when he came to inhabited places.

> When we were seated in the shade of our carts, for the heat was intense, they pushed in most importunately among us, to the point of crushing us, in their eagerness to see all our things [he complained]. And if they were seized with a desire to relieve their stomachs, they did not go away from us farther than one can throw a bean; they did their filthiness right beside us, while talking together, and they did much more.

To the rigours of months of travel were added the strains of the formalities and humiliations of meeting a succession of Tartar chieftains who ruled the vanquished countries and secured communications. Insults and crude treatment could not be openly resented and had to be borne in subservient humility.

The pattern was the same everywhere: on arriving at the seat of a Tartar chief, the traveller was asked if he wanted 'to bow' to the lord, that is to give presents. The intention of showing due respect to the chief was measured by the size of the presents, and since the presents had to reflect the status of the envoys' master, these were usually deemed insufficient. 'You come from a great lord, and you give so little?' they would be asked contemptuously.

If the envoys wanted to do their business satisfactorily and continue their journey expeditiously, they had to increase their offer. Negotiations would then be conducted through inter-mediaries, and when the thorny issue of presents was finally solved, the travellers would be taken to meet the chief in his tent.

Before being admitted into the presence, however, both the travellers and their presents would 'cleansed' by being made to pass between two fires. When Carpine refused to undergo what he thought would be a fire ordeal, it was explained to him that there was no need to be frightened: 'We only make you pass between these two fires lest perchance you think something injurious to our lord, or if you carry some poison, for the fire will remove all harm.'

Although the Western travellers seem to have been startled by this cleansing, the ritual lighting of fires, known as 'living fires' in Eastern Europe and 'need fires' in Germany and parts of the British Isles, was widely used as a protection against outbreaks of plague, evil eye, vampirism and wasting diseases among cattle. The practice was denounced by the Church in the early Middle

Ages as a heathen superstition, but it lingered on until this century in remote areas.*

Assured that the travellers could do no harm to the Tartar chieftain, they would be taken to his tent where they had to bend three times their left knees before entering. They were instructed not to step on the threshold, for those who knowingly tread on the threshold of a chief's tent faced death in the Tartar world.

Inside the chief's tent the travellers were once again made to do obeisance and repeat on their bended knees the purpose of their journey. Only after this symbolic act of submission were they welcomed as guests.

Although these formalities were trying enough in the case of ordinary chieftains, they became even more galling when the travellers reached Batu Khan's nomadic seat near the Caspian Sea. Batu, the grandson of Genghis Khan, was the most powerful Mongol prince after the Khan of Khans, with all the royal trappings of power.

Since he was the warlord in whose service the Englishman was to rise to power and notoriety, the eye-witness accounts of Western travellers calling at his court provide a unique insight into the Englishman's life-style while in Mongol fealty.

Because of Batu's importance, most Western travellers were on arrival not allowed closer than a league to his camp. After the customary cleansing by fire and acts of submission, they would be taken to a cart, positioned beyond the cleansing fires, upon which stood a golden statue of the Mongol emperor, and asked to worship it. Friar Carpine and Friar Benedict refused point-blank, but were made, nevertheless, to bow their heads before the statue. But as clerics they were exempted at least from the more humiliating prostrations required of laymen.

'When I saw the ordu [camp] of Batu I was astonished',†

---

* Sir James Frazer in his *The Golden Bough* adduces startling proof that 'need fires' were kindled in the Scottish Highlands against cattle disease even in the last century. In the island of Mull and in Caithness it was believed that certain rituals following the lighting of bonfires provided cure for the murrain.

† Ibn Batuta, the famous fourteenth century Arab traveller, described his first glimpse of Batu's successors' camp: 'Then the imperial cortege, which they [the Tartars] call ordu, arrived. We saw a great city moving with its inhabitants, containing churches [mosques] and markets, with the smoke of kitchens rising in

Rubruquis wrote, 'for it seemed like a great city stretched out about his dwelling, with people scattered all about for three or four leagues. And as among the people of Israel, where each one knew in which quarter from the tabernacle he had to pitch his tents, so the Tartars know on which side of the ordu they must place themselves when they set down their dwellings'.

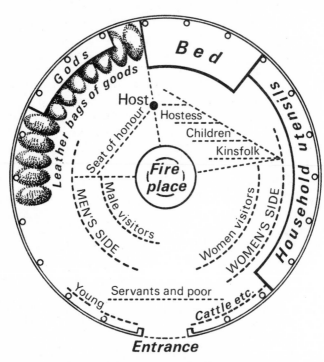

Plan of the interior of a Tartar *yurt*

Continued from previous page.
the air; for they cook their food during the march. Carts drawn by horses transport these people, and when they have come to the camping place they unload the tents which are on the arbas [carts], and put them up on the ground, for they are very light. They do the same with the churches [mosques] and the shops.' (Gibb, *Ibn Batuta*, II.)

This hierarchical order extended to every sphere of Mongol life. In his tent, Batu sat on a raised dais with one of his wives, while everyone else, including his brothers, sons and nobles sat lower down on a bench in the middle of the tent. Lesser people would sit on the ground behind them, the men to his right, the women to the left.

Friar Carpine, after explaining the object of his journey, was made to sit on Batu's left with the women, placing him in a position of inferiority. The French king's envoy, however, appears to have fared better, indicating that Louis' stock was higher than the Pope's due to his warlike reputation and the size of his army.

Rubruquis was duly cautioned, before being taken to the prince's tent, not to speak until invited to do so and on no account to touch the ropes of the tent for these were deemed to represent the threshold of the door. He recalled in his report:

> So we stood there in our robes and barefooted, with uncovered heads, and we were a great spectacle unto ourselves. Then we were led into the middle of the tent, and they did not require us to make any reverence by bending the knee, as they are used to do of envoys. We stood before him the time it takes to say 'Miserere mei, Deus', and all kept profound silence. He looked at us intently, and we at him . . .
>
> Finally he bid me to speak, and our guide told us to bend the knee and speak. I bent one knee as to a man, but he made a sign to me to bend both, which I did, not wishing to dispute over it.

After this revealing episode, Batu questioned the friar closely about himself, his lord and his position in the world and, as a signal honour, he bade him to sit down and drank *kumiss* (fermented mare's milk) with him.

The picture emerging from the reports of the Western envoys shows a man accustomed to rule and exercising his power with dignity. He ate in style and kept his drinks in gold and silver jugs. When he drank he was entertained by singers, or by players of a stringed instrument resembling a guitar.

When he rode out slaves held over his head an umbrella or a little awning, and all the heads of leading families rode with him, providing a retinue of about 500 nobles.

In the opinion of the Western envoys, 'Batu is kind enough to

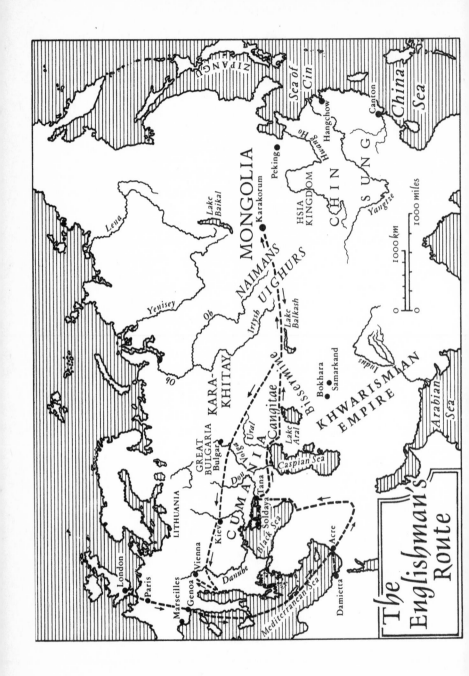

The Englishman's Route

his people, but he is greatly feared by them. He is, however, most cruel in fight; he is also very shrewd and extremely crafty in warfare, for he has been waging war for a long time.' The parameters of the Englishman's career are clearly delineated in these glimpses of the Mongol prince's conduct.

The journey from Batu's *ordu* to the seat of the Khan of Khans in Mongolia took another four months and, as the travellers were duly informed, the cold would be so intense that 'stones and trees split'.

On leaving Batu, the pope's humble envoy and his party wrapped themselves up as warmly as they could and used leggings as a protection both against frost-bite and to bear the strain of endless riding on their legs better. Friar Rubruquis, King Louis' privileged envoy, however, was kitted out in Mongol fashion with fur cap, big sheepskin cloak, sheepskin trousers, felt stockings and curly-toed riding boots.

The 3,000-mile journey across the lands of a succession of conquered nations gave the travellers much food for thought. But more importantly, their descriptions provide signposts for the official route to Mongolia along which the Englishman too had to travel. Although not all the names and places they recorded ring a bell today, they can be identified with considerable certainty.

After the land of the Cangitae, the travellers traversed the country of the Bisermines, a Muslim people who spoke the Cumanian tongue and inhabited the plains of present-day Kazakhstan. Their name is a corruption of the Chinese word *P'u-su-man kuo* — the country of the Pusuman, or Musulman.

Then came the Khwarismian empire, conquered by Genghis Khan shortly before the Englishman crossed it. It stretched from the Aral Sea and Turkmenia right into the Persian plateau. Along the route, Carpine saw 'innumerable ruined cities, overthrown villages and deserted towns'.

The trail then led across the territory of the Black Kitayans, north of Lake Balkash, and the country of the shamanist Naimans, believed by Rubruquis to have been Christians, who inhabited the Altai mountain range near the 'Roof of the World'. The rugged land of the Uighurs and the Tangut came next, and finally Mongolia.

It was a feat of human endurance to have crossed the vast expanses of Asia. Yet it was, as Rubruquis recorded and the

Englishman found, not merely a journey in space but also in time: 'When I found myself among the Tartars it seemed to me in truth that I had been transported into another century'.

TWELVE

The steppe empire
and its Khan

AT THE END OF THE RAINBOW there was no Prester John waiting to welcome the Englishman to his Shangri-la kingdom. Instead of the mysterious Eastern king with a passionate, if inexplicable, interest in the ascendancy of the cross, he found himself facing Genghis Khan, the ferocious nomadic conqueror of Asia.

There was, after his lengthy journey across the ruined heartlands of the continent, hardly any need to explain the true nature of Mongol rule, but Genghis Khan's court must have quickly dispelled such illusions about Prester John as the Englishman may have retained from his crusader days at Damietta.

In 1224, the biggest ever empire on the Eurasian land-mass was less than a generation old. It was created by the ruthless military genius, political acumen and the elementary force of controlled human savagery unleashed by Temuchin.

Temuchin, the unlettered son of a Mongol tribal chief called Yesugai, later took the name of Genghis Khan.* He was born in 1162 on the bank of the River Onon in North-East Asia, with his fist clenched about a blood clot. It was, according to Mongol belief, a sure sign of courage and valour in battle.

The Mongols, like the rest of the cattle and horse-breeding warrior tribes of Central Asia, had for centuries fought each other for better pastures and supremacy in the constellation of petty chiefs. So did their great adversaries the Tartars.

---

* Temuchin was awarded by the council of Mongol tribal chiefs the title 'Zin', ie great, and '-gis' is the superlative ending. Zinghis Khan means the Most Great Khan, or prince; it reached the rest of the world through the phonetically corrupted Persian rendering as Chingiz. But the Mongols pronounced it as Jenghis. The English form of Genghis originates from the eighteenth century French transliteration of Jesuit Mongol experts.

In the changing alliances of Tungusian, Turkik, Altaian, Turanian and Mongolian tribes, always in search of plunder, the lofty Chinese emperors to the south-east provided the constant factor. Their rich, civilised and fertile land drew like a magnet the steppe herdsmen whose simple economy, so dependent on sufficient pastures, condemned them to a life of unimaginable hardships always close to or on the breadline.

When drought burned out the pastures, as it frequently did, and the flocks perished, millet and rice from China had to be acquired to assure the wintering of the steppe herdsmen and their families; the periodic onslaught on China by the barbarians from the north, driven by hunger and greed for booty, was checked by the Chinese Wall. But the attractions of silk, brocade, richly ornamented weapons and clothing proved too strong for the nomad horsemen and their continuing raids across the border elicited a different approach from the Chinese; they fought the barbarians by manipulating and dividing them.

To keep the troublesome Mongols at bay, the Chin emperors of China first forged an alliance with the Tartars, whose hatred of the Mongols offered a fair chance of gainfully exploiting their enmity. But the Tartars grew too strong for the liking of China. After the poisoning and death of Genghis's grandfather, the Mongol paramount chief, the nomadic tribes of Central Asia swore allegiance to the Tartars and began calling themselves Tartars.

To curb the Tartar power, the Chinese switched alliance and, in the spirit of 'divide et impera', encouraged the Mongols to attack the Tartars. Yesugai routed them in a crucial battle and captured their chieftain, Temuchin. In accordance with Mongol custom, he named his first-born son Temuchin to mark the greatest event in his life.

But his victory was short-lived. The Tartars took their revenge, with Chinese connivance, by poisoning Yesugai. At the age of thirteen Temuchin became the Mongol chieftain. It was an honour conferred by the elders with grave misgivings. Tribe after tribe left the clan because they dared not entrust their families and herds to an inexperienced boy. As the enemies of the house of Yesugai gathered for the kill, the future looked very bleak indeed for young Temuchin.

Although the odds were against him, he persevered. After a harsh apprenticeship, he succeeded in reuniting the clan under his undisputed leadership, defeated a hundred rival chieftains within the Mongol orbit and, in an unparalleled carnage, revenged himself of the Tartars for the deaths of his father and grandfather. He crowned the destruction of the Tartars with a decree enjoining their erstwhile steppe allies to call themselves Mongols.

It was a progression that made the savagery and destruction brought upon the world by Attila the Hun look like reasoned acts of statesmanship. Temuchin drowned in blood all the nations that dared to resist him and obliterated towns, villages and *ordus* in his path, leaving no one but the steppe wolves and carrion crows to bury the butchered millions.

'Unchecked by human valour, they were able to overcome the terrors of vast deserts, the barriers of mountains and seas, the severities of climate, and the ravages of famine and pestilence. No dangers could appall them, no stronghold could resist them, no prayer for mercy could move them', is the assessment of the *Cambridge Medieval History* of Genghis Khan and his horsemen.

Within a quarter of a century he subdued all the steppe nations and the *kuriltai,* the council of the Mongol chiefs, proclaimed him Genghis Khan, the Khan of Khans in 1206. It was a fitting name, although the names Mighty Killer of Man and the Perfect Warrior used by the subjects and neighbours of his empire were nearer the truth.

'The merit of an action', he cautioned his sons, 'lies in finishing it to the end'. The empire-building could not be considered completed until three powerful states bordering his realm were destroyed.

But these were not simple steppe kingdoms with armies unable to match the organisation, discipline and massed attacks of Mongol cavalry. The Chin empire, with its well fortified capital city of Peking, then called Yenking, had all the advantages of an ancient civilisation over the Mongol nomads, and furthermore the Chinese army was well versed in the use of sophisticated war machines and gun powder.

The Tangut kingdom of Hsia Hsi, on the upper reaches of the Hoang Ho (Yellow River) was also a state of town-dwellers, while Kara Khitai was a powerful Muslim kingdom.

Genghis chose Hsia Hsi, the weakest of the three, as his first target. In 1207 he invaded part of the Tangut kingdom, but fortifications of the city of Volohai appeared too much for his steppe horsemen. But what he could not get with brute force he won with fox-like cunning. He offered to withdraw if he was given by way of tribute one thousand cats and one thousand swallows. The startled Tangut complied. But instead of withdrawing. Genghis set them alight and released them in one great rush of living fire. The hapless cats and birds set the city on fire in hundreds of places and, while the garrison fought the flames, the Mongols breached the walls.

By the end of 1211 the Tangut empire was subdued and the golden bit of slavery was forced into its emperor's mouth. The following year Genghis invaded the Chin empire and, after battles of gigantic scale and atrocities of terrifying proportions, the Mongol horsemen overran North China to the Yellow Sea. After a prolonged siege, Genghis took Peking in 1215, but by then his reputation was such that, according to a Persian chronicler, some 60,000 Chinese virgins hurled themselves from the city walls to their deaths rather than fall alive into the hands of his soldiery.

With the death of Süan Tsung, the last Chin emperor, in 1223, the rest of the vast empire was occupied and the world's most ancient civilisation lay under the feet of Genghis Khan. The Sun emperor of South China sent envoys with fabulous gifts and offers of alliance, while the Manchus and Koreans readily accepted the crippling bondage of the Mongols as the price of freedom from Chin overlordship. It was a stunning victory that changed the face of Asia.

An act of arrogant folly by Shah Mohammed II, Genghis Khan's powerful Muslim rival in the empire-building business, led to a simultaneous campaign in the west against Khwarism, which united the Muslims from the Persian Gulf to the Aral Sea and from Pamir to the River Indus.

The Mongols, replete with booty from the Chinese war, had become interested in trade links with the fabulously rich Muslim trade centres of Bokhara and Samarkand in the Khwarismian empire. Genghis sent a reasoned message, inviting trade on equal footing, to the Shah, who was of Turkish origin:

> I send you greetings. I know your power and the great extent of your empire, and I look upon you as a most cherished son.
> On your part, you must know that I have conquered China, and all the Turkish nations north of it. You must also know that

my country is an encampment of warriors, a mine of silver, and that I have no need of other lands. I take it that we have an equal interest in encouraging trade between our subjects.

The Mongols began sending caravans of merchants to pave the way for more permanent trade arrangements, but although these were grudgingly accorded the protection and privileges due to merchants, Shah Mohammed did not hide his disdain for the representatives of mere Infidel dogs and their upstart ruler.

When one of these caravans, which included a special Mongol mission, was held at the Transoxiana frontier post of Otrar on suspicion of harbouring spies, the province's governor, wishing to show his contempt for the Infidel nomads, had the envoys, merchants, slaves and servants—150 people in all—put to death.

He then sent the pick of the murdered men's goods to Shah Mohammed as a token of the symbolic humiliation of Genghis Khan.

Genghis demanded satisfaction for this outrage and the extradition of the governor. The Shah, however, added insult to injury by having the chief of the Mongol envoys bearing Genghis's demands beheaded, and sending the rest of the mission back without their beards.

But, as the Persian chronicler noted, 'with this command, the Shah signed his death-warrant. Each drop of the blood he then shed was paid for by floods of his subjects' blood. Each hair of the victims' heads was paid for by a thousand heads, and each dinar was repaid with tons of gold.'

It was a fair appraisal. In Mongol eyes the most heinous crime was the murder of ambassadors, whose person they regarded as inviolable, and in his anger Genghis summoned to war the rest of Asia against the haughty Khwarismian ruler.

Although his battle-hardened main force and the auxiliary troops of over 200,000 were horsemen, Genghis also enlisted Chinese engineers who operated giant catapults, new-fangled battering rams, flame-throwers, explosives and cannon capable of breaching any fortification.

Against this new-type Mongol army, led by the brilliant generals Subotai and Chepe, Shah Mohammed's 400,000-strong army stood no chance, and the Mongol avalanche swept the Khwarismians away. Bokhara, Samarkand, Rai (near Teheran) and dozens of cities were taken and their entire populations massacred, with the exception of the artisans.

After the taking of the city of Parvan, for instance, the massacre lasted for weeks and in the end several hundred thousand people lay dead in the streets and the houses. 'The bones of the slaughtered rose mountain-high, the earth was fat with human fat and the rotting corpses gave rise to a plague', it was reported to Genghis Khan, but he saw no reason to stop the killings.

A captured Khwarismian prince of Afghan stock tried to plead with Genghis against the senseless massacre of innocent millions, by appealing to his vanity. He reasoned that if the Mongols were to drown Khwarism in a sea of blood, 'no one will be left alive to harbour the memory of your bloodshed'.

Genghis brushed aside the prince's reasoning and the underlying plea for mercy: 'What do these people matter to me?', he asked. 'There are other countries and many other races, and among them my fame will live on, even if in every corner of the land to which the hoofs of Mohammed's steed have strayed, such looting and killings should continue with my permission'.

Mohammed had indeed no option but to flee his ruined country, leaving his countrymen mesmerised by the spectacle of Mongol ferocity. His son, Jelal ad-Din, put up an even more valiant fight but he too was eventually vanquished and forced to flee to India, with the Mongols doggedly chasing after him. With the destruction of the Khwarismian empire, the world of Islam was dealt a body blow in Central and Western Asia from which it never recovered.

But the Khwarismian Muslims' misfortune brought in its wake death and destruction for Christendom too, by awakening Genghis's interest in the West, hitherto outside the Mongol sphere of robber wars. Subotai and his fellow 'Dog of War', Chepe, raided Georgia in 1221, then scaled the craggy ranges of the snow-covered Caucasus with their 30,000 horsemen and routed the joint armies of the highlander Chirkassians and Alans, after having skilfully detached their most powerful ally, the Cumanians.*

After this signal victory over the warlike Caucasian nations, the Mongols were confronted for the first time by a powerful Euro-

---

* Among the many names by which the Kipchacks were known to their neighbours at the time — among them Petchenegs and Kuns — Cumanians seem to be the most generally accepted.

King John's effigy in Worcester Cathedral. His despotic rule, corrupt
administration and crushing taxes alienated all estates. Behind his back he was
called 'John Soft-Sword' and 'John Lackland', and these harsh nicknames give
the measure of the man as seen by his contemporaries. In a fit of pique he tried
to convert England to Islam. (*The Dean and Chapter of Worcester Cathedral*)

The Outremer city of Acre, now part of Israel and called Akko, appears to have changed little since the days when the Englishman was gambling in its taverns during the Fifth Crusade. In 1218 the city was floundering under the weight of the crusader armies flocking there. Food shortages and epidemics were common, but there were also diversions and entertainments and, as the Englishman said in his confession, he lost there all his worldly possessions in a game of dice. (*Israeli Embassy*)

A Chinese ink drawing of Genghis, the Khan of Khans of the Asiatic steppes. He was a ferocious war-lover whose empire, built on the bones of butchered millions, stretched from the China Sea to the Dniepr in Europe. His need for qualified people to run the continent-sized empire brought the Englishman to his court. (*By permission of the British Library*)

Genghis Khan in his tent. Although he
believed that his mission was to conquer
the world, he lived like his horsemen
and shared all the hardships of
campaigns with them. 'I hate luxury and
exercise moderation,' he told a Taoist
sage. 'I eat the same food and am
dressed in the same tatters as my
humble herdsmen.' (*British Library*)

Genghis Khan with his chief wife,
Burte, in a Persian miniature. Two
of his sons, Ogodai and Juji, are
kneeling in front of them and two other
wives are on the right of the throne.
According to a Persian chronicle,
Genghis had over 500 wives and
concubines, but the greatest pleasure in
his life was making war. (*British
Library*)

The Tartars in battle. The ferocious horsemen, whose bloodthirstiness became legendary, obliterated all who dared to resist them, leaving the steppe wolves to feast on the slaughtered millions. 'They gloried in the slaughter of men, blood to them was spilt as freely as water', wrote the thirteenth-century chronicler Vincent of Beauvais. (*British Library*)

Execution of a high Mongol dignitary who groundlessly denounced Yeliu Chu-tsai, Genghis's chief minister and the Englishman's protector. Yeliu's privileged position in the court of the barbarous Khan of Khans reflected the high esteem he had earned for himself through his wisdom, integrity and phenomenal intelligence.(*BritishLibrary*)

A page from the written report to Pope Gregory IX on the encounter between the Tartar Khan's Englishman and a Dominican friar named Julian on the Volga in 1236. The friar's superior appears to have realised the importance of Julian's discovery that the Khan's multi-lingual envoy was not a native-born Tartar and included this in his report. These lines are shown in darker ink on the illustration. (*Szechenyi Library, Budapest*)

A Chinese ink drawing of Batu Khan, grandson of Genghis Khan, who was entrusted with the invasion of Europe. His horsemen, seen as beastly, inhuman monsters, instilled terror in the hearts of Europeans. Batu was spoken of as the 'punishing rod of God', sent upon the world, like Attila the Hun, 'by reason of the sins committed among us Christians.' (*British Library*)

A Chinese ink drawing of Subotai, the most brilliant Mongol general, whose victorious campaigns brought devastation to from China to the Danube. Although under Batu Khan's nominal leadership, it was Subotai who worked out the plan of the European campaign. In less than six weeks in the spring of 1241 he laid waste all the countries between the Baltic and the Adriatic, and defeated five armies. (*British Library*)

Tartars roasting and eating their European victims. This graphic account of the invaders' cruelty, found under an entry giving the event of 1243 in the manuscript of Matthew Paris's *Chronica Major,* reflects the widespread contemporary belief that the Tartars were 'monsters rather than men, tearing and devouring the flesh of dogs and men.' (*The Master and Fellows of Corpus Christi College, Cambridge. Photo by courtesy of the Courtauld Institute of Art*)

Tartar horsemen pursuing the defeated King Béla of Hungary; an illustration from the near-contemporary Hungarian *Képes Kronika.* It depicts the fleeing monarch against a background of smoke-covered sky and a burning castle. In fact, the king was relentlessly pursued by the scouts of the Englishman from fort to fort, from Austria down to the Adriatic littoral. (*Szechenyi Library, Budapest*)

The parish church of Little Dunmow, Essex, the surviving portion of the more impressive priory that stood there when Robert FitzWalter was lord of the manor and the Englishman his chaplain. It has changed little since FitzWalter and his chaplain attended mass there, and provides an organic link with the past.

A plaque inside Little Dunmow church, erected near the place where Robert FitzWalter's grave used to be. He left his mark on Little Dunmow, where a legendary tradition has gathered around him. In a suitably romantic form these legends have become entwined with the powerful lore of Robin Hood.

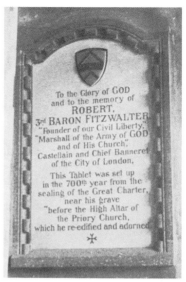

To the Glory of GOD
and to the memory of
ROBERT,
3rd BARON FITZWALTER
"Founder of our Civil Liberty,"
"Marshall of the Army of GOD
and of His Church,"
Castellain and Chief Banneret
of the City of London,

This Tablet was set up
in the 700th year from the
sealing of the Great Charter,
near his grave
"before the High Altar of
the Priory Church,
which he re-edified and adorned

The ceremony of claiming a flitch of bacon has become associated with Robert FitzWalter's memory. His charitable encouragement of stable marriages is now the Little Dunmow church's sole claim to fame, even though the custom of presenting a side of bacon to a couple that had not repented their marriage for a year and a day dates almost certainly from earlier times.

pean ruler—Prince Mstislav of Kiev, who quickly rallied the forces of the Russian principalities of Halich, Kursk, Smolensk and Chernigov against the Eastern horsemen ravaging the lands south of Russia's soft underbelly.

A war against the Russian princes was not part of Subotai's western incursion and, after a swift and deadly attack on the unwary Cumanians, he sent a ten-man embassy to the Russian armies gathered near the River Dniepr, offering to make common cause with the Russians against the Cumanians. 'The Cumanians', the envoys reasoned, 'have frequently plundered the lands of the Russian princes. All the Khan of Khans wants is to punish his disloyal Cuman vassals, yet the Russians are now taking the field with the Cumanians, instead of taking vengeance on them.'

The Russians haughtily rejected the offer of alliance as a cheap Eastern trick, noting that the Cumanians had never been the vassals of the Mongols. And to show their contempt for these uncivilised barbarians, they had the envoys put to death.

The Mongols exacted the most terrible revenge for the murder of their ambassadors. But in order to shame the Christian princes who, contrary to the accepted customs of all nations, murdered envoys, Subotai first sent a fresh embassy to show Mongol observance of internationally accepted standards and declare war. The envoys also invoked divine judgement for the arrogant breach of faith by the Russians, a confusing act by reputedly heathen barbarians. 'You have killed our envoys. Well, as you wish for war you shall have it. We have done you no harm', Subotai's message continued. 'God is impartial; He will decide our quarrel.'

In the 1222 battle of the River Kalka, near the Sea of Azov, Subotai completely wiped out the close-on 100,000-strong Russian host. Among the dead were six royal princes, seventy noble boyars and the cream of Russia's fighting men. With 10,000 Russian dead for every murdered envoy, the Mongols taught a sharp lesson to the arrogant Europeans. But, as the subsequent course of events was to show, the Russians failed to benefit from this lesson.

This signal victory in Europe marked the end of Genghis Khan's unpremeditated western campaign provoked by the Khwarismians' murder of his ambassadors. According to cautious estimates, some eighteen million people were butchered by the Mongols in the years of the empire-building—a holocaust unrivalled in the annals of humanity until the twentieth century.

In 1224, Genghis returned home victorious, having installed his sons and kinsmen as *satraps* to rule the string of newly conquered countries.

A sheer enumeration of the number of countries conquered or a dispassionate account of the scale of his carnage would hardly give a measure of the man.

Although he was an unusually gifted war leader and a brilliant tactician who introduced elements of surprise and innovation into his every campaign, this would only raise him shoulder high above his fellow steppe warriors, but not explain his success in forging the squabbling herdsmen of Asia into an elemental force that changed the course of history and altered the map of two continents.

Like a primeval jolt, his ferocious onslaught upset the balance of the steppes of Asia, and the movement of displaced and warring tribes sucked more and more nations into an avalanche-like progression which kept gathering momentum, almost despite itself. Genghis, who started it all, could no more stop this human avalanche than control the elements. But he could harness it to his purpose. And his purpose—his sole interest in life—was war.

'What is the greatest happiness in life?' he asked his favourite generals whom he had nicknamed 'dogs of war' after the western triumphs. One answered that he could not imagine anything nicer than going hunting on a fresh spring morning and watch his swiftest falcon seize its prey.

'No', said the Englishman's new master, 'this is not true happiness. The greatest pleasure is to vanquish your enemies, to chase them before you, to rob them of their wealth, to see their near and dear bathed in tears, to ride their horses and sleep on the white bellies of their wives and daughters.'

Apart from being a ferocious war-lover, Genghis Khan also had a sense of mission—he wanted to conquer the world. And this sense of mission provided the extra factor in his empire-building career that cannot be quantified, or indeed reduced to religious fervour, since he did not belong to the crusading religions which provided emotional springs for world domination.

The moral justification for the tidal wave of steppe horsemen ravaging the world was his vague shamanist belief in the powers of the 'Eternal Blue Skies', in the name of which he wanted to establish, as he grew older, universal peace on earth. Like so many conquerors after him, he wanted his empire to serve as the ideal of the universal state.

But he had critical faculties and he knew his own and his empire's limitations. He confided in the Taoist monk, philosopher and sage Chang Chun, whom he invited to his court: 'In the space of seven years I have succeeded in accomplishing a great work, uniting the whole world in one empire', he said, looking back on his Chinese and Khwarismian campaigns. 'I myself have not got distinguished qualities . . . But as my calling is high, the obligations incumbent on me are also heavy and I fear that in my rule there may be something wanting. To cross a river we need boats and rudders. Likewise we need sages and must choose assistants to keep the empire in good order.'*

This crying need for qualified people to run the empire brought the Englishman to Genghis Khan's court in 1224. The Khan of Khans was an excessively proud but simple man, quite different in his life style and mode of government from the rulers the Englishman had known in London, Paris or the Holy Land.

'I hate luxury and exercise moderation', Genghis told the Chinese philosopher, and no doubt demonstrated to the Englishman too. 'I have only one coat and eat one [type of] food: I eat the same food and am dressed in the same tatters as my humble herdsmen'.

If this was perhaps a welcome change from the ostentatious luxury of European courts, the way Genghis exercised his power could hardly have been palatable to a politically schooled European like the Englishman, who had devoted his best years to championing individual rights and opposing royal despotism.

But the time of illusions and pipe-dreams was over. The notions cherished in Western Europe did not apply in the Gobi Desert, the principles enshrined in the Magna Carta had no relevance for administration of an empire built on the bones of slaughtered millions. It was the moment of truth in the Englishman's life, demanding an ethical choice when the simple imperative of keeping alive offered no alternative to acquiescence.

Since Genghis Khan brooked no opposition and tolerated no qualms from his officials, the choice facing the Englishman was between faithful service for the Khan of Khans or swift death. He

---

* *The Way and its Power, a study of Tao Te-ching and its place in Chinese thought.*

chose the former, knowing full well that there was no room for doubts or moral reservations in Mongol service.

Yet the very nature of Mongol power and the callous way it had to be exercised by Genghis Khan's officials must have raised doubts in the Englishman about his position. For one thing, the Mongol war preparations were, in the years to come, directed against Europe, not obscure Asiatic steppe kingdoms. Having seen with his own eyes the apocalyptic scenes of destruction wrought by Mongol warfare, he must have sensed that what he was doing was a betrayal of his own civilisation and the world he had grown up in. It was political treason, war crime in modern parlance, a charge hitherto never levelled in Europe.

He could argue, however, in the scholastic spirit of his time, that Genghis Khan had not forced him to betray or abandon his faith, which was the sole criterion of treason in medieval Europe. Furthermore, as a shamanist, Genghis was no enemy of Christendom and, as the scourge of Islam in Asia he was, at a remove, the ally of the crusading princes of Christendom fighting the Infidels.

He could also have countered any Devil's Advocate, if he cared to reason it all out, in the spirit of the Bishop of Winchester, that to serve the Mongol war machine was no treason to Christendom because the destruction of the heretic Nestorian and schismatic Orthodox Christians was a service to the unity of the Church. 'Let those dogs devour each other and be utterly wiped out; and we shall then see, founded on the ruins, the universal Catholic Church'.

With his religious qualms stilled by Genghis Khan's policy of toleration for all creeds, he embarked on his new career with zeal and alacrity, as his activities in Mongol service testified. For, as he emphasized in his confession, whatever he had done he did not desert his faith, and consequently could not have been a traitor.

THIRTEEN

Yeliu Chu-tsai's chancellery

AFTER THE BUSTLE OF ACRE, Paris and London, Karakorum must have seemed to the Englishman a rather unusual place from which to govern a continent-size empire. Originally Genghis Khan's main army camp on the banks of the River Orhon, it was a vast conglomeration of *yurts* (the Mongol felt tents), with camels and cattle ambling along the passageways, children and women riding on shaggy ponies and captive foreign artisans plying their trades in strictly segregated quarters.

In the 1220s, when it suddenly had to cope with the burden of administering the brash new empire, Karakorum was still devoid of the traditional attributes and civilised amenites of city life.

Permanent institutions were needed to rule the conquered territories, courts to mete out justice, financial experts to levy and supervise the gathering of taxes, and a political superstructure to knit into a cohesive unit the extraordinarily disparate collection of vanquished tribes and nations. The task of undertaking this superhuman organisational work fell on Genghis's chancellor, Yeliu Chu-tsai, a former counsellor of the Chin emperor captured in Peking, who had the temerity to tell the Khan of Khans that the empire 'won from the saddle' could no longer be 'ruled from the saddle'.

It was easier for Yeliu to initiate the building of houses to receive the many foreign and provincial dignitaries calling on state affairs, and to finance shops, markets and homes for the officials of the administration than to convince the leading families of the new empire to settle down to an ordered city life.

The Mongols, who had spent virtually their entire lives on horseback, feared and despised houses. In their scheme of things fixed places of abode were for the dead. Houses tied people down, tents did not, so the traditionalist argument ran. The *yurt* could be pitched wherever the fancy took a free-ranging Mongol and his pony; but a house could not be picked up and carted away.

But in this, as in so many other spheres, Genghis overcame his limitations and in spite of the nomad's innate fear of being trapped in a walled city, he proceeded with the transformation of Karakorum into a permanent seat of Mongol power.

Needless to say, it all went against the grain and he himself would not have dreamt of exchanging his imperial *yurt* for a house. Batu Khan, Genghis's grandson and the warlord the Englishman was destined to serve, also showed the same deeply ingrained resistance to living in a house. During his Western campaign the Englishman was charged to commit this sentiment to paper in a taunting letter to the beleaguered King of Hungary:

'For it is much easier for the Cumanians who wander hither and thither to take flight than for you who live in fixed houses, have forts and towns; so how do you escape my hands?'

Craftsmen, stonemasons, gunsmiths and artisans of a wide variety from the conquered cities of Khwarism, and administrators and scribes from China formed the backbone of the resident civilian population of Karakorum at the time of the Englishman's arrival. Arab and Turkish merchants acting as the middlemen between the Far East and the trade centres of the Middle East had their own section of mud-brick houses and warehouses next to the quarter of foreign envoys. Adjoining them lived the mullahs, shamans, bonzes, marabouts and archpriests, with Muslim mosques, Buddhist temples and a Nestorian Christian church coexisting in peace.

But the Mongol aristocrats continued to live in their *yurts,* which they moved as they followed Genghis Khan's court from place to place in accordance with the time-honoured passage dictated by the seasons.

To cope with the rapidly growing needs of his empire, Genghis transferred thousands of Khwarismians skilled in trades and professions to northern China, into what travellers came to describe as the 'Muslim town'. But the shifting of large sections of conquered people from one part of the empire to another could only provide an urban population of certain limited categories.

It was left to Yeliu to recruit, through more subtle means, scholars, astrologers, mathematicians and men of letters for the top posts in the administration. Most appointments went to learned Chinese though some, like the Englishman, were commissioned farther afield. It was their luck to work with and benefit from the protection of Yeliu, a forerunner of the Western Renaissance humanists, to whom civilisation is more indebted than it is credited or realised today.

Yeliu's privileged position in the court of the barbarous Khan of Khans was a reflection of the high esteem he had earned for himself in Genghis's eyes through his wisdom, integrity and phenomenal intelligence.

Their relationship began after the capture of Peking when, along with all the treasures of the Chin emperor, caravans of craftsmen, astrologers, masons and men of letters were sent to Mongolia as booty. One of these captives was Yeliu, the descendant of the powerful Liao family, who was a counsellor of the Chin emperor, but on the list of the Mongols with which the captives were accompanied, his usefulness was catalogued as 'soothsayer and astrologer'.

Genghis, who carefully examined the convoys of useful slaves reaching his court, appears to have singled out the tall, twenty-five-year-old soothsayer for special attention.

'The houses of Liao and Chin have always been enemies', he addressed his captive, in a clever opening gambit, hinting heavily at the Mongol origins of the Liaos who used to rule northern China until ousted by the Chin. 'I have avenged you.'

But Yeliu did not jump at this offer to dissociate himself from the vanquished emperor and the guilt attaching to his service in the Peking court, preferring to show loyalty to his ruler even in adversity.

'My father, my grandfather and I myself were the servants of the house of Chin,' he replied. 'I should be a liar and a hypocrite if I were to feign now hostile feelings towards my father and the Emperor.'

Genghis, who despised the servile attitude of town-dwellers brought in fetters to his court, admired the honesty of the Chin emperor's counsellor and offered him a post as court soothsayer and astrologer. Through his competence and ability to translate Genghis's ideas into government action he soon became the Khan's adviser and eventually his trusted friend.

This friendship brought incalculable benefits to the vanquished countries and saved the lives of millions of people. He stood between the oppressed and oppressor, pleading for justice, order and the sanctity of human life, yet at the same time he was busy establishing the superstructure without which Genghis's empire would have melted away without a trace, like water in the sands of the Gobi Desert.

When Genghis's generals, not knowing what to do with the vast urban population of conquered China, decided to massacre them all, obliterate their towns and turn their well-tended fields into grazing land for the Mongol horses right down to the Yellow River, Yeliu succeeded in convincing the Khan that it was in his very own interest to use the industrious Chinese as a source of regular tax revenue rather than as fertiliser.

His diplomatic reasoning 'why kill the goose that, if well treated, can lay endless golden eggs?' saved the lives of China's teeming millions and won him Genghis's esteem. The barbarous order of 'scorched earth' was retracted and, instead of ruining crops and massacring the population, Yeliu's tax collectors began gathering the revenue to finance Genghis Khan's campaigns.

During the campaigns, while all the Mongols looted, pillaged and robbed, Yeliu concentrated on saving books, geographical maps, musical instruments and paintings and collected drugs and herbs for medicinal purposes. Slowly and subtly, he began to impress upon Genghis and his sons the hideousness of their endless carnage and the importance of ruling rather than butchering the conquered nations.

By the time the Englishman arrived in Mongolia, Yeliu had graduated from divining the future from the shoulder blades of sheep to the all-powerful position of Genghis Khan's chancellor, or chief minister. He was the hub of the nascent administration, the creator of laws and the instiller of order amid the disorder and carnage of Genghis's conquests.

'When one sets up a china factory,' he told the Khan of Khans, 'one must gather the best skilled workmen for the conduct of affairs; we must do the same, and only lettered people are fit for this work. If we do not begin to employ such men the race will become extinct.'

He thus saved the lives and provided employment for thousands of Chinese, Uighur, Persian and Arab scientists and men of letters, to the benefit of the Mongol empire.

Himself a noted mathematician, astrologer and Confucian philosopher, Yeliu tempered the ignorance of the Mongols by making the ancient Chinese civilisation felt in the court. He taught Genghis's sons, and eventually his grandsons, instilling in them love for culture and science.

His friendship with Genghis assured the supremacy of educated men, in the teeth of violent objections by the traditionalist Mongol officer caste, and the closing of the cultural gap between the Mongol warriors and conquered elite of Asia in a very short space of time.

By using the culture and organisational framework of China to create an ordered state, he greatly helped the new empire to survive the death of its creator and continue its progress in the spirit of Genghis. At the same time, the opening of the door for China's men of letters to the controlling positions of the Mongol empire enabled the Chinese to regain, after a long struggle, control over their own country and eventually oust the conquerors.

But Yeliu also knew how to strike a compromise and not to press a point in the face of too strong traditionalist objections. He was, for instance, against the barbarous custom of sending the prettiest girls of the empire in their hundreds to the palace of the Khan, but when he realised that the tradition could not be stopped, he made sure that the 'selection' was even-handed, equally affecting the highest and the lowest of the empire.

According to the Persian chronicle *Tarik Jihankushai*, tributes in girls were exacted by the army. Each home in an occupied territory was inspected by captains, who chose the prettiest maidens for their superior, the commander of the 'thousand', a Mongol regiment-size unit. He in turn chose the prettiest girls for presentation to the commander of the 'ten thousand', the higher divisional formation. It was up to the latter to send the pick of these girls to Genghis's harem and to other Mongol princes. Girls the princes did not want in their beds were presented as serving wenches to their wives or parents.

According to the chronicle, Genghis had over 500 wives and concubines. Yeliu was the only high-ranking official who did not avail himself of the embraces of these miserable captives.

His usefulness to Genghis was underlined by his knowledge of every detail of the situation in the countries occupied by the Mongol army, and by the effortless way he assured vast sums of money and provisions for the frequent campaigns. This seemed to demonstrate to the nomadic warlord that culture had its practical uses, and Yeliu used this powerful source of good will to frame laws and institute wide-ranging reforms.

Parallel with Yeliu's Chinese chancellery, there appears to have been another administrative centre concerned, in all probability, with internal Mongol affairs. It was headed by an Uighur scholar captured by Genghis during his 1205 campaign, whose name—Ta Ta-tong—has only survived in Chinese transcription.*

He staffed his chancellery with fellow Uighur men of letters, highly cultivated people of Turkic race, whose script became the 'Uighur Chancellery's' official writing. Through the medium of Uighur, Buddhist canons and Nestorian Christian teachings reached the nomads of the steppes. Because of its cultural weight among the nomad tribes, Genghis insisted that his sons should also be taught the Uighur script.

Apart from Ta Ta-tong, who introduced Genghis to the use of

The Mongol imperial seal

royal seals and became the keeper of the Mongol seal stone, the Kerait scholar Chinquai also played a vital role in the evolution of the administrative system.

These were the formative years that determined the final shape

* Yuan-che Lei-pien: 'Ta ta-tong', French translation by A. Remusat, *Nouveaux mélanges asiatiques*, II.

of the Mongol superstructure, but no period was more important than 1224-1225, in all probability the only two years when Genghis was not fighting a war. Thus, in a way, the Englishman was lucky in arriving at Karakorum in the days of consolidation, when the stress was on administrative rather than martial skills.

He spent the following years in the chancellery of Yeliu, the dynamic nerve centre of Mongol expansionism. In spite of diligent search in Mongol, Chinese, Persian and Arab archives, no direct mention could be found of the Englishman over these eleven years preceding the crucial 1235 *kuriltai* at which Europe's fate was decided.

But since he could only have survived under the care and protection of Yeliu, the activities of the imperial chancellor provide the best guide as to what filled the waking hours of the Englishman during his stay in Karakorum.

Yeliu's plans for the structural transformation and unification of the occupied countries included sweeping monetary reforms, the issuing of paper money and the introduction of a tax system based on hearth, or family, instead of the Mongol generals' preferred method of indiscriminate wholesale extortion.

He also established a uniform system of weights and measures to replace the arbitrary measures introduced at the whim of Mongol *satraps*.

In an extraordinarily farsighted move, he extended the brief of *darogas* to act not just as mere post station masters but as the fully-empowered bailiffs and commissioners of the central administration. Further, he fixed the number of horses a person of rank was entitled to and introduced the use of travel warrants—still extant in Russia in the form of *putyovka*—which were to be presented at each station when a demand for horses was made. This enraged the Mongol nobles and princes of the royal house, who had been used to taking as many post horses as they wished and to make extravagant requisitions at their will for other supplies, but Yeliu won out.

But Yeliu's most important action, in the long run at any rate, was the introduction of the Mandarin system of examinations for the civil service, establishing proficiency as the test of capacity for public appointment. The examinations were open to everyone and the statutory punishment for preventing slaves from attending was death.

He also founded two colleges, one in Peking and the other at Pin Yang, Shansi province, where the children of the Mongol ruling élite were taught geography, arithmetic, history and astronomy, giving them an excellent grounding for their future commanding roles.

It would be a thrilling enterprise to assess the Englishman's contribution to these reforms affecting continents, but the ascertainable facts only allow the conclusion that his was a junior, subordinate role in his early years in Mongol service.

Yet the evidence of later years indicates that, perhaps because of his political competence and diplomatic aptitude, he soon won preferment and was raised from the rank of interpreter-chancellery scribe to the executive class of Mongol envoys with power to represent and negotiate on behalf of the Khan of Khans.

It is a reasonable assumption, afforded by the inner evidence of the workings of Genghis Khan's 'external' chancellery, that such rapid promotion across the racial divide would have hardly been possible without the good will, and most likely friendly support, of Yeliu Chu-tsai. The belief that a friendship could have developed between the scholarly chancellor and his learned subordinate is not such a far-fetched idea considering their shared interest in linguistics and their similar age—Yeliu was born in 1190 and the Englishman in 1188.

The Englishman's chance came when the ailing Khan of Khans, already in his sixties, decided to divide up his vast empire among his sons, allotting armies and territories. Chagatai was to have the former Khwarismian empire and Kara Khitai; Ogodai the territories east of Mongolia; Tuli the Mongol heartlands as befits the youngest son; and Batu, Genghis's grandson, inheriting the apanage of the dead Juchi, all the lands to the north-west 'as far as the hooves of a Mongol pony can take him'.

It was a vast fief for Batu Khan to rule, with the promise of even more lands to be conquered in the rich plains of Europe. The burden of preparing and spearheading with his diplomatic skill the Mongol drive towards the Atlantic fell on the Englishman.

But before preparations could have started, and organisational changes within the chancellery could be made, Genghis had set out on his last campaign to fulfil his promise of vengeance on the Tangut kingdom of Hsia-Hsi, before death could cheat him of the pleasure of seeing its emperor slain and his kingdom scorched.

Like Carthage for Cato, the destruction of the Tanguts had become an obsession with Genghis. Their ruler's refusal to fulfil a vassal's duty and join Genghis's punitive war against the Khwarismian empire after the murder of the Mongol ambassadors, had filled the Khan of Khans with an all-consuming passion for revenge.

Not unlike Cato's ritual incantation in the Senate ending in 'ceterum censeo Carthaginem esse delendam', Genghis wished daily to be informed, according to the Chinese language *Yüan-chao Pi-shih* chronicle, that the Tangut kingdom had not yet been destroyed, thus keeping his resolve alive.

But in 1226 there were more pressing reasons than an old man's obsession with chastising a traitorous vassal: the new ruler of Hsia-Hsi was actively aiding Chinese rebels in the neighbouring Chin territories, refused to send his son as hostage to Karakorum and, according to Mongol intelligence reports, was busy assembling an army half-a-million strong.

Well before the onset of spring, Genghis set out with an army of 180,000 horsemen to thwart a Tangut-Chin alliance and avenge the Tangut slight. The omens, however, were not good: five planets appeared in a baleful conjunction, foretelling, in the view of the court astrologers, that evil was awaiting the Khan of Khans.

The Mongol horsemen once again defeated the 300,000 strong Tangut army in a cataclysmic encounter on the frozen Yellow River, where the shod hooves of the Tangut horses could find no purchase and slid about wildly, while the unshod Mongol ponies took the ice in their stride.

Although the Mongols embarked on a blood-crazed orgy of slaughter, the much-desired revenge on the Tangut ruler eluded Genghis Khan personally: he was thrown from his horse while out hunting and became mortally ill, according to the thirteenth century *Secret History of the Mongols*.

Before his death, he sent for his sons and grandsons to appoint a successor and to warn them against dissension: 'With the aid of the Eternal Blue Heaven I have conquered for you a huge empire', he told them. 'From the middle of it a man may ride for a year eastward or westward without reaching its limits. But my life was too short to achieve the conquest of the whole world. That task is left to you. Be of one mind and one faith, that you may conquer your enemies and lead long and happy lives.'

He then appointed Ogodai as his successor and ordered him to cut down mercilessly the Tangut ruler and the entire population of his capital when they surrendered.

Genghis died on 18 August 1227. His body was carried back from Hsia-Hsi to Mongolia, and to keep the news of his death from setting alight the empire, every living creature—man, beast and bird—encountered along the route was hunted down and killed.

This gave rise to a multitude of legends as to the 'true cause' of the great khan's death. Friar Carpine was informed in Karakorum that Genghis had been struck down by a bolt of lightning; Marco Polo learnt that he had died from an arrow wound; and Chinese chroniclers, perhaps wishing to avenge with a bit of character assassination the sufferings inflicted on their country by the conqueror, recorded that Genghis died from a wound inflicted by the Tangut ruler's beautiful wife, Kürbeldyshin-Khatun, while dallying in his harem. She caused the mortal wound 'with her teeth' and then threw herself into the nearby Yellow River to avoid capture.

This recurring theme of undignified death in bed can still be found in several seventeenth century Mongol chronicles, which were based on much older works.

One of them, in a graphic description, records that the captive Tangut queen pressed a small piece of metal into her vagina and, on the night Genghis first visited her bed, gravely injured the imperial organ. She then fled from the palace and threw herself into the Yellow River.*

Be that as it may, in order to secure a safe transition of power, Yeliu ordered a two-year mourning and used this breathing space to ensure that the *kuriltai*, the sole body legally empowered to appoint a new Khan of Khans, would respect his lord's choice of a successor.

Genghis's erstwhile captive and soothsayer thus played a crucial role in the election of Ogodai and saved the empire from disintegration through a fratricidal war. More importantly for Europe, he also furnished the new Khan of Khans with the fearsome instruments that would enable him to 'complete the conquest of the whole world', as demanded by Genghis.

* Prof. Walter Heissig in his *Lost Civilisation* devotes a chapter to the sources of this variant of Genghis's death.

FOURTEEN

The power of
Mongol envoys

OGODAI, the new Khan of Khans, was no Genghis. He was kindly and generous, with a greater interest in luxurious living than in war-making, and he totally lacked his father's cruel ferocity. He was also given to excessive drinking, and not even Yeliu's demonstration of how a piece of iron could be corroded away if left in a glass of wine was able to cure his addiction.

However, thanks to the genius of Yeliu and the cohesive force of the *Yassak*, Genghis's set of laws regulating every aspect of life, the empire not only survived the death of its creator but was set to carry out new wars of conquest.

The army, the embodiment of the state's *raison d'être*, was fighting fit, the central administration was functioning smoothly and the 1229 *kuriltai* mapped out, under Yeliu's guidance, the immediate tasks in fulfilling Genghis's behest to conquer the world.

The order of priorities was, first, the silencing of opposition in the territories of the former Chin empire in North China, followed by the completion of the conquest of Western Asia, and finally, the subjugation of Europe.

The campaign against the Chin was led by Ogodai, who proved that he could fight bravely if the need arose. Within a year of ascending the throne he completely destroyed the Chin restoration attempt, and only Yeliu's intervention saved the population from extirpation.

Another army rode to Persia and Asia Minor, completing the conquest of Western Asia. But the third and most challenging enterprise was the invasion of Europe, which required more than simply fielding a seasoned army.

The preparations in the diplomatic field for Batu Khan's western drive fell to the Englishman, who was transferred to the new command. And he had to pick his way gingerly within the system—the army traditions, Yeliu's administration and the precepts of the *Yassak*—without putting a foot wrong. It must have been a difficult, if not an almost impossible, task for a European to perform, but he did it well, for soon he was given the task of spearheading the attack on the West, through diplomatic negotiations as Batu Khan's personal envoy.

There is good reason to believe that he had a hand in the thorough intelligence operation preceding Mongol campaigns, probably in the organisation and evaluation of reports and, as circumstantial evidence suggests, in using the Venetian secret service as an extended arm of Mongol army intelligence.

But his main domain, as he himself later testified, and was observed by startled eye-witnesses, was diplomacy. When the Mongol avalanche eventually reached Europe, sweeping all before it, the majority of kings and princes of Europe believed in their utter ignorance that these Asiatic hordes had no notion of diplomacy. Others simply refused to treat with the representatives of barbarous nomads and had them put to death.

Reflecting Europe's haughty approach, Thomas of Spalato wrote: 'Not being either Christians, or Jews, or Saracens, the Tartars [the name by which the Mongols became known throughout the continent] do not follow any faith, and therefore they do not have any true feeling.

'They keep no faith, nor promise and, contrary to the custom of all nations, they do not receive—nor do they send—envoys or embassies in matters of war or peace.'

In actual fact nothing could have been further from the truth. Diplomacy played a crucial role in the Mongol plans for hegemony. Through his envoys the Khan of Khans expressed his claim to world supremacy and underlined his standing vis-à-vis the rest of the world. The dispatches were clear reflections of the Mongol legal, political and constitutional concepts, but these were completely misunderstood and consequently ignored as the arrogant ramblings of Asiatic savages. The results were terrible, and some of them are still with us over seven centuries later.

The first period of Mongol diplomatic activity, beginning with Genghis Khan's final years to about 1262, when Mongol power was first checked, has never been studied. The attention paid by successive generations of scholars to the second phase of Mongol diplomacy, covering the years after the disintegration of the empire into the successor empires of China, Persia and the Kipchak khanate, has helped to conceal this gap in our knowledge.

Yet the still extant dispatches—some in Persian, other in Latin and Arabic translations*—offer a perfectly lucid guide to the precepts of Mongol diplomacy in its first period and the framework within which the Englishman had had to operate.

These communications from the Khan of Khans were not diplomatic exchanges between equal, sovereign states but simple orders for submission. For Europeans brought up on notions of a world composed of more or less independent sovereign states, this appeared as a preposterous and arrogant insult. Yet as the stereo-typed preamble of all these messages between the years 1221 and 1262 indicates, nothing could have been further from the Mongol imperial chancellery's intentions.

'Through the power of the Eternal Heavens, we, the ocean-like† Khan of the mightily great Mongol people, order . . .'

This formula of the preamble reflected the divine origin of the Khan's power, which automatically raised him above all the other kings and princes. It also justified the intention of securing military and economic domination on earth, since the Mongol empire-building was not an exercise in power politics but the fulfilment of God's will.

The Khan's letter to the French king, for instance, began with a reference to the order of God which 'neither from Genghis Khan nor from his successors came to you' ('nec Chingischan nec ab aliis post ipsum pervenit ad vos').

The legend on the imperial seal, itself the source of mystical power in Mongol eyes, reaffirmed this absolute belief that the Khan of Khans was the sole repository of power on earth by Divine Will: 'God in Heaven, and Genghis [or later, Güyük] on Earth, Khan by the power of God and Emperor of all men'.

This notion, not unlike the contemporary papal dogma of 'one

---

* A collection of the extant Mongol diplomatic dispatches is contained in the *Speculum Historiae* of Vincent of Beauvais. Paul Pelliot's *Les Mongols et la Papauté* provides an incisive analysis of the later period of Mongol diplomacy.

† 'Ocean-like' is a poor rendering of the Mongol word *Dalai*, which is still used to indicate the immense god-given power of the Dalai Lama.

shepherd, one fold', was perhaps the only Mongol tenet showing unmistakable Christian influence.

This metaphysical foundation of Mongol power invested the person of the khan here on earth with rights analogous to those enjoyed by God in the Eternal Heavens, and helped to bridge the gap between the world order envisaged by Genghis and the actual power reality of the first half of the thirteenth century.

Looked at from the Mongol angle, it made the proposed conquest of the world a perfectly natural, legal and, in its intention, peaceful enterprise.

A letter to Pope Innocent, the *primus inter pares* of the Christian world, serenely demanded instant submission:

> . . . Genghis Khan and Güyük Khan have both sent envoys to make God's order on the world's submission to the Mongols well understood . . . Through the power of God, from the rising of the Sun to its setting all the lands have been conceded to us and we possess them. Without the authority of God, how could anyone do anything?
>
> But now you must say with a sincere heart: 'We will be your subjects, we will put our strength at your disposal. You in person, at the head of kings [of Christendom], all together and without exception, must come to us and pay us homage and offer your services. And then we will accept your submission. If, however, you do not observe the order of God and go against our orders, we will know that you are our enemies. This is what we are letting you know. If you go against us, why, who knows what is going to happen? God alone knows.*

Since Genghis's empire was not a mere state among the many states of this world but the earthly reflection of God's rule in Heaven, kings not heeding the order of submission were treated as rebels. And, as the Englishman noted in his confession, the Mongols 'think that there is no cruelty in practising every kind of severity on those who rebel against them.'

The twin source of this concept was the *Yassak* and the Chinese belief in the divine status of an emperor, revealing Yeliu's hand in the formulation of the ideological basis of the Mongol world

---

* In this first ever translation into English of this important document, I used the Persian, French and German versions of the missing original text.

empire. The import of the *Yassak* in formulating submission orders was shown by the phrase in the letter to the Pope which said 'You, the great Pope, must come with the kings to pay us homage and we will then tell you about the prophecies contained in the *Yassak.*'

The divine mandate of the Khan to conquer the world, sanctioned by the *Yassak,* was the source of the legal principle construing all states, even those beyond the immediate reach of the Mongol army, as *intended* members of the Mongol empire.

The Khan's envoys therefore merely performed the ritual function of informing these kings—when their lands came into contact with the expansionist Mongol empire—of their duty to submit and accept vassal status. This was the reason why Mongol embassies could not discuss mutual recognition of power and territories, to the amazement of European rulers. Since the position of the world conqueror was, because of his divine mandate, exclusive and absolute, there was no basis for an equal relationship or alliance, only subservience.

Another aspect of this underlying dogma was that Mongol envoys could neither offer peace nor declare war on independent kingdoms upon first contact with the Mongol empire. It simply depended upon the king's reply to God's order of submission: if he gave in he could secure a position within the empire; if he rejected, he challenged God's order and became a rebel who had to be punished. But there could have been no talk of peace or war, for either was only possible among equals.

To European rulers brought up on ideas that the international community consisted of independent, sovereign states, the demand of a Mongol envoy for immediate and unconditional submission must have seemed arrogant in the extreme and too grotesque to be taken seriously.

This would explain why there was such a strong belief in Europe after the initial contacts with the Mongols that 'contrary to the custom of all nations, they do not receive—nor do they send—envoys or embassies in matters of war and peace'.

As the two worlds, fired by different ideals, were heading for a head-on collision, there was no communication between the two sides. The Englishman who alone could have bridged the gap between the two civilisations, elected to exercise the terrifying power of the Mongol envoy, with the world's most powerful army behind him, in accordance with his brief. His attempts to warn the princes of Christendom of the awful fate awaiting them if they did not submit to his lord were seen as crude intimidation and treated as such. With hindsight, no one could deny his good intentions in painting such a terrible picture of the devastation they faced if they persisted in their foolish resistance to Mongol suzerainty.

Apart from the small Volga nations, who gave in to the Englishman's demand for submission, no self-respecting European power took the message purveyed by Mongol envoys seriously in the 1230s and the beginning of the 1240s.

The Russians had the Mongol envoys put to death; King Béla IV of Hungary refused to reply even after two personal visits by the Englishman; Emperor Frederick of the Holy Roman Empire treated the Mongol submission order with levity and replied with a joke; and King Louis of France saw fit to reduce the Mongol threat to a pun.

The actual letters of the Khan of Khans made perfectly clear in legal terms the alternative to instant surrender—total destruction.

In reply to the Pope's remonstration over the appalling slaughter of Hungarians and other Central European Catholics, the Khan of Khans pointed out, more in sorrow than in anger, that they only got their just deserts, the punishment having been decreed by God to suit the crime.

> These people ignored God's order [of submission]; so much so that they even held a great counsel, behaved very arrogantly in their rejection and they killed our ambassadors. So the Eternal God himself killed and extirpated the people of these lands. But how would anyone, on his own, without God's will, kill and plunder [those lands]?

The self-righteous indignation of the Mongol reply revealed the unshakable belief that nations disobeying God's order had placed themselves outside the community of reasonable, God-fearing men. Their destruction at the hands of the Mongol horsemen was merely an act of divine retribution.

The demarches demanding submission were couched in basically similar terms, allowing a very limited leeway for the chancellery clerk phrasing them. Their work, like that of the translators, was very closely supervised, as we know from Carpine's Karakorum report.

On the feast of St Martin we were again summoned, and Kadac, Chingay, Bala and several others of the [chancellery] secretaries met us, and the letter was translated word for word. And as we translated it into Latin they made us explain each phrase, wishing to ascertain if we had made a mistake in any word. And when the two letters were written they made us read them together and separately for fear we had left out something, and they said to us: 'Be sure you understand it all, for it must not be that you do not understand everything, when you have reached your lands.'

A Latin version of a submission order had preserved the chancellery's standard conditions: 'Quiumque statutum audierit super propriam terram aquam et patrimonian sedeat et ei qui faciem totius orbis continet virtutem tradat. Quiumque autem preceptum et statutum non audierit sed aliter fecerit illi deleantur et perdantur.'

These orders for submission were, however, always elaborated on, commented upon and explained in minute detail by the Khan's envoys. And this offered the Englishman a limited initiative, since there could be no firm rules on how to handle particular situations.

But any tactical compromise, unless done in bad faith, had to be limited by the overriding need to achieve instant submission which made the job of ambassadors an impossible task.

The justifications put forward by the Englishman in the course of his negotiations are most enlightening.

In his confession he admitted that Mongol envoys used 'fictions' in order to prevail 'on some simple kings to make a treaty [of submission] with them, and grant them a free passage through their territories.' He readily agreed that 'the Tartars did not keep the treaties, and those princes perished all the same'.

But he also offered a rare insight into the Mongol negotiating techniques which, in his words, were eminently suited 'to deceive the people and the princes of the countries' as to the true intentions of the Mongols.

To achieve a quick submission the Mongol ambassadors asked for right of passage and gave 'reasons which are no reasons' as an explanation of their campaign in Europe.

He listed several of these diplomatic 'fictions' which, it must be assumed, he used in his own negotiations but which must have formed part of stock explanations prepared in advance by his chancellery.

> At one time they say they left their country [in Asia] to bring back the sacred bodies of the Magi Kings, which adorn the city of Cologne; at another time they say it was to check the avarice and pride of the Romans, who oppressed them of old; another reason was to subdue under their dominion the barbarous Hyperborean nations and tribes; then they said it was their intention to temper the fury of the Teutonics with their own moderation; now it was to learn warfare from the French; now to gain a sufficiency of fertile land on which to maintain their multitudes; and, lastly, they said it was to terminate their pilgrimage at St James's [grave] in Galicia. By these fictions, they prevailed on some simple kings to make a treaty with them . . .

Although some of these negotiating ploys sound rather primitive—and there is good reason to believe that they were deliberately made to appear so in the rendering of the heretic French priest—they reveal an astute appreciation of a number of issues which could have had a popular appeal in the 1230s.

The intention to go to war in order to 'temper the fury of the Teutonic knights' who were then ravaging the north of Russia, would have sounded quite plausible in Eastern Europe, while religious campaign motivations, such as a pilgrimage to the grave of St James or the reclamation of the sacred bodies of the Magi kings from Cologne, would have received a fair hearing in the fervently Catholic countries of Central Europe.

The pressing need to gain a sufficiency of fertile land in order to feed their multitudes, put forward in some negotiations, was an admirably truthful and candid explanation of the Mongols' westward drive. This *Lebensraum* theory has since been used by a great many ideologies to justify invasions, the last time by Hitler's Nazi empire.

But the most intriguing 'fiction' used by the Englishman was the intention 'to check the pride and avarice of the Romans'. Since his tribulations were directly linked to the arrogant interference of papal legates in England's internal affairs, and whose greed and cupidity in settling the Magna Carta rebellion caused great hardships to many participants, the impression that this was an attempt at a personal settling of scores is ineluctable. As a fully-fledged envoy plenipotentiary of the Khan he could safely allow himself the indulgence of revenge on the Romans 'who oppressed' him of old, not his Mongol masters.

The reasons for the Englishman's rise to his high position in the Mongol diplomatic service have already been investigated in the preceding chapter, but his meteoric advance can hardly be appreciated without an inkling of the peculiar blend of dogmatic precepts and down-to-earth realism that characterised the system.

There were many multi-lingual scribes and interpreters working in Yeliu's chancellery. Some of them arrived there as prisoners with 'useful skills', others were attracted by the power of the Khan of Khans. As Carpine recorded in his report, there were in the chancellery 'Ruthenian [Russian] clerks and others who had been with the Tartars—some as long as 30 years—in war and in other events, and who knew all about them as they understood the language, having been continually with them some 20, others 10 years, more or less'.

This thirty-year period covers the entire span of the Englishman's diplomatic activities yet, apart from him, not one of the other interpreters was elevated to the executive class to represent the will of the khans. That was an honour reserved for Mongols and their kith and kin from the Central Asian heartlands, whom they could trust.

A linguistic analysis of the names of sixty Mongol envoys sent to Eastern Europe in the following 200 years shows that exceptions like the case of the Englishman amounted to about one a century.

List of Mongol envoys sent to
East Europe (Russia) in XIII-XVth centuries

Year
1259   Kasashchik
1261   Tetjak
1265   Dzhanibeg
1295   Alexander Nevruy*
1315   Emir Khodzha, Taitemir and Indruy
1317   Savlich and Kasandshchi

* European

Year

1318	Khavghadyi, Astrabil and Ostrev *
1318	Koucha
1318	Achamil (or Kiamil)
1320	Baider (or Paidar)
1321	Sevindzh Buga
1321	Tayandzhar
1322	Akhamil
1327	Shchelkan (or Tchelkan)
1332	Serayshchik
1334	Abdul (or Abdullah)
1337	Kindak and Abdul
1338	Istrotchey
1339	Tavlubeg and Mengkukash
1342	Kinduk
1348	Totu (or Tutu)
1352	Ahmed
1357	Iktar
1357	Koshak (or Kushak: ie 'the Belt')
1360	Urus, Khairbeg and Altunzhibeg
1363	Ilak
1364	Urusmandi
1364	Beiram Khodzha
1364	Hassan Khodzha
1370	Hadji Khodzha
1371	Ssari Khodzha
1374	Seraiko
1375	Hadji Khodzha
1381	Ak Khodzha
1382	Shaikh Ahmed
1383	Ak Khodzha
1383	Karatcha
1383	Adash (or Adam)
1389	Shaikh Ahmed
1392	Allan
1396	Timur Khodzha
1400	Bekshik and Satkin*
1400	Safrak

* European

Year
1403   Aintak
1404   Shadibeg's exchequer (no name)
1412   Loth
1432   Ulan
1448   Kalin
1474   Karaküchük
1474   Botshuk

Even the post of *chapar*, a courier or bearer of official correspondence and orders, was way above the career horizon of Europeans, whereas the Englishman was a *tolmidzh*, an *interpreter of the will of the Khan*. Due to a misunderstanding of the meaning of the Mongol word *tolmidzh* at the court of Béla IV of Hungary, where the Englishman was apparently introduced with this title, it was taken to refer to the court translator-interpreter.

The erroneous meaning of the word first introduced into Central Europe by the Englishman has gained full acceptance as *tolmacs* in Hungarian, *Dolmetscher* in German, *talmaci* in Romanian.

Of course, the Englishman was no ordinary translator, as translators do not head embassies and do not negotiate with kings, and he had his *yarlik,* letter of credence, to prove it. It bore the Khan's seal of gold which, unlike the more common silver seal, placed him in the category of top Mongol envoys. This type of *yarlik* had to be obeyed on pain of death by all subjects of the Khan of Khans; it also secured instant service at the post stations, the pick of horses and mules and priority for all other facilities.

In the annals of our continent there were few, if any, Europeans who had the misfortune to represent such an awesome power with such a limited brief.

PART V

In the Footsteps of the Englishman

FIFTEEN

The 1235 *kuriltai*

AFTER QUELLING THE LAST POCKETS of resistance in China, Ogodai called a *kuriltai* of victory in 1235. The princes, elders and generals attending the great council could hardly recognise Karakorum, which had developed into a city in the intervening years, bearing the unmistakable stamp of Ogodai's style.

His Chinese architects had built him a magnificent palace at the edge of the capital, surrounded by a park and a wall half a league in circumference. Chinese ink drawings, sculptures and objects of art decorated it and it had four entrances—one for Ogodai, one for the royal princes, one for the women of the household, and one for the public.

The splendour of the palace was matched by the Khan of Khan's lavish entertaining. Some 500 carts laden with provisions arrived daily from all over the empire to sustain the imperial household and the royal princes living in adjoining palaces.

Yet Ogodai only spent a month in the spring in his Karakorum palace. He lived the rest of the spring season at Kertchagan, about a day's riding from the capital, where his Persian architects had built him another palace rivalling the luxury of Karakorum.

The hot summer he spent at the cool mountain station of Orketua where, according to Chinese records, he lived 'under a Chinese pavilion made of white felt lined with gold-embroidered silken tissue.' In it he could entertain a thousand people.

In the autumn, he spent a month near Lake Keuke, and in the winter he drank and hunted at yet another residence at Ongki. His luxurious life-style was a far cry from his father's asceticism, but the Mongol war machine which Genghis had set in motion was functioning with consummate perfection even as its supreme commander dallied and drank his waking hours away.

To mark the victory of Mongol arms and Subotai's feat of

generalship in the southern Chin provinces, Ogodai decreed that there should be feasting and carousing for a whole month at his Karakorum palace, with no mention of business. It was a fitting start to the *kuriltai* of victory, but the great bouts of drinking became too much even for a man of Ogodai's drinking habits, seriously affecting his health.

In response to Yeliu's openly voiced concern, he agreed to cut his daily intake of wine by half, but his craving for drink proved stronger than his good intention. In order to avoid having to go back on his word, the Khan of Khans ordered goblets twice their previous size for the imperial household.

Before the grand council could get down to business a clash between Yeliu and the grasping princes and princesses of Genghis's clan cast a grave shadow over the proceedings. The royal kin were demanding entire provinces as presents in the newly conquered south Chin lands and Ogodai, with his customary largesse, was about to hand them the territories when Yeliu stepped in.

He reasoned that taxation was preferable to plunder and since the princes had no interest beyond stripping the newly conquered lands bare, the giving away of territories would harm the exchequer. Ogodai, who had already promised to give his relations the coveted territories, asked his chancellor what to do: Yeliu found a golden formula that saved the inhabitants from slavery and the Khan of Khans from having to go back on his word, and which gave incomes and titles of various provinces to the princes, by insisting that the princes 'must ask no more from the territories than the imperial tax collectors gather in taxes'.

This compromise saved the *kuriltai*, but it did not endear Yeliu to the princes of blood and the generals, who had viewed him with growing suspicion since his last intervention which saved the lives of close on two million inhabitants of the south Chin capital of Kai-feng. When, after a year's siege, that city had surrendered to Subotai, he wanted to put to death the inhabitants and raze every building in accordance with the rule laid down by Genghis that there could be no quarter for those resisting God's will.

But Yeliu had chosen his ground shrewdly to oppose the carnage: 'As soon as a town falls, its inhabitants become your subjects. Among them are the best craftsmen, the ablest artists of the country. Will you have them put to death? Why deprive yourself of the most valuable of possessions?' Ogodai heard him out and spared the inhabitants of the city, but the traditionalists of the ruling élite could not forgive this flouting of Genghis's command.

The *kuriltai* of victors eventually got over these initial clashes of interest and was fully united in working out the directives for four wars of conquest, the fourth enlarging on the previous *kuriltai*'s plan to invade Europe. The campaign plan, under the nominal proctorship of Batu but worked out in detail by the veteran general Subotai, who had explored Southern Europe during the 1221-1222 incursion, gave the army eighteen years to complete the total conquest of the continent.

Remarks made by the Englishman in the course of a chance conversation on the borders of Europe some eighteen months later (see page 158) reveal his inside knowledge of the final objectives of the war plan, which suggests that he had in fact attended the *kuriltai* that sealed the fate of Europe.

There are two contemporary chronicles which reaffirm the directives for the westward drive, although they show some discrepancy over the dates. The Chinese *Yuan-che* chronicle states clearly that 'in the year kia-wou [1234] Ogodai ordered Prince Batu to conquer the Kipchaks, the Alanians, the Russians and other kingdoms of the West.'

The authoritative *Secret History of the Mongols*, however, gives a most stylised account of the plan to invade Europe, presenting it as a straight continuation of Genghis Khan's campaign.

Genghis Khan had sent Subotai Bahadur [the valiant] to the West and he had reached the people of Changlin, the Kipchaks [Cumanians], the Badshigits, the Russians, the Alanians, the Gesut, the Madshars [Magyars], the Circassians and the Kerel and then had forded the water-rich rivers of Idil [Volga] and Dchayah [Ural]; then he had moved against the towns of Meket [Tiflis] and Man Kerman [Kiev], but there he had been held up by those people.

So now [1235] the Khan Ogodai sent as reinforcements for Subotai various princes, such as Batu, Buri, Güyük and Mangu. He gave the following order: over all these campaigning princes Batu should have the supreme command.

[To give a punch to this army] he gave a further order: As far as this campaigning army is concerned, the princes-state governors should send their elder sons to join it in the field.

The princes who are not state governors, ten-thousanders, thousanders, leaders of hundreds and tens, as well as the rank-and-file whoever they may be, should also send their elder sons to join the campaign.

The two campaigns in the Far East—one against the rebellious Koreans, the other against the Sung empire in south China—quickly attained their objectives, and so did the third against the Seljuk Turks in Persia, Iraq and Asia Minor, allowing the Mongol army to concentrate on the thrust into Europe.

In the early spring of 1236, a vast army assembled between the Aral Sea and the Urals, reinforced by the most seasoned troops and commanders and, as the *Secret History* described, by the elder sons of every family, 'because when the elder sons join the campaign, the army has great strength'.

The royal princes too joined Batu Khan's flag in search of glory and plunder, and their presence underlined the importance of the European campaign. Among them were the two sons of the Khan of Khans, Güyük and Kadan; his grandson Kaidu; Tuli's son Mangu; and Jagatai's son Baidar and his grandson Buri. They brought with them crack Mongol troops to augment Batu's 150,000 horsemen.

However, Subotai, the 'chief-of-staff' of the invasion force and the most experienced general of the Mongol army, felt that the forces at Batu Khan's disposal were not quite adequate for the task and he suggested his commander-in-chief should ask Ogodai for more men.

Batu was granted authority to raise new armies from Turkmenian and other steppe people who, under Mongol officers, quickly increased the size of the western invasion force to more impressive proportions. Yet even so the Mongol army was far from being as numerous as Europe took it to be when the continent suddenly became aware of the terrible danger threatening its very existence 'from an infinite number of Tartars who brake forth like Devils loosed out of Hell'.

Batu Khan and Subotai decided that the Kama Bulgars, the Cumanians, the Mordvins, the Magyars of Hungaria Magna and a host of other Volga people inhabiting the southern borders of the

Russian princes' land must be destroyed first in order to safeguard the invading army's lines of communication. It was the Englishman who spearheaded the attack with his negotiations which, in the case of the small Volga nations, resulted in their destruction regardless of their response.

Entering South-Eastern Europe through the 'open steppe gates' between the Urals and the Caspian Sea, Batu Khan's army swept all before it and reached the Volga by June 1236. The first to be annihilated were the Bulgars whom the Mongol horsemen hunted down and butchered, with ferocious bloodthirstiness, almost to a man. The ostensible reason for the excessive carnage was the Bulgars' rejection of Mongol suzerainty during Subotai's brief incursion during the 1220s. However, it was Subotai's policy to leave in his rear no organised groups of people or nations, even if perfectly submissive, who might threaten his lines of communications, thus the promises given by the Mongol envoy urging surrender were broken almost instantly.

There was also a more calculated reason. The Mongols believed that excessive cruelty and terror-instilling carnage at the very beginning of a campaign would paralyse with fear all potential opponents. 'They gloried in the slaughter of men, blood to them was spilt as freely as water', according to the chronicler Vincent of Beauvais.

While Subotai completed the extermination of the Kama Bulgars, Batu's army followed the Englishman's negotiating round with lightning attacks on the neighbouring Mordvins, Mokshans, Circassians and Cumanians.

As the *Yuan-che* recorded, 'in the year ting-yeon [1237], the [Mongol] army arrived at the coast of the Caspian Sea. Batshman, the Cumanian ruler, sought refuge [on an island] in the sea. But a great wind got up and the waves of the sea drew back and the bottom of the sea became dry. Batshman was caught and killed.'

Before the year was out, Batu's army controlled the steppe people between the Caspian Sea and the Sea of Azov, exposing the soft underbelly of the Russian principalities to the fate that had already befallen the Caucasian Christian kingdoms of Georgia, Albania and Armenia. But the agony of these countries, as Batu Khan's horsemen pillaged, raped and butchered the inhabitants, was ignored by the neighbouring Frankish crusader kingdom and the Russian princes.

The Mongol army, which was now slicing into Europe with astonishing ease, was an awesome instrument of war perfectly adapted to its task. It was well trained, strictly disciplined—a virtually unknown facet of soldiering in thirteenth century Europe—and led by experienced officers who knew every aspect of the art of war. Strange as it may seem, in the military field it was the Europeans, not the Mongols, who were the backward 'barbarians'.

Contrary to popular European conception that the invading Mongol hordes were wild, undisciplined nomadic horsemen with no command structure or understanding of the art of warfare, the Mongol army was excellently organised on a decimal system.

A troop comprised ten men, and this basic unit lived and fought together under draconian discipline. If any of the ten showed cowardice or fled from the battle, the rest were instantly put to death unless they had fought with exceptional bravery, in which case only the coward was killed.

Ten troops formed a squadron, and ten squadrons made up a banner, the Mongol equivalent of a regiment. Ten banners formed a *tuman*—the equivalent of a division—and usually three *tumans* made up an army.

The force invading Europe was almost exclusively mounted, divided into light and heavy cavalry. But Batu Khan also brought with him Chinese and Persian artificers who manned siege machines, mangonels, catapults and artillery pieces discharging several containers of burning naphtha simultaneously. There were also engineers well versed in building bridges, diverting rivers to inundate enemy territories and drilling shafts under enemy fortifications. All this was centuries ahead of Europe.

At the centre of Mongol military life stood obedience to orders. The army's standing orders, preserved in the *Secret History*, laid down that soldiers who disobeyed orders were to be flogged mercilessly, while those failing to carry out a personal order from the Khan were to be beheaded on the spot. A similar fate awaited soldiers who became separated from their units and those who left the battlefield to pillage.

Another facet of Mongol soldiering that baffled Europeans was their motivation: soldiers were not paid, as in Europe; in fact, the troops gave their officers once a year handsome presents, including good horses, heads of cattle and lengths of felt. And, as the Englishman stated in his confession, 'when vanquished, they [the Mongol soldiers] never ask for mercy, and themselves never spare the vanquished. In the intention and fixed purpose of reducing all the world under their dominion, they all persist as one man . . .'

The astounding success of the Mongol army in Europe was assured by its mobility and the high rate of fire from deadly bows. Commands were given by flags—at night by lanterns and whistling arrows—and the instructions were followed with agility in complete silence. The sight of large formations of horsemen following complex manoeuvres in utter silence greatly unnerved the Europeans facing them.

The Mongols' ability to effect concentrations and combinations of units and their speed of movement outclassed the cumbersome armoured European cavalry, which was incapable of responding to such an agile foe.

The Mongol horseman virtually lived in the saddle: he ate, drank and even slept on the back of his horse. The shaggy Mongol pony, which made the conquest of two-thirds of the then known world possible, was extremely hardy, subsisted on the sparse vegetation of the steppe in winter and in summer, yet showed stamina of which its oats-fed European cousin was quite incapable. Marches of eighty miles a day for several days on end were nothing out of the ordinary, allowing lightning attacks in the rear of the enemy.

The Englishman was, as his surviving account shows, very well aware of the military significance of the small but hardy Mongol ponies which required little food. With the aid of their 'fleet horses, they [the Mongols] suddenly disperse themselves over a whole province and, falling on the scattered, unarmed and undefended inhabitants, they wreak such havoc that the king or prince of the beleaguered country cannot muster men to take the field against them.'

That the Mongol horsemen proved more than a match for the men-at-arms of the Christian kings, fighting on their own home ground, the Englishman put down in part to 'their mode of fighting' and in part to their savage reputation.

Although they used darts, clubs, battle-axes and swords with great dexterity, their 'chief prerogative' was their use of the bow and their great skill in fighting.

His description of Mongol warriors gives a fairer picture of Batu
Khan's horsemen than the one perceived by the frightened and
biased European chroniclers of the Mongol invasion.

They have hard and robust breasts, lean and pale faces, stiff
high shoulders, and short distorted noses. Their chins are sharp
and prominent, the upper jaw low and deep, the teeth long and
few, their eyebrows stretch from the hair to the nose, their eyes
are black and restless, their countenances long and grim, their
extremities bony and nervous, their legs thick but short below
the knee. In stature they are equal to us, for what they lose
below the knee is made up for in the greater length of their
upper parts . . .

They are clothed with ox-hide, covered with light but
impenetrable armour. They are in war invincible and in labour
indefatigable; their back armour is thin so that they may not be
tempted to run away, and they never retreat from battle until
they see the chief standard of their leader retreating.

But as their awesome reputation spread westward, the people of
Europe endowed them with both superhuman and inhuman
attributes, seeing them as 'the Brood of Anti-Christ' sent upon the
world as a scourge to punish the many sins of Christendom. It was
hardly surprising that resistance against these 'ravenous monsters
of the underworld', reputedly 'thirsting and drinking blood', was
doomed to failure in superstition-ridden Eastern Europe.

SIXTEEN

Encounter on the Volga

THE FINDING of the proverbial needle in a haystack would seem to be child's play compared to the task of tracing the movements on the Eurasian continent and pinpointing the actions of an anonymous Englishman across seven and a half centuries. Chance and the exigencies of religious proselytising, however, engineered a meeting between two Europeans on the Volga in 1236 and their conversation was deemed important enough to be preserved in a report on the shelves of the Vatican Library.

One was a humble Dominican friar sent by King Béla IV of Hungary to re-establish contact with the 'lost Magyar tribes' supposedly living on the borders of Asia. The other was the Englishman who, as the Mongol khan's multi-lingual envoy, made a deep impression on the friar.

The obsessional interest of thirteenth century Hungarians in finding their kin, left behind in their ancient homeland—Great Hungary—when the bulk of Magyar tribes migrated to their present territory in Central Europe in 896, was the motive force behind successive exploratory journeys eastwards. The Catholic Church's interest in converting to Christianity the heathen Cumanians, whose lands extended from the Black Sea to the Caspian, made these missions easier.

The ceaseless raids of the warlike Cumanians had for a long time posed serious problems for the powerful Hungarian kingdom, which then stretched from the Carpathians to the Adriatic, and the Dominican province's decision to send missionaries to the Cumanians was welcomed by the pious Hungarian ruler.

Although his desire to see his neighbours converted to Catholicism cannot be doubted, the shared common ground between the Hungarian Church's proselytising and the country's great-power aspirations lent an extra dimension to these missions.

In the 1220s the friar Paulus Hungaricus, who headed the country's Dominican province, sent several missionaries into Cumania and the Pope's decision to name Theodor, a Hungarian, as the first mission-bishop of Cumania gave a further impetus to this Magyar '*Drang nach Osten*'.

A combination of national interest and missionary zeal made the Hungarian Dominicans look beyond the Cumanian lands where, according to traditional belief and some Hungarian, Greek and Arabic written evidence, lay Great Hungary. King Béla was not slow in realising that, if the missionaries could convert the heathen Magyars of the eastern homeland to Catholicism, Hungary could expand to the Urals and draw into its sphere of interest all the steppe nations in between. Furthermore, basing itself on its vast eastern hinterland, Hungary could make itself felt in Central Europe and challenge the German emperor who dominated the region.

In 1232, four Dominican preachers, led by Friar Otto, set out to fulfil the national dream of finding the ancient homeland somewhere between the Volga and Urals, and to bring the light of the Roman Church to the heathen Magyar brethren.

They 'dressed up as merchants' to ease their passage across the lands of the steppe people, but even so they suffered such hardships that all but Otto died on the outward journey. Otto managed to locate some Hungarian-speakers somewhere near the Volga, who told him how to get to Great Hungary. He returned to Hungary to seek help from the Dominican provincial for the great task of converting the inhabitants of the eastern homeland, but he too died of exhaustion within days of his return to Hungary.

Using Otto's map, four more Dominicans, led by Friar Julian, set out for the legendary Magyar homeland in 1235. They covered up their tonsures and grew their hair and beards 'in heathen fashion' and travelled 'dressed in worldly clothes', according to the annals of the Dominican order.

However, the journey was slow and arduous and, after several months, the money provided by King Béla ran out. It is a lasting memorial to the dedication of these Dominican friars that two of them decided to sell themselves into slavery in order that, with the money raised, the other two should continue the journey.

But the Central European friars, weakened by the year-long

journey, seemed too puny to the nomad slave merchants and found no buyers. One by one they died of the privations and Friar Julian was left to continue the journey alone. After crossing the land of the Bulgars, he reached Great Hungary on the Volga in 1236.*

In his report—made after his return to Benedictus Salvius de Salvis, the Bishop of Perugia and Papal Legate in Hungary—the friar described the rousing reception accorded to him by the heathen Magyars of Great Hungary and the circumstances of his meeting with the Tartars' ambassador.

> When they heard and understood that I was a Christian Magyar, they showed great pleasure over my arrival. They took me from house to house and village to village, asking fervent questions about the kingdom and land of their Christian kith and kin. And whatever I was telling them about, either our faith or other things, they listened to me diligently as their's was a pure Hungarian tongue and they understood me and I understood them.

During this triumphal procession through Great Hungary, he learnt that there was an oral tradition and general awareness that some Hungarian tribes had gone west centuries earlier, but that no one knew what had become of them.

The Tartars, an unknown nation to the Central European friar, loomed large in all the conversations and Julian recorded what seemed to him great unease in the two nations' relations. 'When they first fought [presumably in 1221], the Tartars could not subdue the Magyars in battle and, in fact, in the first encounters the Magyars defeated the Tartars. Because of this the Tartars invited them to become allies and, their two armies together, totally devastated fifteen countries.'

But now the Magyars were allied to the Bulgars against whom the Tartars were taking the field and the palpable anxiety over the presence of Batu Khan's army a mere five days' marching distance from Great Hungary duly communicated itself to Friar Julian.

Although the friar's interest centred entirely on the life-style and condition of the newly discovered heathen kinsmen, he

---

* *Tarikh Ungürüs*, a Turkish-language chronicle in MS form recently discovered in Istanbul and currently translated by Dr Josef Blaskovic, of Prague's Charles University, confirms the eastern journey of Hungarian Dominicans in merchants' disguise on the eve of the Mongol onslaught.

recorded meeting Tartars in the land of the Magyars and made notes on a curious encounter with the Tartar khan's envoy.

Two things struck him about the ambassador of the eastern ruler: one was the envoy's extraordinary knowledge of languages and the other that, although he represented the Tartar khan, he himself was not Tartar.

The role played by the Englishman's diplomacy in the subjugation of the nations of the Volga basin is now patently obvious, but during that summer's day encounter in 1236 Friar Julian clearly had no inkling of it. Yet the Englishman was open and frank about the Mongol war plans, almost as if he wanted to warn the West, through Julian, of the impending holocaust.

Far from using his customary negotiating 'fictions', he told the friar that Batu Khan was only waiting for another army, 'which had been sent by the Great Khan to destroy the Persians', to join him before moving against Germany. He thus intimated that the subjugation of the steppe people was only the first phase of a much wider war plan, and revealed both the focal point and the timing of the onslaught on Europe. The target was Germany and the westward drive would start immediately after the end of the Persian campaign.

He also tried to tell the simple friar, in the hope that he would realise the implications of his words, that the Mongols intended to conquer the entire world 'and destroy all those countries which they could conquer.'

The Englishman's eloquence, or the burden of his message, must have impressed Friar Julian because almost immediately after this conversation he decided to return home, although, as he mentioned in his report, there were several other valid reasons for his departure. One was his fear that if he were to die neither the Dominicans nor the King of Hungary would learn of his discovery and the heathen Magyars would not be converted to Christianity. Another reason was his fear of opposition by the heretic Orthodox Russians to the conversion plan, because 'if the pagan nations and the [Orthodox] Russians whose lands fall between the two Hungaries were to learn of the eastern Magyars' intention of embracing Catholicism, they might object and deny transit rights on their roads.'

He arrived back in Hungary, after a speedy journey across Russia, on 27 December 1236. He was closely questioned about

his discoveries by Friar Ricardus, the provincial of the Dominicans
in Hungary, who appreciated the importance of the meeting with
the Tartar khan's envoy and immediately wrote a separate report
about it to Pope Gregory IX.*

. . . In the land of these Hungarians [on the Volga] the above
named friar met the ambassador of the Tartar prince who spoke
Hungarian, Russian, Cumanian, German, Saracen and Tartar.
[This reference indicates the provincial's realisation that the
Khan's envoy was not Tartar, for there would have been no
point in reporting of a native-born Tartar that he actually spoke
Tartar.]
   This envoy said that the Tartar army, which then was about
five days' march from there, was heading against Germany but
that it was waiting for another army which had been sent by the
great prince to destroy the Persians.
   The envoy also said that beyond the land of the Tartars there
is a very populous nation which is bigger and taller than any
other human species, and that their heads are so big that they do
not seem to fit their bodies.
   He also said that they intend to leave their country and to
fight against all those who dare to oppose them and that they
would destroy all those countries which they could conquer.
When the friar understood all this, he decided to return home
although the Magyars were greatly pressing him to stay on . . .

The Dominican provincial's report to the Pope was the first formal
intimation of the Mongol threat to Europe. The Pope was interested enough to summon Julian to Rome. Soon more dramatic
news was filtering through from the East. However, the reports of
the defeat of the Cumanian state, the fall of the Kama Bulgars and
the destruction of Merovia were not considered of any importance;
they were seen as part of the expansionism of some Asiatic nomad
power and thus, although affecting dozens of European nations,
outside the actual sphere of European interest.
   Even the attack on Russia in 1237 was seen by the rest of
Europe as part of the centuries-old squabble between the steppe
nations and the Russian princes, and therefore ignored. Anyway,

* MS *Liber Censuum Camerae Apostolicae*, No 445.

the Russians were heretics and heretics were hardly better than Infidels in the eyes of Catholic Christendom.

Only King Béla of Hungary showed a little concern about the Mongol threat, perhaps because of his eastern plans, and in 1237 he sent Friar Julian back towards Great Hungary.

As he was making his way east, Mongol envoys were calling on the Russian princes demanding total submission. Their surrender terms were so harsh that no reasonable ruler could even discuss them: all towns and fortresses were to be opened to the Mongol army, a tenth of the population was to become slaves of the Mongols or drafted into their auxiliary troops sent ahead of the regular units. The Russian princes' reply was to murder the envoys of the arrogant Asiatic nomads and fortify their cities which, they knew from experience, the steppe horsemen could not take.

The Mongol response was shattering. Batu Khan took Penza, Tambov and Pronsk and, after defeating the host of the prince of Ryazan, besieged the city of Ryazan. After five days of bombardment from sophisticated war machines the Russians had never seen before, the Mongol army stormed and took the city.

21 December 1237 was a black day for Russia, as a contemporary Russian chronicler wrote:

> The prince, with his wife, mother, sons, his boyars and inhabitants [of Ryazan] were slaughtered with savage cruelty, with no regard to age or sex, by the vengeful Tartars.
>
> Some were impaled, or had nails or splinters of wood driven under their fingernails. Priests were roasted alive and nuns and maidens ravished in the churches in front of their families. No eye remained open to weep for the dead.

The Mongol army battered its way relentlessly into the heart of Russia. It stormed and annihilated the capital of the principality of Vladimir, occupied Moscow and in the space of two months took fourteen other towns.

With the total destruction of the northern Russian principalities the first phase of the Mongol plan for the conquest of Europe, as laid down at the *kuriltai* of victory, had been successfully completed. Batu Khan felt there was cause for celebration, as he informed Ogodai in a letter which has been preserved in the *Secret History*: 'Through the power of the Eternal Heaven and the blessing of the Imperial kin, we destroyed the town of Mzcheti and turned the Russian people into our slaves. We subdued and forced under our rule eleven nations and put the golden bit into their mouths'.

But, as Batu ruefully reported, dissension had reared its ugly head in the Mongol army leadership, endangering the fulfilment of God's will on earth.

We agreed to have a [celebration] feast and set up the great banqueting tent. As we sat down I, who am after all somewhat older than the other princes, took a drink or two from the drinking horn before the others.

Güyük and Buri begrudged this and rode away from the feast without sharing it. As Buri rode away he said: 'Batu is our equal, how dared he drink first? He is just like an old woman with a beard. He should be kicked and trampled on and beaten with a cudgel.'

Thus was I berated by Buri and Güyük when, after the campaign against alien and hostile races, we had come together to discuss the situation. We had to break off the meeting as they left without my assent. Now they should learn the decision of the Emperor, my uncle.

Ogodai acted swiftly to eliminate the rivalry between Batu and his own son, by recalling Güyük to Karakorum and confirming Batu as the supreme commander of the western invasion force. Europe's slim chance of avoiding the holocaust was dashed.

SEVENTEEN

An unwelcome Tartar envoy

As THE CITIES of the Russian forests and steppes burned and the Englishman began delivering his deadly demands for submission to nations in the heart of Europe, refugees in their hundreds of thousands started streaming westward with their flocks and pathetic possessions.

The once powerful Daniil, the Grand Duke of Halich, was forced to seek refuge in Hungary and the Cumanian chieftain Kötöny (or Kutan), sent an embassy to Béla offering to embrace Catholicism in exchange for asylum for the 40,000 families who survived the Mongol attack.

Master Rogerius, the archdeacon of the Transylvanian town of Nagyvarad, whose eye-witness account of the Mongol invasion gives a vivid picture of the mounting tensions in Central Europe, wrote down a précis of the Cumanian envoy's formal appeal for asylum:

> Having fought the Tartars for many years, and twice having been victorious over them [presumably in the 1220s], they broke into Kötöny's country a third time when he was quite unprepared; and not having had an army, he was forced to turn his back to the accursed Tartars, who destroyed the greater part of his country and killed most of his people.
>
> For this reason, if King Béla were to admit him into his country and keep him and his people in freedom, he would be prepared to submit himself and his men—with their relations and friends and kith and kin and all their cattle and chattels—to the king of Hungary and embrace the Catholic faith.*

Béla was greatly pleased with the sudden submission of the

---

* Rogerius's Latin *Carmen Miserabile* has never been translated into any modern European language.

proud Cumanian chieftain and with the prospect of 'winning so many hearts for the Lord Jesus'. He acted as Kötöny's godfather at a mass baptism and gave vast tracts of land to his folk on the Hungarian plains, an area which is called Great Cumania to this day.

But the nomadic Cumanians, used to the freedom of their steppe lands between the Caspian and Black Seas, found the restrictions imposed by the Hungarian peasants' settled existence unbearable and drove their cattle over the wheat crops and pastures of villagers.

These were 'hard, crude and unbending people' and they not only took from the Hungarian villagers what they wanted but also raped their wives and daughters. The hatred generated by the refugees was fanned by the barons who saw the Cumanian army, with its allegiance to King Béla rather than the country, as a dangerous strengthening of royal power.

To defuse the refugee problem, which was rapidly becoming an explosive political issue, the king decided to split up the Cumanians into clans and settle them in various parts of the country, hoping that 'not being many of them together, they would not cause hurt to the Hungarians.'

This tying of the nomad herdsman in smaller groups to confined spaces only exacerbated the situation because it deprived the refugees of their traditional livelihood. 'As the Cumanians were numerous and poor, the Hungarians could get servants from among them for virtually nothing, and their condition was to the Hungarians' benefit rather than harm', Rogerius noted, with unusual perspicacity for the period.

This crude exploitation and despised condition naturally aroused the hatred of the Cumanians against their hosts, with the most dire consequences for the country in the months of Mongol occupation.

Apart from its divisive internal effects, the admission of some 200,000 Cumanian refugees also offered the Englishman a useful lever with which to demand Hungary's submission. Using the fictitious claim that the Cumanians were—perhaps due to their defeat—'the slaves of the Great Khan', he warned Béla that by harbouring the Khan's foes he himself became a foe of the Khan. And the enemies of the divine order must submit unconditionally or be wiped out.

In his confession, the Englishman admitted to having called twice on the King of Hungary with an embassy, 'menacing and plainly foretelling those mischiefs which afterwards happened, unless he would submit himself and his kingdom unto the Tartar yoke'.

His knowledge of Hungarian alone would have qualified him to head these embassies but the importance of winning over Hungary quickly, with its rich plains designated as the recreation ground for Mongol horses used in the drive to the Atlantic, made it unavoidable that Batu Khan's senior ambassador should conduct these negotiations. However, Béla refused even to acknowledge the Tartar envoy's communications, let alone reply to his submission orders.

The Englishman, who succeeded in impressing on Friar Julian the dangers facing Europe, obviously failed, despite the threats of horrors worse than the Apocalypse, to bring home to the Hungarian king that he must submit or perish. Considering the arrogance of suggesting to a powerful European monarch in his own court to submit to some Asiatic nomad chieftain, the Englishman was lucky to escape with his life.

A third and final Mongol diplomatic demarche fell quite fortuitously into the hands of Friar Julian as he was once again trying to reach Great Hungary with three fellow Dominicans.

Because of the rapid Mongol advance in 1237 the Dominicans were held up in Suzdal, whose prince, Yuri Vsevolodovich, broke the news to them that Great Hungary had already been wiped out by the Asiatic horsemen.

Julian's second eastern journey was not totally fruitless, however, because he brought back the latest reports about the Mongol invasion plan of Europe:

Many people assert it as a certainty, and the ruler of Suzdal sent word by me to the King of Hungary, that the Tartars are holding council day and night discussing ways to march on and besiege the Christian Hungarian kingdom.

It is said that there was a proposal to attack Rome and the territories beyond Rome.

This report of Friar Julian's and the news of the destruction of Great Hungary were duly noted in the chronicle of Aubrey of

Trois Fontaines (Albericus Monachus)* in the events of 1237, indicating the close links between the chancelleries and annalists of West Europe.

The most entrancing information contained in the report on Julian's second journey was his personal meeting with the Mongol ambassadors bearing Batu Khan's final message to Béla. These ambassadors had been arrested while travelling across Russia by the Prince of Suzdal and the letter taken from them.

'I myself saw these envoys, together with my honoured brethren in jail', he reported. 'The above mentioned letter was handed to me by the lord of Suzdal to take it to the King of Hungary.'

Apart from the intrinsic value of this Mongol diplomatic communication, preserved in the friar's report to the Pope, the incident briefly focused attention on the Englishman in his native England. Matthew Paris erroneously believed, and recorded in his *Chronica Majora*, that this Mongol demarche was presented by an English Templar in Tartar service to the King of Hungary, probably confusing reports about the Englishman's two earlier rounds of negotiations at Béla's court with this third missive borne to Hungary by Friar Julian. †

However the confusion arose, the St Albans chronicler must have had some report or diplomatic dispatch—now lost—at his disposal to allow the identification of the Mongol Khan's English envoy 'as a Templar'. And this provides a welcome pointer in the quest for the Englishman's true identity, despite his own careful attempts to maintain his incognito.

Batu Khan's letter to Béla, carried by Friar Julian, deserves great attention not only because it is the earliest extant Mongol diplomatic dispatch but because there are sufficient grounds to surmise that it was written by, or under the close supervision of, the Englishman. Although its surviving version contains what would seem to be errors due to the haphazard translation, effected by a chance acquaintance of Friar Julian's instead of the meticulous Mongol chancellery, it is easily recognisable as an ultimatum.

It was written, as Julian stated in his report, in 'heathen characters [probably Uighur], but in the Tartar tongue. Here [in

---

* Albericus Trium Fontium, *Chronicon.*

† The French scholar Cahun noted this fact as a historical curiosity.

Suzdal] the ruler found many people who could read the script but not one who could decipher its meaning. But when we were [on our way back] crossing Cumania, the great heathen country, we managed to find someone who could translate it'.

Although less clear than the later Mongol dispatches translated by Mongol interpreters, nevertheless it contains the standard introductory formula invoking heavenly mandate for the subjugation of the world, and the sanction of total destruction against those who ignore the submission order.

But it also contains such a typical medieval Latin turn of phrase as 'qualiter effugies manus meas' (how do you escape my hands), which only a European trained for the priestly vocation, like the Englishman, would have used to express the patently Oriental meaning of his lord's message. The letter gives a unique insight both into the mentality of its writer and the standards of the early period of Mongol diplomacy.

> I, the Chan, the messenger of the Heavenly King, who has given me authority over the entire world to raise up those who submit and to crush who dare to resist:
>
> I am amazed that you, the kingling of the Hungarians, have taken no notice although I have sent to you thirty [probably a mistranslation of three] embassies; why do you not send me either envoys or replies?
>
> I know that you are a rich and powerful king, who has many warriors and who rules alone in a big kingdom. And precisely because of this you find it difficult to submit to me of your own accord. Yet it would be better for you personally if you submitted to me of your own volition.
>
> I also know that you have given succour to my servants, the Cumanians. Because of this I order you to cease harbouring them from now on and to avoid using them against me because in so doing you are making an enemy of me. For it is much easier for the Cumanians who wander hither and thither to take flight than for you [Hungarians] who live in fixed houses, have forts and towns; so how do you escape my hands?

This ultimatum to Hungary, together with the rest of Friar Julian's report to the Pope, including the Mongol plan to conquer Rome and the rest of Western Europe, was sent by Béla to Berthold, the Patriarch of Aquileia, showing that the King was more disturbed than his stiff-upper-lip stance towards the importuning Englishman could have indicated. The Patriarch in turn sent it to Bishop Egno of Brixen, Count Albert of Tirol and a few more Central European leaders to alert them to the Eastern menace.

But our continent was apparently quite incapable of grasping the magnitude of the peril facing it. As the Mongols resumed their war of conquest, after the recall of the obstreperous Güyük, and smashed Pereyaslavl, Chernigov and the last remaining strongholds of the Nordic Kievan Russia, the rest of Europe could not arouse itself from its all-consuming interest in the petty squabble of the Pope and the Holy Roman Emperor.

Some of the more responsible leaders, like King Louis of France, the Bishop of Paris, the Bishop of the Hungarian see of Kalocsa and King Béla showed a glimmer of awareness and took some elementary precautions, but it was too little and too late.

A letter written to the Bishop of Paris by his Hungarian colleague some time in the autumn of 1240, which has been preserved in the addendum to the St Albans chronicler's *Chronica Majora*, revealed that Béla had sent several Dominicans other than Julian's party, Minorites and 'other messengers' with the express order to 'explore' the strength and disposition of Tartar forces.

These amateur spies, however, were no match for the Mongol professionals: they were all caught and put to death. Some information nevertheless did filter through and the Hungarian bishop collated it in response to his Paris colleague's inquiry:

> I write back to you about the Tartars, how they came near the frontiers of Hungary in five days' march [sic], near to some water named Dniepr which they could not cross in the summer. But being willing to wait for the winter, they sent before them into Russia some spies, two of whom were taken, and sent to our lord the King of Hungary.
>
> I had these in my custody, and learned from them some new things, which I forward to you . . .

The rest of the letter contained a jumble of confused, fourth- or fifth-hand geographical and historical information perfectly suited to confuse the reader.

The Hungarian bishop was also in error in reporting that the

Mongols were five days' march from Hungary. They were actually fifteen days' distance, besieging Kiev, the cradle and centre of Russian civilisation.

Batu Khan, duly observing the rules of war Mongol-style, sent his nephew Mangu with an embassy to ask Grand Duke Mikhail to surrender the city. But the duke had the Mongol envoys thrown to their deaths from the city walls and then rode west to seek shelter at the court of Béla, leaving Kiev's defence to a boyar named Dmitry, a brave and fearless soldier.

As the ring of steel tightened around the city, the inhabitants could hear nothing, according to the *Ipatyevskyaya Letopis*, but the grating and creaking of the wheels of Tartar supply wagons, the bugles instructing the formations of infinite enemy troops, the cries of camels mortified by the Russian winter, and the neighing of 100,000 horses.

Although deafened by the noise of Mongol martial preparations, the Kievans fought bravely. Then Batu Khan ordered the use of battering rams near the Polish Gate, where part of the wall was wooden. According to the Russian chronicler's account of the siege:

> Many rams battered the walls ceaselessly, day and night; the inhabitants were frightened and many were killed, the blood flowing like water.
>
> And thus, with the aid of many battering rams, they broke through the city walls and entered the city, and the inhabitants made haste to meet them. One could see and hear a great clash of lances and clatter of shields; the arrows obscured the light so that it became impossible to see the sky. There was darkness because of the multitude of Tartar arrows, and there were dead everywhere.

On 6 December 1240, the Mongols destroyed the makeshift fortifications thrown up by the defenders around the basilica of the Virgin Mary and, after an unparalleled orgy of blood-letting, destroyed the city. Kiev had virtually ceased to exist, and what eventually rose from the ashes was a different civilisation built on imported autocratic principles and the despotic statecraft of the Mongols.

Six years after the taking of the city, when the papal envoy Carpine passed through it on his way to Karakorum, he found a handful of houses standing in the wasteland that had once been the northern rival of Byzantium.

With their incredible mobility, driving day and night without a halt, eating and sleeping in the saddle and changing horses from time to time, the Mongols gave the impression of possessing armies as numerous as swarms of locusts, to use the contemporary simile. They were also thought to be invincible and the stream of East European refugees became a flood. The people of Central Europe began to show signs of panic.

Whereas they knew virtually nothing about the Tartars, Batu Khan, thanks to the painstaking work of the Englishman and his intelligence staff begun after the 1235 *kuriltai*, had detailed information at his disposal about the internal situation, strength and leadership of the armed forces and even the family connections of the rulers of Central Europe.

As the Mongol army lay poised to strike into Hungary, Poland and Bohemia, scouts and agents recruited from among disaffected elements were sent west to gather the latest information. Some of these must have been rather raw recruits because after the capture of a number of them a spy hysteria swept across the Continent.

The *Dalamil Chronicle* lamented that Tartar spies had penetrated not only into Bohemia but right up to the Rhineland. The Russians accused the Mordva-Finns of acting as Tartar spies, and the Austrian *Annales Claustroneoburgenses* asserted that 'heretics and false Christians', guided by their desire to harm the Christians, were serving the Tartars as spies.

Frederick, the Holy Roman Emperor, found it necessary to warn King Henry III of England of the grave danger posed by the ubiquitous Tartar spies 'who were sent everywhere in advance [of hostilities].' Through them the Tartars learnt of 'the public discord and the unfortunate and weaker parts of the lands; and hearing of the heart-burning of kings, and the strife of kingdoms, are more encouraged and animated'.

In Hungary, the spy mania focused on the alien Cumanian refugees in their midst. Their movements across the length and breadth of the country, tending their herds, was suddenly seen as a clever stratagem allowing the spying-out of the country, and although there were undoubtedly many Cumanians working for the Tartars, the massive retribution against innocent refugees created a crisis.

The barons and the so-called German party, preferring Frederick to Béla, began to put about that the Cumanians had come to a secret agreement with the Tartars against Hungary, and that they would fight against their hosts if the Tartars invaded the country.

Rogerius quotes at some length these claims of the baronial faction, which chose the eve of the country's greatest calamity to weaken the central power of the monarch:

> They said that the aforementioned Kötöny, king of the Cumanians, came into the country a year before the approach [of the Tartars] in order to espy the lie of the country and learn the language; and when Kötöny hears of their entry into the country he is to start to fight the king [Béla] and so make it easier for the Tartars to capture the fortified border posts and waste the quicker a part of Hungary. And attacking the king with glee over his decision to let the Cumanians in, the above mentioned barons thus spoke.

Batu Khan's ultimatum brought back by Julian was used by the factionalists as a proof of the 'close link' between the Mongols and their 'Cumanian servants' and, as the barons whipped up the anti-Cuman hysteria, the burghers and German merchants of Pest took the law into their hands and murdered Kötöny and his retinue of Cumanian nobles.

On hearing of the murder both the Hungarians and the Cumanians reached for their swords. 'Their haters, the Hungarian peasants, rose everywhere against the Cumanians, robbing and murdering them mercilessly; the Cumanians, seeing that thus they all must perish, gathered together not only to protect themselves but to burn the villages of the Hungarians and to overcome bravely the Hungarian peasants'.

The Cumanians fought their way out of the country and promptly joined the ranks of the Tartar army moving against Hungary. On the eve of the Tartar invasion Hungary, the supposed bulwark of Christendom, was in a sorry state of dissension and division, greatly weakened by the Cumanian strife. The ultimatum penned by the Englishman created more mischief than he could have hoped for.

PART VI

The Agony of
a Continent

EIGHTEEN

The fateful year of 1241

IN 1241, the alarm bells began ringing throughout Christendom. Reports of the incredible destruction wrought by the Tartars in Eastern Europe inspired animal fear in the rest of the continent and the omens, to which the terror-stricken people turned for reassurance, were very bad indeed. There were unusual tidal waves, monstrous fishes of the deep with semi-human heads caught in inshore waters, blood-red sunsets and an eclipse of the sun, and those able or qualified to interpret them foresaw nothing but trouble.

The news of the pitiless slaughter of the Russian dukedoms, with which the rulers of Northern Europe then had close ties of kinship, sent such shock waves across Scandinavia that the herring fishermen of Sweden and Friesia dared not sail to their usual fishing grounds off the coast of England. As a result there was such a glut of herrings in England that, acccording to Matthew Paris, forty or fifty of these fishes sold for a shilling.

The fear that the Mongols always sought to instil in their foes at the start of a campaign communicated itself even to the westernmost extremity of Europe as Batu Khan's armies began the second phase of their European war of conquest. It is still palpable in the writing of the St Albans chronicler:

That the joys of mortal men be not enduring, nor worldly happiness long lasting without lamentations, in this same year the detestable people of Satan, to wit, an infinite number of Tartars brake forth from their Mountayne-compassed home, and piercing the solid rocks [of the Caucasus], poured forth like Devils loosed out of Hell, or the Tartarus, so that they are rightly called Tartari or Tartarians.

Swarming like locusts over the face of the Earth, they have brought terrible devastation to the Eastern Confines [of Europe] laying it waste with fire and sword. After having passed through the Land of the Saracens, they have razed cities, cut down Woods, overthrown fortresses, uprooted Vineyards, destroyed Orchards, killing people both of Citie and Countrey.

If perchance they have spared any Suppliants they have forced them, reduced to the lowliest condition of Slavery, to fight in the foremost ranks against their own neighbours. Those who have feyned to fight, or have hidden in the hope of escaping, have been followed up by the Tartars and massacred. If they have fought bravely for them and conquered, they have got no thanks or reward; and so they have misused their Captives as they have their Mares. For they are Inhuman and Beastly, rather Monsters than men, thirsting for and drinking Blood, tearing and Devouring the flesh of Dogges and Men.

Just as Matthew Paris sensed the danger threatening Europe in faraway England, so the spiritual and temporal leaders nearer to the Mongols were aware of this Eastern peril drawing closer and closer.

After all, the ordinary people spoke of nothing but these beastly, inhuman monsters, and in passing wild rumours* about their deeds to their neighbours the terrible cruelties and savage massacres grew greatly in the retelling. Soon the terror-stricken people came to expect the coming of the Anti-Christ and the end of the world.

A contemporary Latin verse captured the true spirit of the superstitious approach to the Tartar menace:

When twice six hundred years and fifty more
Are gone, since blessed Mary's son was born,
Then the Anti-Christ shall come full of devil.

In speaking of the Tartars, the people endowed them with the attributes of animals they feared or admired: they were stong as

---

* Among the best informed chroniclers of Tartar atrocities were the *Annales Capituli Cracoviensis*; *Chronicon Garstense*; *Gesta Senoniensis*; *Chronica Minor Erphordiensi*; *Annales S. Pant. Coloniensis*; *Chronicon Pulkavae*; *Mon. Historia Bohemiae*; Philippe de Mousket, *Historia Regum Francorum*.

oxen, fierce as panthers, artful as serpents, cautious as hares, thievish as mice, mettlesome as horses and frightful as dragons.

The rulers of the continent, although patently aware of the atmosphere of fear, could not assess the true magnitude of the danger partly because of their limited vision and partly due to their ignorance of the Mongols' belief in their divine mandate to conquer the world.

As a result they continued their internecine squabbles and neglected to close ranks in the face of the gravest danger the continent had been confronted with since the Huns.

The papacy and the Holy Roman Empire, the two powers which could have united Europe to stem the Mongol tide, were at each other's throats, locked in an armed struggle for supremacy. Pope Gregory called a crusade against the Hohenstaufen Emperor and accused Frederick of having 'a secret understanding with the Tartars'.

The pro-Pope chronicler Albert of Bohemia* in a letter to the bishop of Ferrara insisted that the envoys of Frederick had been seen in the Tartar camp and that 'they called the Tartars in'. Matthew Paris levelled similar accusations against the Holy Roman Emperor and Philippe de Mousket set it to rhyme:

Et fu par le monde retrait
Que l'empereres par son trait
Flederis [Frederick] les [Mongols] ot fait venir
Pour crestiente ahounir.

In response to the desperate call for help by the rulers of Austria, Carinthia, Silesia and Hungary, the Pope did actually order a crusade against the Tartars, but since he offered the same indulgencies and spiritual rewards as for the fight against the Emperor Frederick, it was no more than a mere gesture without content.

The German clergy at least tried to get the crusade off the ground as the Mongol hordes swept through the gateway of Central Europe to reach the very borders of Germany. They ordered a solemn fast and preachers carried the cross urging all to sign it. The *Chronicon Garstense* even noted that the preachers 'did not exempt either women or children' from the duty of joining

---

* Albertus Bohemus, *Regesta Bohemiae*.

the crusade, but in the end, without the support of the Holy Roman Emperor, it all came to nothing.

For Frederick was so obsessed with his fight against the Pope that instead of levying an army against the Tartars, he gathered forces against the Pope and his Italian supporters and invaded Northern Italy to punish the Lombard 'rebels'. But as a gesture to European opinion, he made his son Conrad take up the cross, complaining at the same time to the crowned heads of the continent that the Pope's backing for the rebels against his authority stopped him from devoting all his forces to the fight against the enemies of Christianity.

France and England, the two other European powers of consequence, were too far geographically to appreciate the true extent and gravity of the Tartar threat, and in any event they were too preoccupied with their own petty territorial squabble over the ownership of Gascogne and Poitou to take an active hand in the defence of the continent. In fact as the Mongol tidal wave reached the borders of the Holy Roman Empire, King Louis was preparing for war against England.

There were, however, a few statesman-like princes among the politically shortsighted leaders of Europe who came to realise that unless Christendom overcame its petty rivalries and closed ranks, they would all be swept away by the Mongol torrent.

On 10 March 1241 Henry, the Earl of Lorraine and Palatine of Saxony, wrote an impassioned letter to his father-in-law, the Duke of Brabant, telling him of the need to act at once, for 'delay is full of danger' when one's neighbour's house is on fire.

After recounting the advance of the Mongols into Poland, he informed his kinsman of the latest intelligence gathered 'by our own Messengers, as by our beloved Cousin the King of Bohemia', that Batu Khan intended to invade Bohemia at Easter.

And if not prevented, [he] will there perpetrate unheard-of slaughter. And because our next neighbour's house is now on fire, and the next Countrey [is] seth open to waste, and some are alreadie wasted, we earnestly and pitifully entreat the ayde and counsell of God and of our neighbour-brethren for the universall Church. And because delay is full of danger, with all our hearts we beseech you that you make all possible speed to arme as well for your as our deliverance, making strong preparations of store of Soldiers; diligently exciting the noble, mightie and couragious, with the people subject to them, that yee may have them in readinesse, when we shall next direct our Messengers to you.

And we, by the ministerie of Prelates, Preachers and Minorites, cause the Cross—because the businesse belongs to Him which was crucified—to be generally preached, fast and prayers to be appointed, and our Lands in common to be called to the warre of Jesus Christ . . .

The need for urgent joint action was borne home to Emperor Frederick by the Mongols' incredible feat of arms who, between Easter and Whitsun, overran seven countries and totally destroyed the mail-clad chivalry of Central Europe.

Although the Holy Roman Emperor did not abandon his punitive Italian campaign, and even found time to extract an involuntary oath of allegiance from the fleeing Hungarian king in exchange for a dubious promise of 'help against the threatening Tartar destruction', nevertheless he began showing signs of awareness that the Mongol invasion was quite different from the wars Europe had known.

He wrote a long letter to King Henry III of England to win him over to a joint defence action in which all the princes of Christendom should participate. Because of his close links with the Arabs of the Levant he had at his disposal more accurate facts about the Mongols than any other European ruler, making his letter the most important document on the state of the continent in this critical period.

Although Frederick addressed his letter to Henry, his brother-in-law, who was highly regarded as a statesman, he soon broadened it into a general appeal for joint action.

Copies were sent 'to Germany, ardent in battle; to France who nurses in her bosom an intrepid soldiery; to warlike Spain; [to England, powerful by its warriors and its ships;] to strap-strong Denmark; to untamed Italy; to Burgundy which never knew peace; to the invincible isles of the Greek, Adriatic and Tyrrhene seas—Crete, Cyprus, Sicily; to Bloody Ireland; to marshy Scotland; to icy Norway; and to every noble and famous region in the West'.

In the letter he informed the English king about the first Mongol invasion of Europe in the 1220s, of the new wave of Mongol attacks resulting in the subjugation of Cumania and Russia, and the current 'sudden assault and barbarous invasion' of Silesia, Poland, Lithuania, Bohemia and Hungary.

He knew of, and recounted to Henry, the Englishman's missions to Hungary, 'whose sluggish King, too secure, being required by the Tartars' envoys and letters that if he desired that he and his should live, he should hasten their favour by yielding himself and his kingdom. Yet he was not hereby terrified and taught to fortify [his country] against the Tartar irruption'. Nor did Béla learn from the fate that had befallen his eastern neighbours, although he 'should have taken warning, but neglected it'.

This accusation of neglect against the king guarding the gateway to Western Europe was certainly true, although in all fairness Béla did take all the routine precautions which would have sufficed against any European army, but which were pitifully inadequate against the Mongols. And of course Frederick's own divisive war with the Pope was equally, if not more, irresponsible.

Frederick also reported at length about the difficulties, posed by the Pope's cruel attacks, on the purposed joint action of Christendom against the common enemy.

Foreseeing all these dangers, often by Letters and Messengers, we are mindful to request your Excellency, as also other Christian Princes, earnestly soliciting and warning, that peace and love may flourish amongst Rulers, and discord being appeased, which often endanger Christendom, agreeing together to set stay to them which have lately shown themselves; forasmuch as fore-warned are fore-armed, and that the common enemies may not rejoice, that to prepare their ways, so great dissensions breake forth amongst Christian Princes.

Oh God, how much and how often would we have humbled ourselves, doing the utmost that the Roman Bishop might have desisted from the scandal of dissension against us, which is gone through the world . . . But Will being to him Law, not ruling the slipperie running of his tongue, and disdayning to abstayne from manifold dissension which he hath attempted; by his Legates and Messengers he hath commanded the Cross to be published against me—the Arme and Advocate of the Church, which he ought to have exercised against the tyrannie of the Tartars or Saracens . . . . And now that our greatest care is to free ourselves from domesticke and familiar Enemies, how shall we also repel Barbarians?

. . . We heartily adjure your Maiestie on behalfe of the Common necessitie, by our Lord Jesus Christ, that taking heed yourself, and to your Kingdome (which God keep in prosperitie) with instant care and provident deliberation, you diligently prepare speedy ayds of strong Knights, and other armed men and Armes; this we require in the sprinkling of the Bloud of Christ, and the league of affinitie in which we are joyned. And so let them be ready with us manfully and providently to fight for the deliverance of Christendom, that against the Enemies now proposing to enter the confines of Germanie by united forces victorie to the praise of the Lord of Hosts may be obtayned.

Neither let it like you to passe over these things with dissimilation, or to suspend them by deferring. For if, which God forbid, they invade the German confines without obstacle, let others look for the lightnings of a sudden tempest at their doors . . . Let your Excellency therefore provide; and whilst the common enemies are outrageous in the neighbour Regions, wisely consult to resist 'them: because they have come out of their Lands with this intent, not regarding the perils of life, that they might subdue to them (which God avert) all the West, and may pervert and subvert the Faith and Name of Christ.

And in respect of unexpected victorie, which hitherto by God's permission hath followed them, they are growne to that exceeding madnesse that they now think they have gotten the Kingdoms of the World, and to tame and subject Kings and Princes to their vile services. But we hope in our Lord Jesus Christ, under whose Standard we have hitherto triumphed, being delivered from our Enemies, that these also which have broken forth of their Tartarian seats, their pride being abated by opposed forces of the West, these Tartars shall be thrust down their Tartara (or Hell). Nor shall they boast to have passed so many Lands, overcome so many peoples, perpetrated so many mischiefs unavenged, when their unwarie Destinie, yea Satan, shall have drawn them to the conquering Eagles of puissant Imperial Europe to their deaths.

This letter shows that not even this giant among the political pygmies of his time could overcome his political limitations, even when the barbarians were already inside the gates of Europe.

In spite of the sincerity of Frederick's rallying call against the Tartars, it was taken as yet another ruse to unite the continent against the Pontiff. In the atmosphere of fear and mistrust in divided Europe, nothing one side proposed could be acceptable to the other. Thus Frederick was accused by his opponents of having invented 'this plague of Tartars' and the Church used his letter as further evidence of the Holy Roman Emperor's intent to cause mischief.

As a result, no West European ruler backed Frederick's action plan, preferring to limit their vision to the familiar landmarks of Western politics: the Pope's quarrel, the fight against heretics and the recovery of the Holy Land from Islam. The Tartars and the noisy clamour of Central Europeans were ignored.

If there was no spirit of Christian solidarity there was, at least, a sense of self-preservation among some West Europeans who could see that, once Germany had fallen, there would be nothing between the Tartar hordes and the Atlantic. The French Templar Grand Master, Ponce d'Aubon, wrote to warn King Louis of France that although the nobles, the clergy and the lay-brothers of Germany had taken the cross against the Tartars, these forces would be no match for the Tartars. 'Should it be the will of God that the Tartars conquer the Germans, the burden of the war will fall on the King of France', he told King Louis.

When Queen Blanche, the King's mother, heard of the Tartar threat, she tearfully asked her son if there was any hope of delivery from 'this terrible lava of the Lord's wrath', wondering if they were all 'sentenced to die' at the hands of the Tartars.

To which the King replied, according to the St Albans chronicler, in a sad voice but not without divine inspiration:

May the Grace of Heaven sustain us, Oh Mother of mine. For whether this nation comes to us, or whether we go to where these Tartars, as they are called, live, it all comes to the same — we'll all go to the Heaven. Whether we kill them or we will be killed by them, we all go to our Maker, either as believers or as tortured souls.

According to the chronicler, these words restored the spirits and greatly heartened not only the barons of France but also the inhabitants of neighbouring lands. Beyond the pious hope of spiritual salvation the West had nothing to offer the terror-stricken people of the continent, and since it lacked the will to unite and fight for its very existence it interposed prayers between its defenceless cities and the Mongol war machine.

NINETEEN

Subotai's feat of arms

WHEN, EARLY IN THE SPRING OF 1241, the armies of Central Europe took the field against the invading host of Batu Khan, and Mongol horsemen and armoured European knights came face to face for the first time, the odds, in the view of the rulers of the region, were against the Mongols.

They were fighting, or so the traditional view ran before the Mongol fury taught them otherwise, in a hostile world and on unknown terrain; the European knights, on the other hand, were on their home ground, with well-fortified cities to back them up; the Mongols had over-extended and therefore vulnerable supply lines and an insecure hinterland, while the Christian host had no such handicaps.

More importantly, the monarchs of the region — stretching from the Baltic to the Adriatic — were closely linked by marriage and kinship and could not be destroyed piecemeal, like the Russian dukedoms or the Volga nations. And in spite of later claims to the contrary, the Mongols were numerically weaker than the Central European forces opposing them.

Boleslav the Chaste, the suzerain of Poland, fielded a strong army, backed by the Palatine of Cracow with extra forces; Duke Henry of Silesia mobilised a still stronger army, strengthened by Bavarians and an élite Templar unit from France; the Margrave of Moravia, with a force of mercenaries, and Mieczyslav, the Duke of Oppeln (Opole) aided by a contingent of Teutonic knights, assembled the third host in the north. All in all, a force close on 100,000 men.

To the south-west, good King Wenceslas of Bohemia was mustering a 50,000-strong army, backed by contingents from Saxony, Brandenburg and Austria.

And finally King Béla of Hungary mobilised an army of about 100,000 men to fulfil the role allotted to the 'bulwark of Christendom'. He also instructed his Lord Palatine to have the passes blocked in the Carpathians, which formed an almost impenetrable barrier in the east, and called up the warlike frontier-guard Szekely highlanders of Transylvania. On completing his preparations he convoked the National Assembly to discuss the situation but events soon overtook both king and his sluggish parliamentary procedure.

The rulers of the region, although not under a joint command because of the political divisions of Europe, were at least acting in concert, denying the Mongols the chance to take them on singly. For if Batu had attacked Béla, he would have had the Poles at his rear, and if he had ventured with all his forces into Silesia, he would have had Béla at his exposed back.

According to Mongol, Chinese and Turkish chronicles, Batu's invasion force consisted of 160,000 seasoned troops transferred mainly from the Chinese and Khwarismian theatres, plus a large number of freshly conquered steppe peoples and Cumanians press-ganged into auxiliary forces.

This differs greatly from the exaggerated numbers given by the contemporary European sources which, perhaps to justify the defeat of the Central European armies in a mere six weeks, spoke of about a million invading Tartars.

It is not without interest that the Englishman felt compelled to correct this misconception in his confession, insisting that his lord's army did not number a million soldiers ('nec possunt tamen millia millium computari'). He said that the Mongols had 600,000 'satellites', probably freshly formed troops and auxiliaries, and this accords with recent studies* which found that Batu Khan's forces in Russia and Central Europe around 1240-1241 numbered 600,000 people and that this number included all the supply, auxiliary and non-combatant units.

But if the Mongol invaders were not as numerous as swarms of locusts, they had the military genius of Subotai to make the most of the military potential.

Subotai, one of Genghis Khan's 'Dogs of War' and the victor of countless campaigns from China to Khwarism, was the planner

* Ivanov, *Mü*.

and cool-headed commander of the European campaign under Batu Khan's nominal leadership. He was probably the ablest of the Mongol generals, with the most comprehension of Genghis's art of war and the greatest aptitude for carrying it into effect in vastly differing circumstances.

The general also put to maximum use every aspect of contemporary warfare, including psychological warfare, and was light-years ahead of the European monarch-cum-army commanders in the use of tactics and strategy.

At the centre of his life stood obedience, both to orders he received and to those he gave. Discipline, instilled with a mixture of terror and motivation, gave him total control over huge formations of men. He applied Genghis's code of law to every aspect of military life, imbuing his campaigns with a fanaticism worthy of later, ideologically motivated, wars.

His Central European opponents were kings who, without the advantage of a life-time of war-making, could hardly differentiate between Subotai's tactical feints and strategic thrusts. Their armies consisted of heavily armoured knights, cumbrous and slow, followed by undisciplined mobs of peasant retainers fighting, more often than not, with their sharper agricultural implements.

Against the high fire-power and clockwork-like precision of Mongol deployment, the European soldiery pitted its personal bravery rooted in the ideals of chivalry. Individual valour and challenges to single combat, however, were useless against the massed attacks of superbly disciplined Mongol formations.

By personally leading the charges, the European princes gave yet another hostage to fortune: for the Mongol commanders commanded from a suitable distance with signals and retained perfect control of operations, instead of being swept about by the tide of the battle.

In addition to these advantages, Subotai knew everything about the war preparations of Central Europe. Mongol intelligence from Russia had penetrated every corner of the target countries and provided detailed information about forts, army strengths, preparedness, internal dissensions, external treaty and family connections, topographical descriptions and a wealth of other data, allowing the Mongol command to form a perfect picture of the opponents.

The information brought back by King Béla's spies and the

reports sent to him by Russian princes, on the other hand, gave the Europeans the sketchiest information about the Mongol army. The scene was thus set for the biggest military disaster Europe had known in the Middle Ages.

Subotai's war plan was classical in its simplicity, yet it took account of all the complex details of the Central European situation. He divided his forces into four armies and engaged the five Central European armies simultaneously, denying them the chance to go to each other's aid.

He sent an army under Baidar and Kaidu, Ogodai's grandsons, on a diversionary attack into Poland; another army led by Kadan, Güyük's brother, attacked Moldavia, Bukovina and Wallachia to the south in a deadly pincer-movement against Béla; while Subotai himself and Batu led the two élite armies against Hungary, the main target.

Military experts, aided by neatly drawn maps, adorned by coloured arrows and pretty flags, have ever since been mulling over the battles of Subotai's *Blitzkrieg*, making anything beyond the stating of straight facts superfluous. But then, the facts spoke for themselves.

In the diversionary attack on Poland, Baidar and Kaidu first took Sandomir then, on 18 March 1241, decisively defeated Boleslav the Chaste and on 24 March burnt the city of Cracow. Within days Breslau (Wroclaw) fell and its population was driven into slavery chained together in groups.

On 9 April the Mongols clashed with and annihilated the second army led by Duke Henry of Silesia at Liegnitz (Lignice), before the arrival of the allied Bohemian forces. Up to 40,000 Polish and German soldiers were butchered. Duke Henry and his barons died, and so did the Grand Master of the Teutonic Knights, the Hospitaller contingent and nine French Templar knights with 500 men-at-arms.

Appalled European chroniclers recorded that the Mongols cut off an ear from each slain soldier at Liegnitz and sent them to Batu Khan, filling nine sacks with the grisly proof of victory.

Then Baidar and Kaidu swiftly defeated the third Polish army and, with a tactical diversion, tricked the army of the Bohemian king into marching north, while they swung south to join Subotai and Batu's attack on Hungary.

Béla, although he had duly mobilised, was not ready. The

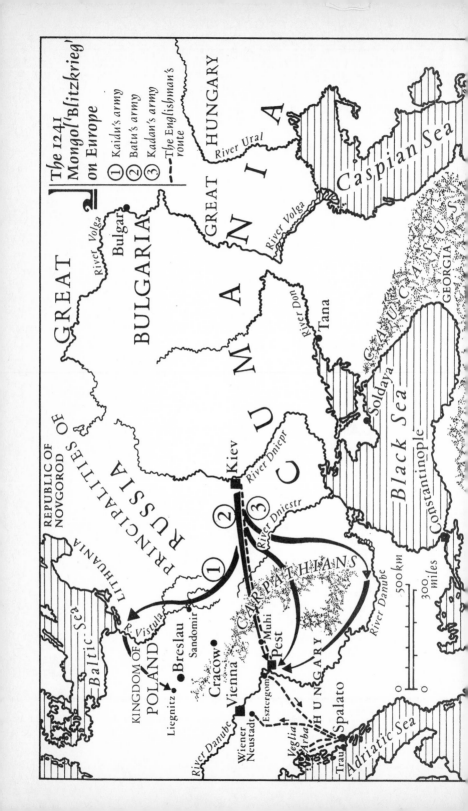

The 1241 Mongol ('blitzkrieg') on Europe

① Kaidu's army
② Batu's army
③ Kadan's army
---- The Englishman's route

country was in a turmoil after the Cumanian massacres and the Hungarian nobility, angered by the curtailment of their feudal rights, responded with a marked lack of enthusiasm to their sovereign's call to arms. They showed up for the war against Batu Khan's host 'equipped as though they were going to a hunt' to show their contempt for the Asiatic horsemen, and also because they felt that a 'bit of a humbling' at the hands of the Tartars could do more good than harm to Béla.

Europe watched with bated breath as the Mongol torrent swept into Hungary after 40,000 prisoners armed with axes cleared away the fortifications from the Verecke pass in the Carpathians.

The feeling that these monstrous horsemen of Satan were aided by demonic forces became a firmly held belief in the wake of reports of the speed of Batu's advance. Only fiendish, superhuman agency could explain the fact that, three days after the forcing of the pass, the Tartar advance guard could reach the Danube, over 200 miles to the west, and that in another two days Subotai's main force too set up camp on the river.

Concepts of logistics and the perfect manoeuvring of hundreds of thousands of men and beasts across wild mountain ranges and hostile countries were notions that Europeans could not fit into the ordinary scheme of things, and when Kadan's army from Poland also joined the main force at the Danube, everyone saw this as proof of Satan's aiding hand.

Even Vincent of Beauvais, that level-headed chronicler and shrewd observer of the European scene, shared the prevalent superstitious beliefs and wrote about the invasion of Hungary in a strange hyperbole:

> Before Batu invaded Hungary, he sacrificed to demons. One of them, who lived in an idol, addressed him and bade him march on hopefully, promising that he would send three spirits before him—the spirits of discord, the spirit of mistrust and the spirit of fear.

Heeding the sound military advice of Subotai rather than waiting for the mischievous spirits to do his job, Batu Khan withdrew from the Danube when Béla took the field to give battle. It was a clever tactical withdrawal aimed at testing the reactions and responses of the Hungarian army. For four days Batu and Subotai lured Béla northwards, away from the protection of the

Danube and the chances of reinforcements.

Then they stopped beyond the River Sajo and Béla's big army set up camp on the wide, open heath of Muhi, surrounding itself with a bulwark of wagons chained together for safety. Subotai and Batu set up camp on the other side of Sajo, in a triangle of land bounded by the River Hernad, where their position was perfectly hidden by brushwood from the Hungarians.

On the eve of the Muhi battle that dealt a death blow to the 'bulwark of Christendom', Batu Khan inspected from a vantage point the Hungarian laager and then drew his generals' attention to how ill-chosen the enemy's position was.

Like all generals preparing for a decisive battle, Batu too addressed his troops to give them encouragement and dispel an unusual spirit of despondency that prevailed, particularly among the fresh Muslim troops from Central Asia unnerved by the size and extreme confidence of the Magyar army.

'My comrades', Batu said, 'be of good cheer. Although the Hungarians are numerous, they are led by unthinking counsel and they are not going to escape from our grip. For I have seen with my own eyes that their army is like sheep, driven into tight little pens.'

The battle itself is of particular interest for the purposes of this narrative, not so much because of the magnitude of the Hungarian defeat or its effects on the defences of Central Europe, but because the Englishman was there.

He was acting, there is reason to believe, as Batu's European intelligence expert and he probably devised, and certainly carried out, a 'black deception', of which every dirty tricks and physcological warfare chief of our advanced civilisation would be proud today. It caused as much damage and more casualties than the battle itself, which ranks as one of Hungary's greatest national disasters.

TWENTY

The Englishman's
letter ruse

THERE COULD BE FEW BETTER EXAMPLES of the superiority of the Mongol art of war over the amateurish mode of fighting of European chivalry than the battle of Muhi. With their fertile military minds, Batu and Subotai immediately grasped the potentials of the situation, improvised accordingly, introduced elements of surprise and unexpected shock tactics, and used gun-powder for the first time in Europe.

Béla's army, on the other hand, was led into battle by two fiery Catholic archbishops and three bishops, with a better understanding of prayers than combat, and the King's brother, Duke Coloman.

On seeing the crowded Hungarian wagon laager, cluttered up with heavy baggage, the noble's household retinues, private food supplies and kitchens and the forest of tents housing the armoured knights, Batu decided that his best bet would be to deny the Hungarians the chance to get out and deploy their troops and finish them off in their 'little pens'.

He sent Subotai during the night, while the Hungarians and the French and German Templar knights slept, as was the wont of European armies, in a wide circle to ford the river way below Béla's camp, and at dawn on 11 April he himself attacked the bridge, which was guarded by about 1,000 troops. With the aid of seven giant catapults and some fire-belching war machines, he bombarded the bridgehead and soon forced a passage across.

The panic-stricken guards of the bridge rapidly retreated into the laager from the fire-breathing 'devilish sorcery' of the aliens. Archbishop Ugolin (or Ugrin) and Coloman led charge upon charge against the Mongols who were advancing in a semi-circle around the camp, doing great damage with their sabres.

However, many nobles refused to leave the safety of the camp and go into action on seeing the Mongols' terrible standard, 'a gray face· with a long beard' of yak tails 'giving out noisome smoke'. The silence in which the Mongols fought and their grouping and regrouping in response to flag signals in deadly formations also helped to unnerve the knights, used to a completely different kind of warfare.

Then Batu began investing the tightly enclosed camp, bombarding it with a hail of stones, canisters of burning naphtha and discharges of gun-powder resembling thunder flashes.

The Hungarians fought on with great bravery and desperation, as Chinese chronicles confirm, even after Subotai's army appeared as if from nowhere at their back, completing their encirclement.

'People fell right and left like leaves in winter', according to a Magyar chronicler of the battle, and Archbishop Ugolin and Duke Coloman, the two most aggressive and fearless generals, were themselves gravely wounded. With no effectual leadership to rally the big army, a section broke out of the narrow confine and fled.

The Mongols, just as they did in China and in Khwarism, opened their ranks as if to allow a brave enemy to retreat in dignity. They did so, however, because they knew that pent-in soldiers facing certain death will fight to the last, whereas fleeing troops are· easy game.

The Hungarians began streaming out of their wagon camp through the gap in the Mongol ranks, throwing away their armour, possessions and even their weapons to speed their escape. The Mongol horsemen pursued and harried the running army, cutting down stragglers and hunting down soldiers overcome by exhaustion. For two days and nights the Eastern horsemen butchered the remnants of Béla's grand army.

On 13 April there were about 70,000 dead on the heath of Muhi and along the bloody escape trail, among them two archbishops, three bishops and the flower of Hungarian nobility.* Béla himself managed to escape in disguise, thanks to his swift horse, and sought refuge in his fortified town of Pozsony on the Austrian border. Organised opposition to the invading army had ceased and the systematic plunder and butchering of Hungary began. It was a

---

* The Hungarian chronicler Thurocz and the Austrian *Annales Claustroneo-burgenses* put the casualties at one hundred thousand, while the abbot of the Benedictines of Hungary in a report (contained in Paris's Addendum) put the dead at sixty-five thousand, including three archbishops and four suffragans.

holocaust infinitely more terrible than the cruel reprisals threatened by the Englishman in the course of his 'negotiations' with Béla.

The treasures of the dead of Muhi and the riderless chargers with their rich trappings were gathered by a special squad. 'The gold and silver, still covered by the blood of the slain' wrote Rogerius, 'were stacked like stones or wheatsheaves in readiness for sorting and eventual sharing out [by the victors].'

Béla's magnificent golden tent went to Batu Khan with his share of the booty. It became the symbol of Batu's prowess, and when he eventually settled down in southern Russia at Sarai, on the Caspian Sea, his Kipchak-Mongol state was named the Golden Horde after Béla's golden tent.

During the search of the dead for valuables, the Mongols found the royal seal on the headless body of the Chancellor. As Archdeacon Rogerius reported to the Bishop of Pest, his ecclesiastical superior, after his escape from Tartar captivity a year and a half later, someone in the Tartar camp who realised the importance of the royal seal, 'concocted a ruse'.

He wrote a proclamation in the name of King Béla, calling on all the nobles, castellans and people of Hungary not to flee the country or attempt a general muster.

The counterfeit proclamation, bearing the royal seal for all to see, said:

Do not fear the ferocity and wildness of these [Tartar] dogs; do not leave your houses. For although, due to chance, we have lost both our tents and our camp, we shall soon, with God's help, recapture them both, and resume the fight. Therefore you should not cease to pray to the merciful God to allow us to smash in our enemies' heads.

Significantly, the brains behind this deception chose 'some Hungarian priests who had been left alive' for this purpose, to make many copies of this phoney proclamation in a letter form. These were entrusted to 'some renegade Hungarians' who took them to towns and villages throughout the county.

In the words of Rogerius, the counterfeit proclamation not only prevented a general muster but 'led both myself and the whole of Hungary into disaster'. He was not exaggerating.

We gave the letter [of the King] great credence, although daily we saw events contradicting its content; for in the spreading chaos of war, we could not send out messengers to check the truthfulness of the letter's news and so we could not assume that the contrary was true. And so, poor blinded Hungary could not flee.

The circumstances of Rogerius's capture in the Transylvanian town of Varad and his subsequent tribulations at the hands of the Mongols, recorded in his *Carmen Miserabile*, fully bear out the contention that who ever had invented the counterfeit royal proclamation, successfully 'blinded' poor Hungary, causing literally hundreds of thousands of casualties.

Master Rogerius did not know who that person was apart from the fact that he had been present at the battle of Muhi. As for the veracity of his statement, he assured his bishop that 'you will find in this present report of mine that which I saw with my own eyes, felt with my own hands, or else I learnt from men of credence who witnessed them'.

The weight of circumstantial evidence points to the Englishman as the brains behind the royal letter ruse. He was at Muhi with his lord, Batu, in his capacity as European intelligence expert. He spoke Hungarian and, as a former Catholic priest, he would have been perfectly aware of the traditions and responses of a Catholic society.

One of the most significant aspects of this black deception was the perpetrator's decision to employ Catholic priests especially spared to write the copies of the proclamation. No Mongol member of Batu Khan's chancellery would have known about the literacy or spiritual guiding role of priests in European society, as their own shamans were not literate. On the other hand, the former chaplain of baron Robert FitzWalter would naturally have sought out men whose function in society he understood and who were conversant with Latin, the official language of the medieval Hungarian state.

The grasp of overall Mongol strategy reflected by the letter excludes all the renegade Hungarians who chose to join the ranks of the victors as these were, without exception, semi-nomad animal husbandmen and herdsmen in whose hearts the nomadic Mongol way of life struck an atavistic chord.

An analysis of the style and rhetoric of the letter, the semantic choice and significance attached to words would greatly strengthen the conviction that it was the work of a shrewd European with higher education. The reasoning was not unlike that of the Englishman's negotiating 'fictions'. Together with the rest of the available evidence, it would bring a verdict of guilty against the Englishman in any British court basing itself on the notions of justice laid down in the Magna Carta.

Simultaneously with the letter ruse, Batu Khan's chancellery divided up the territories north and east of the Danube among the Mongol aristocracy serving in the invasion army, and sent word to Karakorum, to the other noble families not yet represented in the carving up of Hungary, to 'make haste as there is no more opposition'.

Genghis Khan's tenet on how to treat a 'rebel' nation which chose not to submit to the Khan of Khans' heavenly mandate to world dominance was now put into application by his dreaded 'Dog of War'. Subotai remembered his lord's warning that 'when the enemy is vanquished, it does not mean that he is pacified', and he used the two tested tools of Pax Mongoliana to achieve this: wholesale massacre and indiscriminate destruction.

Villages and towns were systematically razed, the men butchered and their families and chattels taken as booty. Churches were demolished, nuns and women raped in front of congregations before being put to the sword. 'The young and the beautiful, spared to serve the Tartars during the day,' an eye-witness wrote, 'were starved and miserable. And during the night, they were treated as the basest animals.'

It is noteworthy that in this orgy of blood-letting and destruction the Mongols' first target was not Esztergom, the kingdom's capital city and military and administrative centre, but the German trade emporium of Pest. Its merchants had grown rich on the lucrative Danube trade linking the Black Sea with the Bavarian staging posts of the Hanseatic cities. The depots and storehouses of Pest fulfilled the same function as Venice's Black Sea colonies, arousing the envy and animosity of the 'Pearl of the Adriatic'.

In a carbon copy of the attack on Kiev, the other challenger of Venice's monopoly of East-West trade, this thriving Danube town was invested and, after a desperate fight, totally destroyed, almost as if in response to a specific request from the Mongols' chief European trading partner.

Thomas of Spalato's chronicle saved for posterity the eye-witness accounts of the terrible day, when the blood-crazed Mongols massacred 100,000 people in the street of Pest.

In the Dominican monastery of the town alone some 10,000 people lost their lives. They had thought that the thick walls of the monastery could save them, but the Tartars set it on fire and the refugees all perished.

In order to frighten into submission the people living on the other side of the Danube, they 'heaped the bodies of the butchered multitudes on the embankment; others skewered little children on their lances and carried them along the dykes as if they were speared fishes. There is no measure to state the size or value of their booty.'

To provide pastures and revitalise the strength of their horses, the Mongols systematically devastated vast tracts of land on the Hungarian plains. The devastation was a simple precaution to assure complete security. It was achieved in the most barbarous manner and with extreme cruelty, as shown by Archdeacon Thomas of Spalato's account.

> They lined up the women, children and the aged of the villages and towns in groups and, in order to save trouble for the executioners and avoid spoiling their clothes with their spilled blood, they forced them to undress. Then the executioners plunged their knives into the hearts of the miserable people and extirpated them from this world.

He also shed light on the role of the Mongol women, who apparently accompanied their men on the European campaign, in these grisly massacres. They were dressed and armed masculine fashion and accompanied their men fearlessly into battle.

> They showed even greater cruelty against women prisoners than their men; for when they saw women of more pleasing appearance and attractive faces, who aroused their jealousy, they unsheathed their swords and killed them instantly. Those who were found fit to be used as slave servants, they disfigured by cutting off their noses.

The blood-thirsty Tartar leaders, like hunger-crazed wolves seeking their victims in sheep pens, next turned on Esztergom and 'considered ways in their wild hearts of luring out the Hungarians or, else, to get the sharp ends of their swords in among them.'

It was a big city of mixed Frankish, Italian, German and Hungarian population whose numbers were swelled by streams of refugees, including 'very rich burghers, valiant warriors and noble ladies'. The old city was protected by earthworks, stone ramparts and high wooden towers, giving the inhabitants the conviction that 'they could resist the entire world'.

Batu, who led the attack on the city, subjected it to a terrible bombardment from thirty war machines, positioned behind a wall of faggots higher than the town's earthworks.

The ceaseless bombardment created such confusion in the city covered by a pall of murky smoke [wrote Rogerius] that the people could not even think of defending themselves and, as if they were blinded, tottered hither and thither. And when the Tartars destroyed their wooden towers and began catapulting with their machines sacks of earth to fill in the trenches and earthworks, they did not even dare to show themselves on the ramparts because of the hail of Tartar stones and arrows [raining down].

Seeing the hopelessness of the situation, the inhabitants destroyed their treasured possessions, large stores of cloth and other merchandise, slaughtered their horses and buried their gold and set fire to the wooden outskirts of the city, withdrawing to the more defensible stone inner quarters. The enraged Tartars, seeing their booty go up in smoke, stormed the inner city and 'fought from palace to palace, hardly leaving fifteen people alive, the rest they wickedly slaughtered'.

Scores of cities and thousands of villages suffered the same fate. The harrowing news from Hungary shocked the West but did not unite it or elicit an effective response. Pope Gregory wrote to Béla to express his regrets over the great sufferings of Hungary 'this favoured daughter of the Holy Church', and urged him to fight on. He offered some cash and the same indulgencies as for the crusaders.

Venice's reply to Béla's plea for aid was even more revealing. The Doge, hinting darkly about the two countries' dispute over the possession of the Dalmatian coast, smugly announced that 'out of consideration for the Christian religion, [Venice] refrained from doing harm to the King at this juncture, although it might have undertaken a great deal.'

Duke Frederick of Austria was even less inclined to come to the aid of his neighbour and saw fit to lure Béla out of his fort of Pozsony 'to the safety of Austria' and arrest him on account of some old debt. Béla was forced to hand over his gold and silver plates and precious stones, saved from the Tartars, and pledge three border counties to Frederick before being allowed to proceed to seek aid for his country.

But Frederick, 'seeing that the Hungarians keep running away [from the Tartars], sent his troops into Hungary to occupy the town of Győr, and so it happened that, while one side of the Danube was being destroyed by the Tartars, the other was being pillaged and burned by the Germans'. The Pope raised his voice against the Austrian ruler's appalling behaviour, but this did not stop Frederick from extorting huge sums from the rich Hungarian nobles who had sought refuge in his kingdom. A carrion crow would probably have shown more mercy.

In December, the Tartars crossed the frozen Danube and put to the sword the whole of Transdanubia. Hungary was bleeding to death, but with Pope Gregory's sudden demise there was no hope of uniting Christendom to mount a rescue operation. The Mongol invasion was left to run its course and Western Europe's chances of escaping the fate of the rest of the continent looked slim indeed.

A Bavarian chronicler, writing at the monastery of Niederaltaich, wrote the epitaph for the 'bulwark of Christendom' destroyed by the Tartars: 'Hoc anno [1241] regnum Hungariae quod 350 annis duravit a Tatarorum gente destruitur'.

But it was the Mongol generals who had participated in the Central European campaign who gave the most devastating verdict on Europe's feeble performance in its own defence. In a conversation with the Papal envoy Carpine in 1246, they ridiculed the ineptitude of their Western adversaries who, they scathingly noted, had locked themselves into their forts: 'these were our little pigs holed up in pens'.

So they had to mount a war of sieges and assaults on big cities, raze small towns and blockade isolated fortresses, and then the little pigs could be served up as roasts.

Carpine took to heart the Mongol analysis and, however

belatedly, urged the European monarchs to model their mode of fighting on the Mongol system.

Our armies ought to be marshalled after the order of the Tartars, and under the same rigorous laws of war. The field of battle ought to be chosen, if possible, in a plain where everything is visible on all sides. The army should by no means be drawn up in one body, but in many divisions. Scouts ought to be sent out on every side. Our generals ought to keep their troops day and night on the alert, and always vigilant as devils.

If the princes and rulers of Christendom mean to resist their progress, it is requisite that they should make common cause and oppose them with united council.

Carpine's sound advice was ignored.

TWENTY-ONE

Confrontation at
Wiener Neustadt

THERE IS A SUFFICIENT NUMBER OF POINTERS, afforded by the focal concerns of Mongol intelligence operations, to follow the Englishman's movements in Hungary.

While Batu Khan's armies smashed the remaining forts and other pockets of resistance, the intelligence and scout units concentrated all their efforts on capturing the fleeing King Béla to bring him to book in accordance with Genghis Khan's laws. Since there was little scope for diplomacy, the Englishman's knowledge of Europe was now put to good use in the search for Béla. Another task of his was the preparation of the attack on Austria with probing raids and taking of 'tongues'.

Batu sent Kadan and his whole army in pursuit of Béla and there is good reason to assume that it was the Englishman's intelligence section that tracked the luckless King from fort to fort, from Austria down to Dalmatia.

With the Englishman's scouts in the vanguard, Kadan's army relentlessly hunted the King, like Batu had hunted the king of the Cumanians at the Caspian Sea at the start of the European campaign.

Béla eluded his pursuers at Verbac, near Spalato, and Kadan butchered a great number of captives to relieve his anger. Instead of joining most of his nobles, his wife and the leading clerics in the well-fortified city of Spalato, Béla fled along the Adriatic seaboard and sought refuge on the island of Trau (Trogir, now a mere promontory). Kadan's scout units, guided by the Englishman's intelligence reports, found him in the whorl of islands off the Dalmatian coast and chased and defeated his fleet in locally requisitioned boats. But Béla once again escaped capture.

His next refuge was on the island of Arba (Rab), but the Tartars again ran him down and the king fled to the island of Veglia (Krk).

(In an attempt to identify these old place names and to seek an explanation as to how the Englishman's scouts could track down the king among close on 700 islands, I went last spring to the island of Lesina [Hvar], where old maps in the possession of a Franciscan monastery indicated that Béla was simply following the east-west sea route towards Venice. According to Don Jure Belic, of the bishopric of Hvar, this was the natural line of communication along the Dalmatian coast, and the grasping of this must have enabled the Englishman to pursue Béla so successfully in this strange terrain for Mongol horsemen.)

On Veglia the king, bereft of his lands and people, waited for the day when he could return once again to his devastated kingdom and pick up the pieces. As a reminder of his former power he had with him St Stephen's crown, the symbol of Hungary's dedication to Christendom.

In the spring of 1242 the hungry peasants were lured out of their hiding places in marshes, forests and other inaccessible places with more forged letters, bearing King Béla's name and his royal seal, assuring them that it was safe to return to sow their fields.

The Mongols also sent out newly taken prisoners to tell the refugees that anyone prepared to adopt their mode of life— Rogerius mistakenly claims 'prepared to embrace their faith'— could return home without fear.

And since the people were dying [in their hiding places] due to a terrible famine, they gave credence to these words of promise and, those still alive, returned to their houses.

And since the forests are vast, there were many people hiding there, so that in a region of three days' walking from my hiding place [Rogerius reported], the villages began to be populated. Each village chose its own Tartar ruler.

From the report it transpires that some kind of an administration was set up, headed by *balivs* and *kenez** who dispensed justice and, in exchange for sexual favours of the prettiest Hungarian maidens, gave cattle, horses and other implements to restart life.

---

* The word *baliv* was clearly the title of the Mongol overlords, while *kenez*, a word of Slavonic origin (from *knyaz*) was probably brought in with the lower administration established in Russia a few years earlier by the invading Mongols.

A *baliv* had about 1,000 villages under his control, aided by about a hundred *kenez*.

> The Tartars and the Cumanians lived with us [in the villages] and many watched with approval how fathers redeemed their lives with the services of their daughters, husbands with their wives and brothers with their pretty sisters, surrendering them to the mercy of the Tartars; and they found some consolation in this even though wives and daughters were defiled in front of husbands and fathers.

The people, glad to be alive, harvested the grain crops and made hay for the Tartars, but after the harvest, which is towards the end of June in Hungary, the *balivs* ordered that men, women and children must gather at a given spot with presents. Archdeacon Rogerius found this ominous and hid with his servant.

The villagers, their usefulness exhausted, were taken to a valley, ordered to strip and then massacred. It was a pattern followed throughout the country, revealing the outlines of the Mongols' 'final solution' for Central Europe.

In the wake of the Mongols' extermination policies, the lot of the survivors became desperate. They had no food, epidemics were rampant and life in their remote hiding places was not fit even for animals.

When, a few months later, King Béla succeeded in returning to his country as the head of an army of Templar and Hospitaller knights from Rhodes, he was met by a panorama of death and destruction of such vast proportions that he despaired of his country.

In previously densely populated regions, he rode for days on end without seeing a living soul. There were hideously mutilated and half decomposed bodies lying in their thousands everywhere, slowly disposed of by packs of wolves and other wild animals.

Wolves appeared to infest the whole country, roaming the villages in broad daylight, attacking the survivors in their homes and 'snatching children from the bosom of their mothers'.

Hunger took a terrible toll and, according to a neighbouring Austrian chronicler, 'more people had died of hunger than from the weapons of the pagans [Tartars]'. People were reduced to eating dogs and cats, and human flesh was being openly sold. Worms and roots counted as delicacies.

The belief that the Tartars were cannibals was firmly held by all European chroniclers of the period. The Austrian, Hungarian, Bohemian and Polish annalists could draw on facts observed by the survivors of the Mongol invasion, but the fear and hatred of these Asiatic horsemen was such that they were endowed with beastly, sub-human characteristics.

As it was the accepted norm of the period to send reports of important events from monastery to monastery and copy them out, the fallacies of the East and Central European chroniclers were compounded by the annalists of the West. A factual investigation of this and similar claims was not possible and anyway, the wholesale massacres perpetrated by the Mongols from the Elbe to the Adriatic appeared to confirm their lowly, barbarous habits.

Yvo of Narbonne, the heretic French priest who was an eyewitness of the Mongol incursion into Austria in the summer of 1242, is greatly responsible for the prevalence of this belief in Western Europe, as his report to his ecclesiastical superior in Bordeaux was the primary source of all Western chroniclers.

He informed Archbishop Malemort in his letter that the Tartar officers were feeding 'their brutish and savage followers' with the carcasses of the butchered people.

Old and deformed Women they gave, as if it were for daylie sustenance, unto their Dog-headed Cannibals; the beautifull devoured they not, but smothered them, lamenting and scritching, with forced and unnatural ravishments. Like barbarous miscreants, they deflowered Virgins until they died of exhaustion, and cutting off their tender Paps to present for dainties unto their chiefs, they engorged themselves with their Bodies.

The Mongols, of course, were no cannibals*. This is attested by the contemporary Chinese and Persian chronicles and the observations of the papal envoys, who traversed the length of the Mongol empire in their journey to Karakorum. But they were in the habit, when on a long campaign with no supplies, of opening a

---

* The epithet 'dog-headed Tartar' became a generally used expression to describe bloody-mindedness or a tearaway in several Central European languages, and I heard it frequently in Transylvania.

vein and drinking the blood of their horses, then staunching it. This habit of theirs, common to all nomadic horsemen of the Asiatic steppes of the time, appeared like clinching proof to the horror-stricken Europeans.

Their constant epithet of 'dog-headed Tartars' similarly reflected Europe's bias rather than factual observation, since the Mongols, with their flat faces and snub noses, were most unlike dogs with big snouts. Nevertheless, the pejorative 'dog-headed' adjective used by Yvo caught on and was duly used by Matthew Paris in Hertfordshire.

In his *Chronica Majora*, the St Albans monk described the Tartars as 'monsters rather then men, thirsting and drinking blood, devouring the flesh of dogs and men.' His prompter was, without much doubt, Father Yvo. But as befitting a chronicler of his stature, Paris used other sources too, and one of them, which informed him that the Tartars 'drank the blood of their beasts for dainties', was much nearer the mark.

But in the warm early summer days of 1242, when Kadan's army threatened northern Italy and Subotai and Batu were poised to invade Germany from two directions, the Mongol army was suffering from grave food shortages due to their improvident scorched-earth policy in Hungary, their European base. It is quite possible that the Mongols, like the Hungarians hiding in marshes and forests, were reduced to occasional cannibalism.

Meanwhile, the probing raids into Austria provided the Englishman with ample intelligence material for Subotai's main thrust into Germany. These raids, some of them undoubtedly under the personal guidance or participation of the Englishman, confirmed that the Austrians were, just as their neighbours, incapable of defending their land against the Mongol invaders. Western Europe now faced imminent destruction and in all the churches fervent prayers were offered up for a delivery from the Tartars.

The annals of the Austrian monasteries show that Duke Frederick, much given to boasting of his military prowess after the Mongol withdrawal from Central Europe, offered no effective resistance against the incursions.

'The Tartars broke into Austria with a big body of men without encountering any resistance, took with force a great many prisoners and then they returned with their prisoners and their cattle to Hungary', the monastic chronicler of Zwettl wrote in the summer of 1242. His Heiligenkreuz colleague recorded another raid which devasted part of Bohemia and Austria, and the Tartars, 'after massacring many people, returned to their camp'.

A third raid along the Danube right up to Korneuburg ended, according to the Garsten chronicle, 'without any casualties for the Tartars, who then returned to Hungary.' There was only one raid, in the district of Theben, where the Duke of Austria succeeded in defeating a Tartar force and this small reverse was, with the passage of time, built up into a major victory.*

Duke Frederick realised the reason behind the probing raids and gathered an army to confront the invasion force on Austrian soil. He was joined by Prince Bernard of Carinthia, King Wenceslas of Bohemia, Patriarch Berthold of Aquileia, Count Hermann of Baden and Duke Otto of Dalmatia, with their forces. It was a fair-sized army but, after the dismal destruction of so many bigger and more seasoned hosts in Europe, it did not stand a prayer's chance in Hell against the Mongol war machine.

At the end of June, literally in the last minute before Batu unleashed his horsemen for the final assault on Western Europe, an imperial messenger arrived from Karakorum having brought post-haste across two continents the news that the Great Khan Ogodai had died in December. Batu, eager to compete for the throne, knew that his presence in Karakorum was vital but, with the entire European continent virtually within his grasp, he hesitated.

Having quarrelled with his cousins Güyük and Buri during the European campaign, he knew that he could not afford to be away from Karakorum while the succession was being decided if he was to stand a chance. In any event, the *Yassak* required that every member of Genghis's clan must attend the *kuriltai* that elected the new Khan of Khans.

The lure of the crown proved stronger than the quest for glory and Batu Khan decided on interrupting his campaign. He ordered a withdrawal from Central Europe, while maintaining strong garrisons in occupied Russia. The West escaped the Mongol holocaust by the skin of its teeth.

---

* This small-scale Mongol defeat is also mentioned in Chinese chronicles and in the annals of Prince Haithon of Armenia.

The Mongol wagons, laden with the fabulous booty of half a continent, began rolling eastwards. 'On the orders of the bigger chiefs, we [the prisoners of the Tartars] began to withdraw from the devastated lands, with wagons full of loot and furnishings, and herds of cattle and sheep', wrote Rogerius about the evacuation of Central Europe.

Although driven eastwards by his guards, he rejoiced because he knew that 'the total ruin of Christendom had been avoided and the conquest of Germany given up.'

The Mongol withdrawal was methodical, as the invaders were determined to take everything with them. 'Step by step, every coppice and all the caves were searched by the Tartars so that what was missed during the advance should not escape them during the retreat.'

Nothing was missed, and the prisoners who helped to cart the riches of Central Europe across the Carpathians were massacred on the eastern slopes. Rogerius survived because he escaped at the last minute.

Batu wanted the German princes to know that this was no retreat from the puny forces they had fielded against him. Thus while Subotai withdrew with the main army, he sent Kadan and Kaidu to mount diversionary raids in Austria.

One raiding party, spearheaded by the Englishman's scouts, pillaged and burnt Lower Austria and probed the defences of Wiener Neustadt. Father Yvo, who was taking refuge in the town from the attentions of the Papal Inquisitor, said that the town had a small garrison of fifty men-at-arms and twenty crossbowmen.

They could do nothing to protect the peasants against 'the many thousand soldiers' of the enemy and the Tartars embarked on their usual butchery. 'The hideous lamentations of his [the Governor's] Christian subjects, who suddenly being surprised in all the Provinces adioyning, without any difference or respect of condition, Fortune, Sexe or Age, were by manifold cruelties all of them destroyed . . .'

That this was a diversionary raid, not a proper Mongol siege, was unwittingly underlined by Father Yvo's report. He wrote that the lookouts of the Tartars, having espied 'out of a high promontory' the approaching Christian armies, turned tail and disappeared as quickly as they came into Hungary. Since it was not the Mongol habit of turning tail on sighting an opposing army, the reason for this quick withdrawal was that the Englishman's scouts were never meant to give battle.

The emboldened Christian forces, led by the Duke of Dalmatia, pursued the Tartars and captured eight of their leaders. One of them was the Englishman. He was the most astonishing captive of this war of extermination waged on Europe by 'the brood of Anti-Christ'.

His fair skin and European features set him apart from his moon-faced Mongol comrades-in-arms, making him extremely conspicuous in the unlikely situation at Wiener Neustadt. Frederick recognised him and there was no chance of a mistaken identity.

'One of the captives the Duke of Austria knew to be a native of England, who was perpetually banished from the Realm of England in regard of certain notorious crimes by him committed', Father Yvo wrote of this astonishing encounter.

It must have impressed Matthew Paris too, for he included the whole episode related by Father Yvo in his great history. The Elizabethan antiquarian Purchas was similarly taken by the puzzling presence of an Englishman in the Tartar host ravaging Europe and gave, in his *Pilgrims*, a fair amount of space to Yvo's report. 'This Epistle following, as containing both the strange adventures of an Englishman and his relations of the Tartars from bitter experience, I could not but adde here, making so much to the Readers' purpose and ours.'

He was further identified as 'the Englishman', who had negotiated as Batu Khan's ambassador with King Béla. Yvo's report leaves no doubt about the positive identification: 'This fellow, on the behalfe of the most tyrannical king of the Tartars, had been twice, as a messenger and Interpreter, with the King of Hungary, menacing and plainly foretelling those mischiefs which afterwards happened, unlesse he would submit himselfe and his kingdome unto the Tartar yoke.'

His phenomenal command of foreign tongues, his distinguishing mark as it were, was duly noted, and the languages listed by Father Yvo tallied exactly with the ones mentioned in Friar Julian's report on the Tartar Khan's non-Tartar envoy he met on the Volga in 1236. In a period of limited social mobility this was clinching evidence.

The Englishman's luck had run out at Wiener Neustadt. But to judge by the drift of Father Yvo's eye-witness account, he must have felt that he stood a sporting chance to talk his way out of that tight corner, and so he played for time.

PART VII

A Traitor to Christendom

TWENTY-TWO

Europe's first
'war criminal'

AS IN A NIGHTMARE, the past suddenly caught up with the Englishman. With his protective anonymity lifted, the excommunication imposed by a meddling papal legate twenty-five years earlier in another world became relevant again.

His challenge to papal authority, his actions in the Magna Carta rebellion and in the Holy Land were all raked up and held against him even though he was being tried, if that is not too precise a word for it, for siding with the Tartar enemies of Christendom. The wheel had gone full circle and he was once again in the hands of the most bigoted followers of the Roman Pope.

His chances of surviving the most dangerous first day or two of his captivity were linked to his ability to humour his captors and keep their interest alive, and that meant talking. As long as his information was deemed to be of sufficient importance he would not be put to death and meanwhile Batu Khan would, he must have been absolutely sure, ransom out his chief diplomat.

First, he reported of himself, according to Father Yvo, the facts and circumstances of his banishment from England, when he was a youngish man of thirty. Then he related his unfortunate game of dice and his tribulation in the neighbouring lands as a result of his expulsion from the Holy Land.

He spoke at length of his recruitment by Tartar intelligence on account of his linguistic flair, but there is a ten-year gap in the chronological order of his career in Mongol service. It is safe to assume that this was due not so much to his reticence as to Father Yvo's belief that it would not enhance his purpose to report to the Archbishop of Bordeaux that the Tartars had a well-structured central administration and a diplomatic service in which able men could advance rapidly.

Father Yvo's short-sighted 'selective reporting' has deprived us of the Englishman's intimate, inside knowledge of the Mongol hierarchy in its crucial formative years.

However, the heretic French priest found the Englishman's admission, that he had called on King Béla as the Great Khan's envoy to pressure the Hungarians into the Mongol yoke, sufficiently important to include in his letter. The Englishman's account of the Tartar's style of diplomacy and their negotiating ploys was also saved for posterity.

The Englishman's eagerness to talk can be gauged from the wide range of information he provided about the Mongols which was wholly irrelevant to the charges. Tantalising snippets survive about their manners, moeurs and superstitions: 'He swore that they are greedy, passionate, deceitful and merciless beyond all other men . . . The founders of their tribes are called gods, and they celebrate their solemnities at certain seasons; they have many especial celebrations, but only four regular ones.'

The blame for a garbled geographical account of their Asiatic homeland and a confused description of the historical origins of their empire must be laid at Father Yvo's door, but even in the priest's faulty rendering the reflections of the Mongols' extreme arrogance survive intact: 'They think that everything was made for them alone . . . In the intention and fixed purpose of reducing all the world under their dominion, they all persist as one man.'

As a proof of his sincerity the Englishman also volunteered military information about their numbers, dispositions, arms, armour and mode of fighting. But the most interesting part concerned his reasons for Mongol discipline: 'the vigour and ferocity of the punishments which were inflicted on them by their chiefs is that which restrains them from quarrels, or from mutually cheating and injuring one another.'

In spite of his clearly demonstrated eagerness to talk, he was tortured in accordance with the contemporary procedures of dispensing justice.

His full confession fell short of explaining how a former champion of England's charter of rights could have served so wholeheartedly the Mongol tyrant bent on world domination, but at least it linked together the two halves of his career which must have had few rivals in thirteenth century Europe.

The trial documents have not survived but the drift of his confession indicates, despite Father Yvo's tendentious rendering, that his prime concern was to justify his actions and rebut the charge of 'traitor to Christendom'.

The known political views and religious attitudes of his captors make for an easy reconstruction of the drumhead trial that was the lot of such traitors.

Because of the high Mongol rank and extraordinary background of the Englishman, the trial was, no doubt, chaired by the princes. Two of them, Duke Otto of Dalmatia and Patriarch Berthold of Aquileia, were close relations of King Béla and their kinsman's appalling tribulations alone would have been enough to make them want to exact a swift retribution. But the atmosphere of fear then prevalent in Central Europe, something even Father Yvo found necessary to mention, could hardly have inspired the other judges to give the Tartars' dreaded envoy a fair hearing.

Since the ordeal which he had to undergo would have assured in the minds of his captors that he was speaking the truth and nothing but the truth, the oaths and protestations—such 'as the Devil himself would have been trusted for'—must have served a special purpose.

In the light of the main charge against him, it is not too difficult to guess what the Englishman had tried to achieve. By under-pinning his confession with the strongest and most emotive Christian oaths, he was indirectly affirming that these set forms of incantations of Christianity mattered to him, whereas they would have been irrelevant for a proselyte.

This emphasis on his having remained faithful to his religion could also be found in further remarks and in the admission that during his long years outside the pale 'every day by rashness of speech and inconsistency of heart, he endangered himself to the Devil'. It was a delicately phrased admission of ordinary fallibility, with the intrinsic implication that his actions had never carried him beyond redemption.

In support of his defence he could point out that he did not sell out to Islam, like so many of his crusader comrades at Damietta, and that he never embraced 'the fetishism of his Tartar masters' religion'.

His claim that he was no traitor to Christendom, although caught in the company of 'the brood of Anti-Christ', was apparently rejected, if Father Yvo's own well-reflected scepticism is anything to go by.

In an age when religious loyalty was the motive force of political life transcending national boundaries and feudal fealty, every local rebellion, act of defiance or political challenge could be construed as treason against Christendom, since Christendom was indivisible and its rulers ruled as vassals of Christ's infallible earthly representive. With religious treason the only indictable violation of natural allegiance, the Englishman's judges must have felt keenly that this tool of the Tartar onslaught was guilty of betraying his roots and culture, but the correct charge had yet to be invented.

In challenging the main charge, the Englishman seemed to demand to be tried on a charge that actually fitted his crimes. Today, he would be called a war criminal.

There were other political renegades and defectors in war-ravaged Europe in the 1240s, but none so important or with such a list of 'war crimes' against his name as the Englishman. He was probably the first war criminal in Europe put to death by the victors* for his signal services to the enemy.

The Russian princes who swore allegiance to the Tartars were collaborators, the crusaders who went over to the Muslim side were renegades, but only the Englishman qualified in this class as a war criminal.

But the known facts about his diplomatic activities and the guile with which he prepared the Mongol domination of Europe must have outweighed his much-protested religious loyalty in the eyes of his judges. With his vast array of negotiating ploys he could hardly have claimed, like latter-day war criminals, that he was merely carrying out orders.

Within the frame of the Mongol 'no peace, no war' situation following the delivery of submission orders, he used deception, war of nerves, subversion, enlistment of disaffected groups for 'fifth column' roles, diplomatic pressure and plain threats of destruction, as well as occasional blandishments, to further his master's goal—world domination.

As all the threads of negotiation merged into a single spectrum in his hands and he alone knew the stage that had been reached with these marked-down nations at any one time, he bore full responsibility for their destruction. And this could not have escaped

---

* Because of their sudden withdrawal the Tartars were deemed the losers.

his judges who, in their impotent rage at Europe's humiliation at the hands of the Tartars, were so determined to exact at least a symbolic retribution for the massacred millions.

The verdict on the Tartar Khan's powerful envoy and European intelligence chief could only have been death, cruel and lingering, in accordance with the customs of the time and the inclination of the Central European princes. It could hardly have come as a surprise to the Englishman. But Batu Khan's tardiness in opening negotiations to ransom him out must have been a shock.

There are no surviving documents which could shed any light on why Batu Khan took no steps to secure the release of his chief diplomat. In all probability he had already left Hungary with the central army when the Englishman was captured. Even for the 'arrow men', the fast imperial messengers, it would have been an impossible task to find Batu Khan somewhere east of the Carpathians and bring back instructions in time for Kadan to select a suitable negotiator and establish contact with the Christian princes.

Thus, the decision was left to Kadan, who knew very little about the foreign-born ambassador and cared even less about his fate. With the usefulness of his diplomatic role in Europe eclipsed by the starker needs of the Mongol power struggle played out in Karakorum, no one could spare time and effort to ransom him out.

The Englishman's fate was sealed. He was executed towards the end of July 1242, and buried in an unmarked grave as befitting a traitor to Christendom.

The movements of the Central European princes in the summer of 1242 offer useful evidence corroborating the date of the Englishman's execution. Duke Frederick of Austria had, according to contemporary records, no allied forces in his camp towards the end of June. He was, however, in Wiener Neustadt on 31 July, and miles to the south in Styria on 12 August.

Patriarch Berthold was in Austria in July, but on 21 August he was back in Cividale, in Friuli (Northern Italy), which was about twenty days' march for an army. Thus the nodal point would be the very end of July, when at least two of the princes were ascertainably in Austria.

Father Yvo's report also furnishes sufficient information to establish the place of the Englishman's capture and eventual execution. After describing the siege of Wiener Neustadt, he mentioned that a Tartar reconnaissance unit penetrated further to probe the country's defences.

> After a while the spies of the Tartars spotted, from the summit of a mountain [*promontorium*] with a wide view, the armies of the Duke of Austria, the King of Bohemia, the Patriarch of Aquileia, the Duke of Carinthia, the Margrave of Baden, with the very numerous levies of the neighbours, forming up in battle order. On seeing this, the entire abominable Tartar army disappeared at once and rapidly retreated into poor Hungary.

Since the Latin *promontorium* denotes a headland jutting out from a mountain chain or into the sea, the geographical features of the region make the identification of the place fairly easy: Leopoldsberg in the Vienna Woods fits the description perfectly.

The Englishman and the other Tartar captives were then taken to Wiener Neustadt, and that was how Father Yvo came to witness the confession of the Tartar Khan's envoy.

Wiener Neustadt had been the Austrian ruler's seat until 1239, thus he would have had his quarters in the town; but it could hardly have accommodated the allied armies.

The trial itself could equally have taken place in the town or in the camp of the Duke of Dalmatia close by. Tradition has it that the execution of criminals used to take place near the St Ulrich church, not far from the 'Hungarian Gate' in medieval times, and there would have been little reason to make any changes or exceptions in the case of the Englishman.

After a life of adventures that shook the world, the Englishman was thrown into a ditch near St Ulrich's church and interred outside God's Acre. No cross or monument marked his grave, to relate to travellers passing by the deeds of his extraordinary life, or to ask for a prayer for his soul.

The Pope and the Holy Roman Emperor, whose petty fight for supremacy left Christendom defenceless in its hour of peril and in effect exposed European civilisation to total destruction, were just as deserving of the title 'traitor to Christendom'. So was the Doge of Venice, who directly profited from the destruction of that city's East and Central European trading rivals. But they all died peacefully in their beds, knowing that they would have honoured places in the annals of our continent.

The Englishman was not so lucky, and he paid with his life for his actions at Wiener Neustadt. A victim of circumstances, one could charitably say, and make it his epitaph.

TWENTY-THREE

Dénouement

THRILLER WRITERS OF NOTE, with an ability to create and sustain suspense, and the eminent craftsmen and craftswomen of the historical 'whodunit' genre, usually end their stories with a grand dénouement. The master detective gathers the protagonist, deuteragonist, the suspects and the walkers-on of the drama in a comfortable drawing room, where he unravels the plot, names the villain of the piece and, occasionally and where necessary, reveals the real story behind the story.

This final scene is a traditional device of the genre allowing the writer to eliminate, without offending the intelligence of the reader, all the red herrings and clear up the confusion shrouding the case.

All the evidence is once more reassembled, the motive of the crime is clearly established on the basis of hard facts, the loose ends are neatly tied up and the guilty party is duly named. Occasionally, the failure to solve the crime is admitted, with a soothing apportioning of blame to groups of people or organisations beyond the reach of the master detective.

The grand dénouement has an equally justified place in a historical investigation like the Englishman's case.

Having followed in the footsteps of the Englishman across three continents and re-created, with the aid of documentary evidence, his extraordinary career, the most striking realisation is that one started one's investigation into the identity of the man with a preconceived idea.

Like a red herring, this preconceived idea about the criminal background of the Englishman led to many dead ends and false trails. The prejudice of Father Yvo's assertion that the Englishman 'was perpetually banished from the Realm of England in regard of certain notorious crimes by him committed', made one take for granted certain received notions instead of allowing the facts to speak for themselves.

Since a contemporary eye-witness branded him as a criminal, the investigation got off to a false start and it took painstaking search in contemporary documents to establish the true reasons for his banishment. It was a detective work full of excitement but, perhaps because of the meticulous attention to detail and the unglamorous, scholarly tools of historical investigations, it could not be captured in writing, so it was left out of this present account.

Once this preconceived idea, like a malevolent ghost, was laid and the true reason of the Englishman's banishment was established, the search for his identity could begin in earnest.

However, even then nothing was taken at face value among the contemporary documents and every piece of evidence was carefully examined for hidden bias.

The facts of the Englishman's involvement in the Magna Carta rebellion provided the key to his banishment and his station in England, and, through a process of elimination, to his identity.

He could have been one of the leading barons (pages 41, 43, 44) one felt on reading Wendover's list of nobles, in the vanguard of the struggle against King John, and this impression grew when the list was compared with the thirty-one named rebels excommunicated by the Pope. There were several extremely likely candidates who featured on both lists, among them Robert FitzWalter, the Marshal of the 'Army of God', the Earl of Winchester and Eustace de Vesci. But any other of the twenty-five baronial executors of the charter of rights granted at Runnymede could equally have fitted the bill.

But the terms of the peace concluded between Louis and Cardinal Gualo, the Papal Legate, at the end of the barons' rebellion removed from the list of candidates the excommunicated barons and the commoners of London and the Cinque Ports.

Although Robert FitzWalter and the Earl of Winchester, together with a handful of gravely compromised barons, found it necessary to go on a pilgrimage to the Holy Land in order to rehabilitate themselves, they were certainly not banished in perpetuity and, in due course, the survivors returned home.

Thus the circle of candidates was narrowed to one section of the defeated rebels by the Papal Legate's stipulation that bishops, abbots, priors, secular canons and other political clerics who had sided with Robert FitzWalter's 'Army of God' and Louis' invasion force must be excluded from the absolution. The peace of Henry III's new reign did not apply to these political outcasts.

The highest echelon of the victimised political clergy could buy, at a price, an absolution from the excommunication and even the middle-ranking abbots and priors, who 'were made paupers by the Papal Legate, who swallowed everything they owned', were left alone once stripped of their office and cash.

It was the 'priestly ring-leaders', the political clerics who celebrated Mass or caused excommunicated priests to say Mass for the excommunicated rebel army, who were made the real victims of the Magna Carta rebellion by Cardinal Gualo.

On his insistence they were perpetually banished from England. It was the very punishment, as we know from the confession, that started the Englishman off on the long road to Karakorum.

There were two political priests singled out for especial punishment: one was 'R[obert], chaplain to Robert FitzWalter', the other 'W[illiam], archdeacon of Hereford'. Both were included, in spite of their relatively humble social position, in the list of excommunicated leading barons (page 44), and by being anathemised in such illustrious company, they rocketed to a disastrous notoriety.

The terms of the 1217 Lambeth Palace peace absolved the barons but left the two priests high and dry. Their defiance of the Pope could not be forgiven. William, the Hereford archdeacon was older than twenty-nine, the age of the Englishman in 1217, and this effectively excludes him from the short-listed candidates for the Englishman.

The process of elimination thus places Robert in the focal position of chief suspect, and a juxtaposition of the chaplain's and the Englishman's movements between 1217 and 1220 bears out that the investigation is on the right track.

The banished chaplain went, with his lord, on a pilgrimage to the Holy Land to purge himself of the papal excommunication; so did the Englishman. Robert's role in the Magna Carta rebellion on the side of Robert FitzWalter fits the 'crime', and punishment, of the Englishman; furthermore, the timing of his pilgrimage and its stations in the Holy Land tie in perfectly with the Englishman's recorded presence there.

The chaplains's progress from named excommunicant to penitent pilgrim to the Holy Land raised the tantalising prospect that Chaplain Robert and the Englishman were one and the same person, allowing the investigation to graduate from the plausible to the factual.

Further evidence is provided by the ascertained fact that the Englishman moved in the highest circles in Damietta in 1218, for otherwise the Austrian ruler would hardly have taken notice of him and his son would hardly have had any recollection of the encounter twenty-four years later.

The company of Robert FitzWalter, the former Marshal of the 'Army of God', the Earls of Chester, Winchester and Arundel and the English king's son would, however, have assured the Englishman the attention and social position that no ordinary excommunicated priest could have commanded. And this was the entourage with which Chaplain Robert arrived in the Holy Land. It would count as clinching evidence in any court of law.

In order to remove any lingering doubt, it is worth recalling that in 1220 the sick Robert FitzWalter returned to England, without his chaplain. This was, of course, hardly surprising since the Englishman had been perpetually banished from his native land, while the former Marshal of the 'Army of God' had not.

FitzWalter's return to England removed Chaplain Robert's sole protector and when he ran into trouble with the Templars on account of his gambling, there was no one to stand up for him. Had he not been expelled from the Holy Land, Robert FitzWalter could have secured a free pardon for him in England, and eventually Robert too could have returned home like the other exiled, political clerics.

But he was unlucky and, due to fortuitous circumstances he remained the victim of the barons' rebellion to his dying day. With his last link with England severed, his metamorphosis into the Khan's Englishman began.

There are no surviving contemporary documents—either in the church archives at Little Dunmow, Robert FitzWalter's Essex seat, or from Baynards Castle, FitzWalter's London home— which could shed some light on the origins and early adult life of Chaplain Robert.

During his truly extraordinary career, people perceived different impressions of him. To Robert FitzWalter and the other champions of the charter of rights, he was a committed fighter against King John's tyranny; to Cardinal Gualo, he was a dangerous nationalist challenger of papal authority, so depraved as to cause excommunicated priests to say Mass to the excommunicated baronial rebels; to the new administration of King Henry III, he appeared as a dangerous political wrong-doer.

In the Holy Land, his linguistic interest revealed a hitherto unknown intellectual side, but his compulsive gambling put his scholarly pursuits in a broader context, showing him as a clever and capable man who was, at the same time, prepared to take almost unacceptable risks to satisfy his passions.

This complex man showed further contradictory traits in his search for the legendary Prester John and, on not finding him, in his acceptance of service in Genghis Khan's chancellery. Although his participation in the barons' rebellion against the tyrant John showed his ability to differentiate right from wrong, he went on serving the Khan of Khans who trampled on everybody's rights and mercilessly destroyed all who dared to resist him. The two worlds—the fight for a charter of human rights and Genghis Khan's blood-drenched drive for world domination—were æons apart, yet Chaplain Robert could serve both.

If he had any reservations about the nature and form of Mongol power, he did not show it; because of his absolute loyalty he rapidly rose in Mongol service, and he showed no wavering even when the awesome Mongol war machine turned against his own civilisation.

To the nations of Eastern and Central Europe ánd to King Béla he represented an alien power bent on Europe's annihiliation. He negotiated harshly and paved the way for the destruction of millions of people whose beliefs and ideals were the same as his own. Yet he saved the lives of Roman Catholic priests in occupied Hungary amidst the indiscriminate wholesale massacre of the young and old, of men and women.

To his captors, he was a traitor to Christendom, a charge he vehemently contested. And this revealed his ability to divorce, in the scholastic fashion of the time, his faith in Christ and priestly loyalty from being instrumental in the destruction of millions of innocent Christians.

His character, shaped by the events of his formative years, holds the key to the mystery of the Englishman. The glimpses caught of him in the course of the present investigation appear to indicate that there is no telling what a human character is really like, until it is put to the test.

In the turmoil of the English civil war he was confronted, like many other idealistic and honest person, with the need to stand up to evil and face the dangers manfully. His excommunication proves that his choice was impeccable.

Yet some years later—and perhaps after great disillusionments in the practice and power of Christianity as exercised by the Pope and the crusader leaders—his line in dealing with difficult moral decisions was pragmatic or, less charitably, downright opportunistic. But by then he understood better not only his own frailties and limitations but also the ways of the world. He who has succeeded in retaining his moral integrity, after comparable adverisities, should throw the first stone at the Englishman.

It is this inner evidence of almost cynical pragmatism and political unscrupulousness that raised the tantalising prospect that Chaplain Robert and Master Robert of London could be identical.

It was supported by the two Roberts' unusual linguistic flair and recorded diplomatic ability. Master Robert's outstanding diplomatic skills were duly noted even by the hostile St Albans chronicler of King John's embassy seeking to convert England to Islam. It was therefore only natural that, in the years of adversity after his banishment from England, he should have taken up the trade that he 'understood so well'.

Another identical trait in the two Roberts was their blatant switching of alliances. Master Robert, or Robert de London as he is named in the contemporary *Rotuli Litterarum Patentum* in connection with his St Albans appointment, changed sides in 1214 in as cool and calculating manner as Chaplain Robert did after his expulsion from the Crusader Kingdom.

Although the clever London priest was King John's own cleric, he had no scruples in destroying his lord's plans of a new alliance when the tide was turning against John.

After his brief but lucrative presence at St Albans he found his only hope of advancement was in the ranks of the rebel baronial army. Their leader, Robert FitzWalter, was not only an implacable opponent of King John, who so callously took away St Albans from his erstwhile envoy after a suitably big bribe from the monks, but also a great adversary of the rich and powerful abbey.

Due to a bitter dispute over the ownership of huge forests in Northawe and to FitzWalter's armed enforcement of his feudal right to appoint the prior of Binham, a cell of St Albans, he was described by the abbey chronicler as 'Robert, our adversary'.

Thus Master Robert would have found a natural ally in Robert FitzWalter, who shared both his hatred of King John and of the scheming monks of St Albans, and the post of personal chaplain would have suited him admirably.

Chaplain Robert's total commitment to his lord and his cause, even under papal anathema, is perfectly understandable in the light of Robert of London's background: having burnt his boats before joining FitzWalter's 'Army of God', he had no option but to soldier on to the bitter end.

And the close link between the two Roberts and the Marshal of the 'Army of God' only reinforced the conclusion that the two Roberts were identical.

Indeed their identity of background, condition and motivation and the inner logic of their actions make this conclusion inescapable. Yet, in spite of long and diligent search, no documentary evidence could be unearthed to prove it.

But having spent my waking hours in the last three years researching and writing the story of the Englishman, and having thus seen it, as it were, from the inside, I became absolutely convinced that Chaplain Robert and Robert de London were one and the same person—the Englishman. Nothing has come to light to shake this conviction.

TWENTY-FOUR

Epilogue

NOTHING COULD BE MORE TRANQUIL than the parish church and graveyard of Little Dunmow on a fresh spring morning. Its massive flintstone walls and Norman buttresses, scoured by the spring showers and autumnal rains of nine centuries, blend into the green Essex countryside naturally, providing an organic link between the dead and the living, the past and the present.

This continuity brought me to Little Dunmow, where Chaplain Robert's one time lord and confederate, Robert FitzWalter, was buried on 9 December 1235.

The little church is a mere wing of the impressive priory that stood here when Robert FitzWalter was the lord of the manor. It is, nevertheless, solid and its stones speak of permanence. Mistress Ailish, the freewoman who owned the manor by the grace of Edward the Confessor and founded the priory, would still recognize it.

Along an ancient path between the church door and the grave-yard gate countless generations of honest local farming folk have walked, every Sunday since the days of Robert FitzWalter, to say their prayers and sing grateful hymns.

They were baptized here. Along the same path they walked to be married and, when their time was up, they were carried to be buried. Nothing disturbed the peaceful rhythm of life, the sure changing of seasons. The big events of history, the upheavals and dramatic changes, took place in faraway outlandish parts. They reached Little Dunmow through travellers' tales and were earnestly discussed, together with the more pressing problem of the price of wheat, after Sunday service in front of the church.

Seated on a moss-covered tombstone near this focal point of village life, it is not too difficult to conjure up the succession of generations—dressed in medieval garb, Elizabethan cloaks, or steeple-topped hats—gossiping with self-righteous rectitude and putting the world to rights.

The surviving portion of the priory has hardly changed since the days when FitzWalter and Chaplain Robert attended Mass there. The carved oak chair in which the lord of the manor used to sit is still next to the altar, a tangible witness of Robert FitzWalter's position between parishioners and God.

Master Robert would be seated right behind him, defining his worldly station, with the rest of the congregation deferentially gazing at lord and learned chaplain between prayers.

This harmonious picture of lord, chaplain and people, all solidly rooted in the English countryside, made the subsequent adventures of Master Robert in Tartar service seem monstrously implausible. Nothing could be more remote from reality in the peace of Little Dunmow churchyard than thoughts of a Mongol empire, built with the active help of a prominent local parishioner on the bones of massacred millions.

Yet the manor house of Little Dunmow, together with Baynards Castle in London, were his homes before the vengeful papal legate set him on the road to Karakorum; they would have provided a frame for his recollections of home, the final links with the past, if he had cared to remember his roots.

His life's voyage ended in a ditch at Wiener Neustadt, not in the Little Dunmow priory like his lord, and one cannot help wondering whether he would welcome resurrection. Would he wish to heed Archangel Gabriel's summons to wake and see again the dread faces of Genghis Khan and Cardinal Gualo, his torturers at Wiener Neustadt, or the agony of the victims of his diplomacy? Or would he wish that nothing should disturb the peace of his earthly bed, to have no dreams of a fleeting life?

Whatever his preference would be—a chance to defend his actions or to salve his soul—the effects of his actions are still with us in Europe.

The thirteenth century Mongol onslaught was one of the most terrible calamities to befall the Eurasian continent. Even if the number of human beings slaughtered by the Mongol horsemen was somewhat exaggerated by the chroniclers of the time, they ran into tens of millions. This unprecedented slaughter of scores of nations daring to resist the Mongol dream of a world empire has left an indelible mark: it transformed the thriving Khwarismian empire into a desert, gave further impetus to the westward drive of the Ottoman Turks into the lands of the weakened Greek empire, recast the shape of China and sowed the seeds of India's present division.

In Europe, the effects of the Englishman's diplomacy resulted in the destruction of the Turkic and Finno-Ugrian Volga nations and the eventual Russian domination of the southern steppes from the Caspian to the Carpathians.

In Central and Eastern Europe—west of Russia—the terrible destruction wrought by the Mongol horsemen was but an awful interlude, which lives on in the folktales and national consciousness of each of the affected nations.

But the impact of the Mongol invasion on Russia was much more dramatic and lasting. It was directly responsible for the destruction of the Nordic Kievan civilisation, and since the attack on Kiev followed directly upon a meeting between Batu Khan's personal envoy and the Venetian consul in the Crimea, the awful responsibility for the ensuing consequences lay in part with the Englishman.

The downfall of the free political institutions of Kiev led, during the two centuries of Mongol sway, to the growth of absolutism and serfdom and the emergence of Moscow as the focal point of Russian power. The rulers of Muscovy borrowed the tools of their statecraft from the tyrannical Mongol system. It took the Russians centuries to rid themselves of the Mongol yoke, but its spiritual legacy is still active today.

Since the general principles of government, diplomacy and administration of the Golden Horde, which ruled Russia, were laid down by Genghis Khan, without a study of the Mongol legacy the present-day Russian system of government and body politic can hardly be understood.

In the light of these unexpected and surprisingly lasting effects of Master Robert's diplomacy, he may well go down in history as the man who helped to destroy the fabric of medieval Europe without, as he insisted, losing his faith or becoming a traitor to Christendom.

He will also be remembered, when the balance sheet of Europe's second millennium is drawn up, as the diplomat who helped to consign the thriving Volga nations and steppe kingdoms to oblivion and thus, however unwittingly, to open up the region to eventual Russian domination. The destructive force of his actions has altered the ethnic balance, and the map, of South-Eastern Europe; the echoes of the shock-waves occasioned by him are still discernible in the tangled affairs of the region.

Robert FitzWalter, his confederate, has left an altogether different legacy. He left his mark on Little Dunmow, where a large legendary tradition has gathered around his figure endowing him with all the heroic traits fit for the first champion of English liberty. In a suitably romantic form these legends became entwined with the evergreen lore of Robin Hood.

Matilda, the fair and chaste daughter of FitzWalter, has become in the mind of the local people strangely mixed up with the fair Maid Marian, Robin Hood's mistress. Several poems and plays have been based on this romance. The best among these—'The Death of Robin Hood with the Lamentable Tragedy of Chaste Matilda, his faire Maid Marian, Poisoned at Dunmowe by King John'—clearly draws on the romantic tale recorded in the manuscript of the *Dunmow Chronicle*.

For the year 1216, this chronicle has an entry recounting that Robert FitzWalter had a very beautiful daughter, called Matilda, who aroused the passion and lust of King John:

> King John coveting this fair and precious lady, and her father not consenting to his immoral desires occasioned a war between him and the barons . . . Matilda abode at Dunmow, where a messenger [from the King] came to her under pretence of love, and because she would not consent, he poisoned her and so she died.

The story has had a great following and even today an alabaster figure on an altar-tomb in Little Dunmow is claimed, however erroneously, to be the effigy of the chaste maid Matilda.

The ageing lord of the manor himself is now chiefly remembered for his good works, and is credited with starting the custom of giving a flitch of bacon yearly to the couple that had not regretted their marriage or had a household brawl for a year and a day.

The *Dunmow Chronicle*, written in 1270, records that

> Robert FitzWalter, living long beloved of King Henry, the son of King John, as also of all the Realme, betook himself in his latter dayes to prayer and deeds of charity, gave great and

bountiful almes to the poor, kept great hospitality and reedified the decayed prison at Dunmowe, which one Juga, a most devout and religious woman, being in her kinde his ancester, had builded.

In which prison arose a custom, begun and instituted eyther by him or some other successor of his, which is verified by a common proverbe or saying, viz. 'That he which repents him not of marriage eyther sleeping or waking in a year and a day, may lawfully go to Dunmowe and fetch a gammon of bacon'.

The oath with which each couple had to support their claim was heard in a solemn ceremony by the church elders and townspeople. One recorded in 1640 read:

You shall swear by custom of confession
If ever you made nuptial transgression,
Be you either married man or wife,
If you have brawls or contentious strife;
Or otherwise at bed or at board
Offended each other in deed or word:
Or since the parish clerk said Amen,
You wished yourselves unmarried again;
Or in a 12-month and a day
Repented not in thought any way;
But continued true in thought and desire,
As when you joyned hands in the quire;
If to these conditions without all feare,
Of your own accord you will freely sweare,
A whole gammon of bacon you shall receive
And bear it hence with love and good leave:
For this is our custome at Dunmow well known
Though the pleasure be ours the bacon's your own.

Thus the memory of Robert FitzWalter lives on, and the priory's sole claim to fame today is its association with the former Marshal of the 'Army of God' and his charitable encouragement of stable marriages in the region.

There is no moss-covered grave, nor the memory of good works to remember Chaplain Robert by. But the nations of Europe that were drowned in blood by the savage Tartar horsemen have good reason to remember the Tartar Khan's Englishman.

APPENDIX I

The Englishman's confession

An Epistle written by one Yvo of Narbona unto the Archbishop of Bordeaux, containing the confession of an Englishman, as touching the barbarous demeanour of the Tartars, which had lived long among them. Recorded by Matthew Paris in the year of our Lord 1243.

To Gerald, by the grace of God, archbishop of Bordeaux, Yvo, named from Narbonnes, formerly the lowliest of his clerks, Health and strength to render account of the talents intrusted to his care.

The souls of reprobates, engaged in terrestrial affairs, do not regard the threatenings of divine justice, nor does terror find its way into their obstinate hearts until they are smitten with the sentence of awful damnation. For, I wonder that, when so terrible an extermination threatens all Christians, such stubbornness should have universally seized on kings and other potentates of the earth, that you, who are said to have zeal for God, do not attempt to move the hearts of the obstinate, by the weight of your influence, seeing that many wise people would abide by your authority, and believe in your words.

But experience alone shows what great danger threatens the Christians through the invasion of the Tartars. For, touching the cruelty and cunning of that people, calumny itself could not lie; and, in briefly informing you of their wicked habits, I will recount nothing of which I hold either a doubt or mere opinion, but what I have with certainty proved, and what I know.

Having formerly been accused, as you know, by my rivals, on account of heretical depravity, in the presence of Robert of Curzun, the legate of the Roman court, from no scruple of conscience, but blushing at the baseness of the cause, I declined the judgment, and for this became still more an object of suspicion.

When, therefore, I heard the threats of that man of authority, I fled from the face of the persecutor. Compelled after this to traverse many provinces, I uttered my complaint to the Paterinians, who dwelt in the city of Como, how that on account of their faith, which, as God is my witness, I had never learned, or followed, I was now in exile from the sentences that had been pronounced against me!

They were pleased at hearing this, and said that I was to be envied, for having suffered persecution for righteousness' sake. I was entertained there among them three months, in splendour and voluptuousness; and every day listened in silence to the many errors — ay, horrors — which they uttered against the apostolic faith.

They so bound me to them by kindnesses, that I promised from that time I would endeavour to persuade all Christians with whom I should have serious talk, that no one could be saved by the faith of Peter, and would boldly persist in teaching this doctrine.

When I had promised, on my word of honour, to do this, they began to disclose to me their secrets, and told me that from almost all the cities of Lombardy and some of Tuscany, they had sent apt scholars to Paris, some to study the intricacies of logic, and others theological disquisitions, for the purpose of maintaining their own errors, and refuting the profession of the apostolic faith.

For the same purpose, also, they send many merchants to the markets, to pervert rich laymen, their companions at table, and their hosts, with whom they have an opportunity of conversing familiarly, and so, driving a double traffic, get into their own hands the money of others, and at the same time gather souls into the treasury of Antichrist.

I at length obtained leave to depart from these apostate brethren, and was sent by them to Milan, to be there entertained by their fellow professors. In this manner I passed through all the cities of Lombardy on the banks of the Po, always residing among the Paterinians, and always at my departure receiving an introduction to others of the same sect.

I at length reached Cremona, a celebrated town in Friuli, where I drank the most noble wines of the Paterinians, ate their preserved raisins, cherries, and other exciting meat, deceived the deceivers, and professed myself a Paterinian, though I still continued to be, so help me God, in faith, though not in perfect works, a Christian. I stopped three days at Cremona, and received safe conduct from the brethren, but malediction from one of their bishops, named Peter Gallo, who held me in suspicion; afterwards, however, as I heard, this man was deposed by them for fornication.

I then set out with a lay brother, and, in the course of my travels, came to the canals of Aquileia; proceeding thence onwards, we took up our quarters with some brethren in a small town at Frisac. The next day the lay brother left me, and I remained alone.

I passed along through Carinthia, and continued my route into Austria, put up at a town called in the Teutonic tongue Neustadt, ie New-city, where I was hospitably entertained by some religious of a new order, called Beguins.

I next concealed myself for some years at the neighbouring city of Vienna, and the adjoining districts, confounding—alas! that I should say so!—right and wrong together, for I lived incontinently by the instigation of the devil, and was a deadly enemy to my own soul, though at the same time I recovered many from the error of the Paterinians, of which I have already spoken.

In consequence of their heresy, and many other sinful things arising among us Christians, the Lord has been roused to anger, and become an angry devastator, and most fearful avenger. This I say, because a fierce race of inhuman beings, whose law is lawlessness, whose wrath is fury, the rod of God's anger, is passing through and dreadfully ravaging a wide tract of country, horribly exterminating with fire and sword everything that comes in their way.

In the course of this very summer, these people, who are named Tartars, left Pannonia, which they had got by treachery, and with numberless thousands fiercely besieged the town above named, in which I perchance was then residing.

There were no soldiers on our side in the town, to oppose them, except fifty knights and twenty cross-bowmen, whom the duke had left in garrison. These, mounting on some neighbouring promontories, saw the immense army that lay round them, and shuddered at the fierceness of those satellites of Antichrist.

Miserable groans were now heard ascending to the Lord of the

Christians, from those who had been surprised in the neighbouring province, and, without distinction of rank, fortune, sex or age, all perished alike, by different kinds of death.

The Tartar chiefs, with the houndish cannibals their followers, fed upon the flesh of their carcasses, as if they had been bread, and left nothing but bones for the vultures. But, wonderful to tell, the vultures, hungry and ravenous, would not condescend to eat the remnants of flesh, if any by chance were left.

The old and ugly women were given to their dog-headed cannibals—anthropophagi, as they are called—to be their daily food; but those who were beautiful, were saved alive, to be stifled and overwhelmed by the number of their ravishers, in spite of all their cries and lamentations.

Virgins were deflowered until they died of exhaustion; when their breasts were cut off to be kept as dainties for their chiefs, and their bodies furnished a jovial banquet to the savages.

Meanwhile those who were looking out from the top of a promontory, saw approaching the duke of Austria, the king of Bohemia, the patriarch of Aquileia, the duke of Carinthia, and, as was said, the marquis of Baden, with many princes of the neighbouring states, drawn up for battle.

In a moment all that execrable race vanished, all those riders returned into wretched Hungary. As suddenly as they had come, so suddenly did they disappear; a circumstance which creates the greater fear in the minds of those who witnessed it.

The prince of Dalmatia took prisoner eight of the fugitives, one of whom was known by the duke of Austria to be an Englishman, who, for certain crimes, had been banished for ever from the kingdom of England.

This man had twice come as an envoy and interpreter from the king of the Tartars to the king of Hungary, and plainly threatened and warned them of the evils which afterwards happened, unless he should give himself and his kingdom to be subject to the Tartars.

The princes persuaded him to speak the truth about the Tartars, and he, without hesitation, under every form of oath, made his statements so strongly that the devil himself might have been believed.

First, he told about himself, that immediately after his banishment, that is, before he was thirty years old, he lost all he had at gambling, in the city of Acre; and in the winter-time had nothing but a shirt of sackcloth, shoes of ox's skin, and a cape made of horsehair.

In this shameful state of want, and in an enfeebled state of body, with his hair cropped as if he were a buffoon, and uttering inarticulate cries like a dumb man, he passed over many countries, and met with great kindness from his entertainers, wearing out his life somehow or other, though he daily, in the levity of his tongue and the foolishness of his heart, had wished himself at the devil.

At length, from the excessive toil, and continual change of air and diet, he was seized with a severe illness, among the Chaldees, and became weary of his life.

Not able to go farther, or to come back, he stopped where he was, breathing with difficulty, and, being somewhat acquainted with letters, he began to put down in writing the words which were there spoken, and afterwards pronounced them so correctly that he was taken for a native, and he learnt several languages with the same facility.

The Tartars heard of him through their spies, and drew him over to their interests: when they had got an answer about their claim of subjugating the whole world, they bound him to be loyal in their service, by bestowing on him many gifts; for they were in much need of persons to be their interpreters.

Concerning their manners and their superstitions, the disposition and dimensions of their persons, their country, and mode of fighting, he swore that they are greedy, passionate, deceitful, and merciless beyond all other men.

The vigour and ferocity of the punishments which were inflicted on them by their chiefs, is that which restrains them from quarrels, or from mutually cheating and injuring one another. The founders of their tribes are called gods, and they celebrate their solemnities at certain seasons; they have many especial celebrations, but only four regular ones.

They think that everything was made for them alone, and they think that there is no cruelty in practising every kind of severity on those who rebel against them.

They have hard and robust breasts, lean and pale faces, stiff high shoulders, and short distorted noses; their chins are sharp and prominent, the upper jaw low and deep, the teeth long and few, their eyebrows stretch from the hair to the nose, their eyes are black and restless, their countenances long and grim, their extremities bony and nervous, their legs thick but short below the knee. In stature they are equal to us, for what they lose below the knee is made up for the greater length of their upper parts.

Their native country is that great waste, formerly a desert, lying beyond the Chaldees, from which they expelled the lions, bears, and other beasts, with their bows and other warlike weapons. Out of the tanned hides of these animals they made for themselves armour of a light description, but impenetrable.

They have horses, not large, but very strong, and that require little food, and they bind themselves firmly on their backs. They use darts, clubs, battle-axes, and swords in battle, and fight bravely and unyieldingly.

But their chief prerogative is their use of the bow, and their great skill in fighting. Their back armour is thin, that they may not be tempted to run away; and they never retreat from battle until they see the chief standard of their leader retreating.

When vanquished, they never ask for mercy, and themselves never spare the vanquished. In the intention and fixed purpose of reducing all the world under their dominion, they all persist as one man; nor yet can they be reckoned at a thousand thousand.

Their satellites, in number six hundred thousand, are sent forward to prepare quarters for the army, on fleet horses, and perform three days' journey in one night. They suddenly disperse themselves over a whole province, and falling on the inhabitants, unarmed, undefended, and scattered, they make such havoc, that the king or prince of the beleaguered country cannot muster men to bring into the field against them.

In time of peace they deceive the people and the princes of the countries, on reasons which are no reasons. At one time they say they left their country to bring back the sacred bodies of the Magi kings, which adorn the city of Cologne; at another time they say it was to check the avarice and pride of the Romans, who oppressed them of old; another reason was, only to subdue under their dominion the barbarous Hyperborean nations and tribes; then they said it was their intention to temper the fury of the Teutonics with their own moderation; now it was to learn warfare from the French; now to gain a sufficiency of fertile land on which to maintain their multitudes; and, lastly, they said it was to terminate their pilgrimage at St James's, in Gallicia.

By these fictions, they prevailed on some simple kings to make a treaty with them, and grant them a free passage through their territories; the Tartars did not keep the treaties, and those princes perished all the same.

Seeing, then, that such dangers are arising to the whole of Christendom, what are these holy brothers doing, with their new religious rites, and fresh from the fire of the furnace out of which they have been fashioned, who wish it to be believed that they alone have found out the way of perfection beyond all others?

By confession, and other intimacies, they should gain the favour of the princes and nobles, and earnestly and importunately cry into their ears against the Tartars: they do badly, if they do not so cry; they do worse, if they only make pretences; but worst of all, if they assist the enemy.

What are the Black and White friars doing? And the Norbertine canons, who wish to be thought dead unto the world? Why do they not preach a crusade against the Tartars, when they see all these perils approaching?

Oh the foolish counsel of kings! the supine silence of bishops and abbats! the unheard-of fury of the Tartar cruelties! Six Christian kingdoms have already been destroyed, and the same fate hangs over the others; whilst the example of those who have perished does not serve as a warning to the survivors, but we neglect our worst enemies at home, and attack those who are harmless beyond the sea.

These reasons have led me, who owe to your fatherly care that I am what I am, to advise you in the Lord, that you should persuade the kings of France, England, and Spain, between whom you hold a middle place, by every means in your power, to lay aside all their private quarrels, for ever, or at least for a time, and hold wise and speedy counsel among themselves, how they may be able safely to encounter so many thousands of such savages.

For I call to witness the faith of Christ, in which I hope to be saved, that if all are united, they would crush those monsters, or singly, will be crushed by them. Farewell.

APPENDIX II

The letter of excommunication

Pope Innocent III's letter backing King John and excommunicating the barons and priests of the Magna Carta rebellion, from Roger of Wendover's Flores Historiarum *(1216).*

'We bring to your knowledge that at our late general council, we, on behalf of the Almighty God, the Father, Son, and Holy Ghost, and by the authority of the Blessed Peter and Paul his apostles, and by our own authority, excommunicated and anathematized the barons of England with their aiders and abettors, for their persecution of John the illustrious king of the English, a king who has assumed the cross and is a vassal of the Church of Rome, inasmuch as they are endeavouring to take from him the kingdom which is known to belong to the Roman church.

'Moreover we excommunicate and anathematize all those who have lent their assistance or money in attacking that kingdom, or to hinder those who go to the assistance of the said king, and we lay the lands of the said barons under the interdict of the church.

'We also lay our hands more heavily on them if they do not desist from their designs, since in this respect they are worse than Saracens; and it is our decree that, if any priest of any rank or order shall dare to violate the aforesaid sentences of excommunication or interdict, he may rest assured that he is struck with the sword of the interdict, and will be deposed from every office and benefice.

'Wherefore we, by these apostolic letters, entrust it to your discretion to publish the aforesaid decrees throughout all England, and with our authority to cause the same to be observed inviolate notwithstanding the interposition of any condition or appeal.

'It is, moreover, our will and command, that you, by the

apostolic authority, publicly throughout all England denounce as excommunicated, and cause to be strictly avoided by all, certain barons of England, whom our venerable brother the bishop of Winchester, and our well-beloved sons the abbat of Reading, and master Pandulph our sub-deacon and familiar, by us delegated, have personally declared excommunicated, because they found them guilty in the aforesaid matters.

'To wit: those citizens of London who have been the chief promoters of the aforesaid crime, and Robert FitzWalter, S. earl of Winchester, R. his son, G. de Mandeville, and William his brother, R. earl of Clare, and G. his son, H. earl of Hereford, R. de Percy, E. de Vesci, J. constable of Chester, William de Mowbray, William d'Albiney, W. his son, R. de Roos and FitzRobert, R. earl Bigod, H. his son, Robert de Vere, Fulk FitzWarren, W. Malet, W. de Montacute, W. FitzMarshall, W. de Beauchamp, S. de Kime, R. de Mont Begon, and Nicholas de Stuteville, and also several others expressed in the decree by name as guilty of the aforesaid offences, together with their accomplices and abettors; and that on each Sunday and feast day you solemnly republish this sentence, and order it to be strictly observed; and that you lay the city of London under the interdict of the church, putting aside all appeal and checking the opposition of all gainsayers, under penalty of the church's censure.

'We also command that you publicly denounce, as excommunicated, master Gervase chancellor of London, who, as we have heard from the aforesaid arbiters, has been a most open persecutor of the said king and his followers, and that you threaten him with more severe punishment unless he make a meek reparation for his offences. And if all do not, etc. Given at the Lateran, the 16th day of December in the eighteenth year of our pontificate.'

The aforesaid sentence enforced.

On receipt of the above-mentioned letters the arbiters wrote to all the churches of England, cathedral and conventual, to the following effect:

'Innocent, bishop, etc. We strictly command you by authority of this mandate to denounce as excommunicated, the barons of England, together with all their aiders and abettors, who are persecuting their lord, king John of England, and all those who have lent their assistance or money to seize or attack the said kingdom, or to obstruct those who go to the assistance of the said king, and to make it public that the lands of the said barons are laid under the ecclesiastical interdict.

'Also that you denounce as excommunicated all the barons, who are personally mentioned in the above letter of our lord the Pope, together with all others mentioned by name in the sentence of the aforesaid arbiters, namely, Walter de Norton, Osbert FitzAlan, Oliver de Vaux, H. de Braibrock, R. de Ropele, W. de Hobregge, W. de Mauduit, Maurice de Gant, R. de Berkley, Adam of Lincoln, R. de Mandeville, W. de Lanvaley, Philip FitzJohn, William de Tuintuna, W. de Huntingfield, Alexander de Puintune, R. de Munfichet, R. de Gresley, Geoffrey constable of Meantune, W. archdeacon of Hereford, J. de Fereby, *R. chaplain of Robert FitzWalter* [author's italics], Alexander de Suttune, W. de Coleville, R. his son, Osbert de Bobi, Osbert Giffard, Nicholas de Stuteville, Thomas de Muletune, the citizens of London, and master G. the chancellor, and that you publicly declare the city of London as laid under the ecclesiastical interdict.

'And you will cause these sentences of excommunication and interdict to be published and solemnly renewed on each Sunday and feast day in the churches, as well conventual as parochial, which belong to you, strictly fulfilling each article of the apostolic mandate, and duly observing it yourselves on your own part, that you may not incur the censure of the church, which is due to the contumacious. Farewell.'

When these sentences of excommunication and interdict were published throughout England, and became known to all, the city of London alone treated them with contempt, inasmuch as the barons determined not to observe them, and the priests not to publish them; for they said amongst themselves, that all the letters had been obtained under false representations and were therefore of no importance and chiefly for this reason, because the management of lay affairs did not pertain the Pope, since the apostle Peter and his successors had only been entrusted by the Lord with the control and management of church matters; they therefore paid no regard at all to the sentence of interdict or excommunication, but held worship throughout the whole city, ringing bells and chanting with loud voices.

Selected Bibliography

Abel-Remusat, M. *Mémoires sur les relations politiques des princes chrétiens avec les empereurs mongols* (1822).

Addison, C. G. *The History of the Knights Templar* (1842).

Albericus Trium Fontium. *Chronicon* (*MGH Series Scriptoris*, XXIII)

Altan Tobci ('The Mongol Chronicle') (1955).

Altaner, Berthold. *Die Dominikanermissionen des 13. Jahrhunderts* (1924).

Altunian, Georg. *Die Mongolen und ihre Eroberungen in Kaukasischen Ländern in XIII-en Jahrhunderts* (1911).

Annales Claustroneoburgenses (MGHS IX).

Annales Cremifaneuses (MGHS XXV).

Annales de Dunstaplia (*Annales Monastici* III).

Annales Stadenses (MGHS XVI).

Anonyme de Béthune (in Bouquet, XXIV).

Bendefy, L. *Fontes authentici itinera (1235-1238) fratris Juliani illustrantes* (1935).

Az Ismeretlen Juliánus (1936).

Berezin, Ilya Nikolai. *Sheybaniada* (1849).

Tarchannye yarliki Toktamysha (1850).

Bohemus, Albertus. *Regesta Bohemiae.*

Bouquet, Martin. *Recueil des historiens des Gaules* (1904).

Bratianu, G. I. *Recherche sur le Commerce Genois* (1929).

Bretschneider, E. *Medieval Researches from Eastern Asiatic Sources* (1888).

Brown, Horatio. *Studies in Venetian History* (1907).

Cahun, Leon. *Introduction à l'Histoire de l' Asie* (1896).

Carpine, John de Piano. *Historia Mongolorum* (1913).

Texts and Versions of John de Piano Carpine and Rubruquis (1963).

Caxton, W. *The Book of Eracles* (1481).

Heraclius— Emperor of the East.

Charol ('Prawdin'), M. *Tschingis-Chan und seine Erbe* (1938).

Chronica Majorum Londoniarum (1846).

Chronica Regia Coloniensis (1880).

Comisso, G. *Tribunale degli Inquisitori (Agenti secreti Venetiani)* (1945).

Cornava, Ignaz. *Jaroslav von Sternberg der sieger der Tartaren* (1813).
al-Din, Rashid. *Jami al-Tawarikh.*
Doerrie, Heinrich A. *Drei Texte zur Geschichte der Ungarn und Mongolen* (1957).
D'Ohsson, Mouradja. *Histoire des Mongols depuis Tchingiz Khan jusqu'à Timur* (1834).
Domesday of St Paul's of the year MCCXXII (1858).
Donovan, J. P. *Pelagius and the Fifth Crusade* (1950).
Endlicher, Stephen F. L. *Rerum Hungarorum Monumenta Arpadiana.*
Eracles. *Recueil des Historiens des Croisades.*
Fedden, Henry R. *Crusader Castles* (1957).
Félegyházi, J. *A tatárjárás történeti kútföinek kritikája* (1943).
Folda, Jarolslav. *Crusader manuscript illumination at Acre* (1976).
Formaleoni, Vincenzo. *Storia filosofica e politica della navigatione* (1788).
Fotheringham, John K. *Marco Sanudo* (1915).
Francisque, Michel. *Les Chroniques de Normandy* (1839).
Gaubil, Antoine. *Histoire de Genghis et de toute dynastie des Mongous* (1739).
Gesta Ungarorum.
Gestes des Chiprois (1887).
Gibb, Sir Hamilton. *Ibn Batuta* (1929).
The Damascus Chronicle of the Crusaders (1932).
Gibbon, Edward. *The History of the Decline and Fall of the Roman Empire* (1908).
Gleich, Aloys. *Geschichte der Stadt Wienerneustadt* (1808).
Grousset, R. *L'empire des steppes* (1941).
L'empire mongol Ière Phase (1941).
Gurtler, Nicolaus. *Historia Templariorum* (1703).
Haenisch, E. *Die Letzten Feldzüge Cingis Khans und sein Tod* (1932).
Hammer-Purgtall, J. von. *Geschichte der Goldenen Horde in Kipschak* (1840).
Hantos, Elemér. *The Magna Carta of the English and of the Hungarian Constitution* (1904).
Hazlitt, William. *The Venetian Republic* (1915).
Heissig, Walter. *A Lost Civilization.*
Heyd, Wilhelm von. *Geschichte des Levantehandels in Mittelalter* (1879).
Histoire de Normendie (1558).
Histoire des ducs de Normandie et des rois d'Angleterre (1840).
Historia Diplomatica Frederici Secundi (1852).
Hormayr-Hortenburg, Joseph von. *Die Goldene Chronik* (1842).
Howorth, Sir Henry Hoyle. *History of Mongols* (1876).
Hyacint, Archpriest. *History of the First Four Khans* (1829).
Ipatyevskaya Letopis.
Ivanov, Vsevolod. *Mü* (1929).
Joinville, John. *Histoire de Saint Louis* (1874).
Kantemir, Demetrius. *The History of the Growth and Decay of the Othman Empire* (1734).

Karamzin, N. *Istoriya Gossudarstvo Rossiyskogo,* III (1818).

Kézai, Simon. *Gesta Hungarorum (De originibus et gestis Hungarorum)* (1272).

Khara-Davan, Yerenyen. *Chingis Khan kak Polkovodets* (1929).

al-Khuli, Amin. *Svyazy mezhdu Nilom i Volgoy v XIII-XIV vekov* (1962).

Krause, F. E. A. *Cingis Khan. Die Geschichte seines Lebens nach der Chinesischen Reichsannalen.*

Lamb, Harold. *Genghis Khan: Emperor of All Men* (1927).

La Primaudaie, F. Ellie de. *Etudes sur le commerce au moyen-âge. Histoire de Commerce de la Mer Noire et des Colonies Genoises et de la Krimée* (1848).

Lattimore, Owen. *High Tartary* (1928).
  Silks, Spices and Empire (1968).

Lavrentyevskaya Letopis.

L'Estoire de Eracles (Académie des Inscriptions et Belles Lettres) (1841).

Liber Censuum Camerae Apostolicae (445, Vatican Library).

Liber de Antiquis Legibus (Chronica Majorum et Vicecomitum Londoniarum 1188-1274).

Lister, Richard P. *The Secret History of Genghis Khan* (1969).

Luard, Henry R. *On the relations between England and Rome* (1877).

Magrisi. *Histoire des Sultans Mamelouks* (1837).
  Histoire d'Egypte (1902).

Magyar Történeti Szemle (1911).

Marek, Jan. *Tschingis-Chan und Sein Reich* (1963).
  The Jenghis Khan Miniatures (1963).

Matthew of Westminster. *Flores Historiarum* (Rolls Series, 1890).

McKechnie, W. *Magna Carta* (1905).

Norgate, Kate. *John Lackland* (1952).

Novgorodskaya I-aya Letopis.

Obshchestvo Istorii Drevnostey. *Zapiski.* 30 (1844-1860).

Ob otnoshenyakh Rossiyskikh knyazey Mongolskim i Tatarskim Khanem ot 1224 do 1480 (1823).

Olschki, Leonardo. *Guillaume Boucher* (1946).

Oliver of Paderborn. *Historia Damiatana* (1894).

Palacky, Frater. *Der Mongolen Einfall in 1241* (1842).

Palfy, Ilona. *A Tatárok és a XIII Századi Europa* (1928).

Panis, Ogerius. *Annales Januenses* (s.a. 1218).

Paris, Matthew. *Chronica Major* (Rolls Series, 1872-1884; Corpus Christi, Cambridge MS 16; Cotton Collection MS Nero D5; Harleian Collection MS 1620).
  Historia Major Matthei Paris Monachi Albanensis (1571).

Pelliot, Paul. *Les Mongols et la Papauté* (1923).
  Chingiz Kahn (1951).

Pfeiffer, Nikolaus. *Die Ungarische Dominikanerorderprovinz* (1913).

Pilgrim Trust. *Survey of Ecclesiastical Archives* (1952).

Powicke, Sir Frederick. *The Compilation of the Chronica Majora* (1944).

Pray, György. *Annales veteres Huunorum, Avarorum et Hungarorum* (1716).

Purchas, Samuel. *Purchas—His Pilgrims* (1625).

Radulphus, (Ralph) of Coggeshall. *Chronicon Anglicanum*: *Radulphi opera quae supersunt* (1856) *Radulphi Coggeshale Abbatis Chronico* (1858).

Ragg, L. M. *Crises in Venetian History* (1928).

Rapin-Thoyras. *Acta Regia* (1732).

Rauch, Adrian. *Rerum Austriagarum Scriptores* (1793).

Regesta Honorii Papae III (1888-1895).

Ricardus, Frater. *Relatio fratris Ricardi de facto Hungariae Magnae* (Vatican Library).

Rishanger, William. *The Chronicle of William de Rishanger of the Barons' War* (1841).

Roehricht, Reinhold. *Der Kinderkreuzzug* (1876). *Geschichte des Königreichs Jerusalem* (1891). *Studien zur Geschichte des Fünften Kreuzzuges* (1891).

Roger of Wendover. *Flowers of History* (1847). *Chronica* (Rolls series, 1886).

Rogerius, Archdeacon. *Carmen Miserabile super destructione regni Hungariae temporibus Belae IV per Tataros facta* (in *Fontes Historiae Hungariae Domestici*).

Rotuli Chartarum in Turri Londinensi Asservati (Record Commission, 1837).

Rotuli Hundredorum (Record Commission, 1812).

Rotuli Litterarum Patentium in Turri Londinensi Asservati (Record Commission, 1835).

Rubruquis, William. *The Journey of W. Rubruck to Eastern Parts of the World 1235-1255* (Hakluyt Society, 1900).

Rymer, T. *Foedera, Conventiones, Literae et Acta publica inter Reges Angliae et alios* (1816).

Saad ad-Din, Juwaini. *Une source pour l'Histoire des Croisades* (1950).

Sacerdoteanu, A. *Marea Invazie Tarară şi sud-estul European* (1933).

St Bernard, Abbot of Clairvaux. *De laude novae militiae.*

Shcherbatov, Mikhail. *Istoriya Rossiyskogo* (1794).

Schwammel. *Der Anteil des österreichischen Herzogs Friedrich des Streitbaren in der Abwehr der Mongolen und seine Stellung zu König Béla von Ungarn* (1857).

Shirley, I. *Royal and other historical letters*, I.

Siestrencewiz, Stanislas. *Histoire de la Chersonèse taurique* (1824).

Silberschmidt, Max. *Das Orientalische Problem* (1923).

Sinor, Denis. *Les relations entre les Mongols et Europe jusqu'à la mort d'Arghoun et de la Béla IV* (1956).

Spuler, Bertold. *Die Aussenpolitik der Goldenen Horde* (1940). *Geschichte der Mongolen* (1968).

Ssanang Ssetzen (1893).

Strakosch-Grassmann, Gustav. *Der Einfall der Mongolen in Mitteleuropa* (1893).

Tatischev, Vasily N. *Istoriya Rossiyskaya s samykh drevneyshikh vremyon* (1768-84).

Theiner, A. *Vetera Monumenta Historica Hungariam Sacram Illustrantia* (1860-   ).

Thiriet, Freddy. *La Romanie Venetienne au Moyen Age* (1959).

Thomas of Spalato, Archdeacon. *Historia Salonitarium pontificum atque Spalatiensium* (in Lucius, *De regno Dalmatiae et Croatiae*) (1666).

Thurocz, Johannes de. *Thuroczy Kronika* (1488).
   Illustrissima Hungariae Regum Chronica.

Tout, Thomas F. *The History of England from Henry III* (1905).

Troitskaya Letopis.

Vámbery, Armin. *Die Geschichte Bucharas und Transoxaniens* (1872).
   A Magyarok Eredete (1882).

Vernadsky, G. *A History of Russia* (1948).

Villehardouin, Geoffrey de. *La Conquête de Constantinople* (1938-9).

Vincent of Beauvais. *Speculum Historiale* (1624).

Vitry, Jacques (Jacobus de Vitriaco). *Histoire des Croisades* (1823).
   The History of Jerusalem (1897).

Walter of Coventry. *Memoriale.*

White, Joseph. *Timur, Great Khan of the Mongols* (1783).

Wolff, Otto, Pastor zu Grunberg. *Geschichte der Mongolen* (1872).

Yahia, Ahmad ibn. *Das Mongolische Weltreich* (1969).

Yakubovsky, A. Yu. *Zolotaya Orda ilyo padenye* (1950).

Yüan Chao Pi-shih. *Histoire secrète des Mongols* (1240). (French translation by Paul Pelliot, 1940; German translation by Erich Haenisch, 1931.)

Yule, H. *Cathay and the Way Thither* (Hakluyt Society, 1866).

Zwettel. *Zwettel Chronicle* (1743).
   Urkunden und Geschichtliche Notizen (1848).

Index

Acre, 14–15, 64, 67, 68, 73–76, 82, 83, 88, 232
al-Adil, 53, 55, 69, 77
Albericus Monachus: *see* Aubrey of Trois Fontaines
Albert, Count of Tyrol, 167
Albert of Bohemia, 175
Albigenses, 7, 51
Alexander (Mason), Master, 20
Alexander III, Pope, 89
al-Kamil, 77, 81, 82, 85, 87
Al-Makrizi, 97
al-Mikdam ibn Shammas, 97
al-Muazzam, 77
Andrew II, King of Hungary, 56, 72–3, 79
Annales Ceccan, 74
Annales Claustroneoburgenses, 169, 190n
Annales de Dunstaplia, 80
an-Nassir, 97
Arthur of Brittany, 63
Attila the Hun, 11, 115
Aubrey of Trois Fontaines, 164–5

Baibar, 96
Baidar, 150, 185
Batshman, 151
Batu Khan, 10, 13, 17, 29; onslaught on central Europe, 58; uses English-man as envoy, 78; success of his army in Russia, 95; sells 12,000 slaves, 97, 107; receives friars, 109; dislike of fixed abode, 124; chooses Englishman as envoy to West, 133–4; plan to invade Europe, 149; granted authority to increase army, 150; decision to annihilate Volga

peoples, 150–1, 152; his army five days' march from Great Hungary, 157; informs Ogodai of victory in Russia, 160; dispute with Güyük and Büri, 161; final message to Béla, 165–6; sends Mangu to Grand Duke Mikhail, 168; takes Kiev, 168; his spies, 169; intention of invading Bohemia, 176; his force, 183; leads army against Hungary, 185; withdraws from Danube, 187; addresses troops at Muhi, 188; attacks bridge over Hernad, 189; his booty, 191; attacks Esztergom, 194–5; pursues Béla, 198; poised to invade Austria, 201; hears of Ogodai's Karakorum, 203; mounts diversion-ary raids in Austria, 204, 209; fails to ransom Englishman, 213
Baynards Castle, 40, 219, 224
Béla IV, King of Hungary, 10, 16; refuses Tartar demand for sur-render, 17, 138, 164; mistakes Englishman's role, 143; sends Friar Julian to Volga, 155; idea of Hungarian expansion, 156; shows concern about Mongol threat to Europe, 160; receives submission and conversion to Catholicism of Cumanians, 162–3; splits Cuma-nians into clans, 163; letter from Batu Khan, 165–6, 170; sends letter to Berthold, 166; takes ele-mentary precautions against Mongols, 167; Frederick III prefer-red as leader, 170; inadequate pre-parations taken against Mongols,

Hardington, Thomas, 29–32
Henry III, King of England, 9, 12, 15, 29, 45, 57, 59, 91, 169, 177, 218
Henry, Duke of Silesia, 182, 185, 231
Henry of Lorraine and Saxony, 176
Hermann, Count of Baden, 203
Hernad, River, 188
Hervé de Donzy, Count of Nevers, 64
Historia Majora, 167
History of England, 79
Hoang Ho: *see* Yellow River
Honorius III, Pope, 45, 56, 64, 73
Hsia Hsi, 115, 131, 132
Hugh, Bishop of Lincoln, 47
Hugh de Lusignan, Count of La Marche, 64
Hugh, King of Cyprus, 72
Hugh the Iron, 54
Hungary, 2, 9, 10, 11, 16, 56, 72, 78, 79, 155, 157, 158, 159, 169, 170, 175, 187, 188–92, 196, 202

Ibn Batuta, 107n
Ibn Hadzhar, 97
Ibn Iyas, 97
Ibn Tagribardi, 98
Innocent III, Pope, conflict with King John, 19; orders King Philip to embark on crusade against John, 20; sends Pandulf to John, 24; approached by John, 39; declares Magna Carta null and void and detains Archbishop Langton in Rome, 42; excommunicates Louis of France, 43; his death, 45; his crusade, 52–6; instant submission demanded by Mongols, 136; his letter of excommunication, 235
Isabella of Angoulême, 21

Jagatai, 130, 150
Jelal ad-Din, 118
John, King of England, 15, 17; his tyranny and conflict with Innocent III, 19; despotic rule, 20; tries to conciliate people, 21; his nicknames, 22; meets papal legate and submits to Rome, 24; demands scutage, 25; defeated at Bouvines, 26; decides to embrace Islam, 28; dislike of Langton, 35; appeals to Innocent for help against barons,

39; challenge of barons, 40; rejects their demands, 41; signs Magna Carta, 42; dies 44–5; and Templars 59; murders Arthur of Brittany, 63, 217
John de Cell, 34
John of Brienne, King of Jerusalem, 72, 82
Juchi, 130
Julian, Friar, sets out for Great Hungary, 156–7; hears of Tartars, 157; meets the Englishman on the Volga, 158, 205; arrives back in Hungary, 158–9; summoned to Rome, 159; sent back to Great Hungary, 160; reports destruction of Great Hungary, 164; meeting with Mongol ambassadors, 165; takes letter from Batu Khan to Béla, 170

Kadan, 150, 185, 187, 198, 202, 204, 213
Kaidu, 150, 185, 204
Kalaun, Sultan, 97
Kalka River, battle of (1222), 119
Kalocsa, Bishop of: *see* Berthold of Meran
Karakorum, 16, 96, 102, 122, 123, 124, 131, 132, 147, 161, 192, 201, 203
Khwarismian empire, 87, 111, 116, 117, 118–19, 131, 190, 225
Kiev, 95, 96, 103, 168, 193, 225
Kipchaks: *see* Cumanians
Kötöny, 162, 170
Kürbeldyshin-Khatun, 132
Kutan: *see* Kötöny

Langton, Master Simon, 47
Langton, Stephen, Archbishop of Canterbury, 35–8, 42
Lateran Council (1215), 54, 60
Leopold of Austria, 13, 56, 72, 73, 75, 78
Leopoldsberg, 214
Liegnitz (Lignice), battle of (1241), 185
Little Dunmow, 80, 219, 223
Louis VIII, King of France, 26, 43, 44, 46, 217
Louis IX, King of France, 102, 109, 167, 176, 180